# TOUGH TOWNS

# TOUGH TOWNS

## True Tales from the
## Gritty Streets of the Old West

ROBERT BARR SMITH

**TWODOT®**

GUILFORD, CONNECTICUT
HELENA, MONTANA
AN IMPRINT OF THE GLOBE PEQUOT PRESS

A · **T W O D O T**® · **B O O K**

Copyright © 2007 by Robert Barr Smith

TwoDot is a registered trademark of Morris Book Publishing, LLC.

Text design by Lisa Reneson
Map by Melissa Baker © Morris Book Publishing, LLC

**Library of Congress Cataloging-in-Publication Data**
Smith, Robert B. (Robert Barr), 1933-
Tough towns : true tales from the gritty streets of the Old West /
Robert Barr Smith. — 1st ed.
p. cm.
Includes bibliographical references and index.
ISBN 978-0-7627-4004-8
1. West (U.S.)—History—1860-1890. 2. West (U.S.)—History, Local.
3. Vigilantes—West (U.S.)—History—19th century. 4. Outlaws—West
(U.S.)—History—19th century. 5. Law enforcement—West (U.S.)—
History—19th century. 6. Frontier and pioneer life—West (U.S.) I. Title.
F594.S655 2007
978.4'04—dc22
2006029789

Manufactured in the United States of America
First Edition/Seventh Printing

# CONTENTS

# ACKNOWLEDGMENTS

Nobody writes alone. I owe thanks to a great many people, most especially including my patient wife; my excellent editor, Mr. Patrick Straub; Ms. Dawn Tomlins, The University of Oklahoma College of Law, Norman, Oklahoma; Dr. John Lovett, The Western History Library, The University of Oklahoma, Norman; Ms. Lisa Bowles, The University of Oklahoma College of Law Library, Norman; and Mr. Gregory Lalire, editor, *Wild West*.

I have listed below all of the other kind people who gave of their time and wisdom to help me—all those, at least, whom I can call to mind. If I have omitted anybody, the omission was inadvertent, and I much regret it.

Ms. Phyllis Adams, Oklahoma Historical Society Research Division, Newspapers, Oklahoma City, Oklahoma

Ms. Sharon Brock, Western Manuscript Collection, The University of Missouri-Columbia

Mr. Jim Chipman, Staff Archivist, Colorado State Archives, Denver

Ms. Letha M. Clark, The Johnston County Historical Society, Tishomingo, Oklahoma

Mr. Richard W. Crawford, Preservation Specialist, Special Collections, The San Diego Public Library

Ms. Barbara Dey, Reference Librarian, Stephen H. Hart Library of the Colorado Historical Society, Denver

Ms. Ardis Douglas, Curator, The Rio Blanco Historical Society, White River Museum, Meeker, Colorado

Mr. Dan Felsenthal, Education Coordinator, The Gregg County Historical Museum, Longview, Texas

# ACKNOWLEDGMENTS

The *Fort Worth Star-Telegram,* Fort Worth, Texas, especially Pat

Mr. Harold Dean Garrison, Mill Creek, Oklahoma

Mr. Steven B. Guy and Mr. Herman Thompson, the *Morris News,* Morris, Oklahoma

Ms. Jo-Ann Palmer, Secretary, Sutton County Historical Society, Sonora, Texas

Mr. Chuck Parsons, Luling, Texas

Mr. Jack Penner and Ms. Roberta Penner, Mill Creek, Oklahoma

Ms. Ramona Rand-Caplan, The University of New Mexico

Mr. John Russell, *Wisconsin Lore & Legends,* Menomonie, Wisconsin

Ms. Lois Schultz, Menomonie, Wisconsin

Ms. Judy Shofner, Librarian, The Texas Ranger Hall of Fame and Museum, Waco

Ms. Jeanie Streets, the *Rocky Mountain News* Library, Denver

Mr. Jim Wetzel, The Delta Museum, Delta Colorado

# PREFACE

This is a book about good men and bad men, upright citizens and vicious outlaws in the American West. It's a collection of true tales about towns that fought back when criminals tried to push them around. Sometimes the fighting was done by lawmen, but frequently many or all of the defenders were ordinary people. This book is mostly about them, and how they stood up against the toughest outlaws in the West.

Most Hollywood movies about the West are moonshine, fun, and good entertainment, but historical nonsense. Occasionally somebody makes a good western: Clint Eastwood's *Unforgiven* is such a film. But generally, although Hollywood may prate about historical accuracy, moviemakers pay no attention to it.

*The Great Northfield Minnesota Raid*, for example, is an exciting tale about the James–Younger Gang's last great raid. It's fine entertainment, but it ignores readily available historical fact. Instead of portraying the citizens of Northfield for what they were—tough, brave, and enduring—Hollywood chose to cast them as venal and cowardly. Nothing much has changed in Hollywood since the first movie about the James boys, which starred Tyrone Power and Henry Fonda and made the brothers out to be good boys driven to outlawry, instead of the hoodlums they were.

One of the worst films in terms of accuracy is the much praised, well-acted *High Noon,* in which the citizens of a little western town abandon their lawman, turning their backs on him in his hour of need and forcing him to face a band of killers alone. In fact, western men and women were not generally that craven and pathetic, as the stories in this book will tell. In town after town, the ordinary people who lived there were willing to step up and defend their homes, help their local peace officers, and lay their lives on the line against heavily armed bullies. Some of them died fighting for their town and their neighbors.

They were, in the words of the Bard, "warriors for the working day," who fought against evil and then went back to their stores and farms and families. This book is dedicated to their memory.

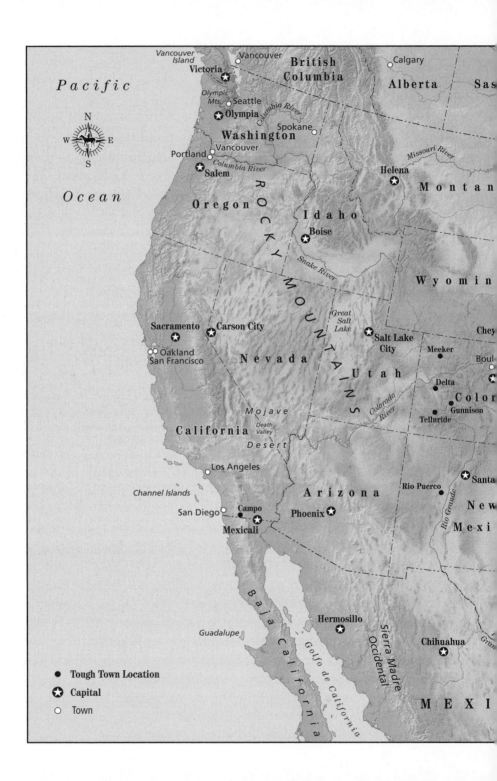

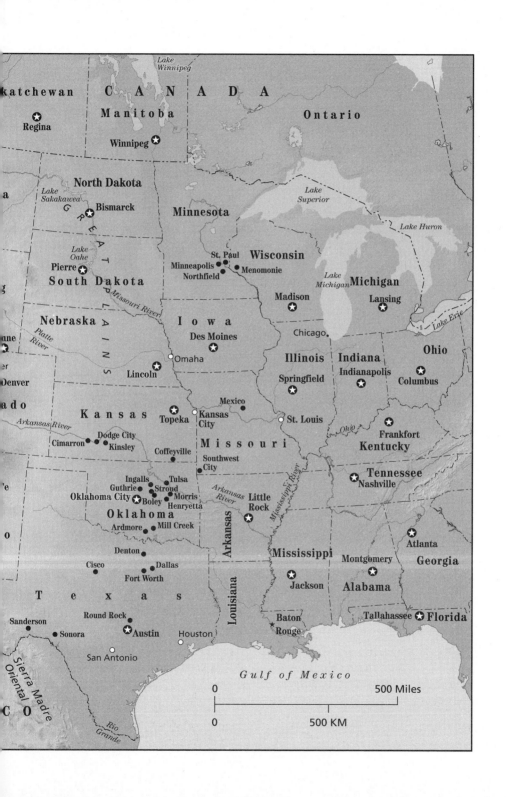

# TUESDAY AFTERNOON IN MEEKER

## *The Wrong Town*

*Thus was justice meted out to three bold bandits who struck
the wrong town in which to ply their villainous trade.*

THUS SPAKE THE *Meeker* (Colorado) *Herald,* and it was so.

October in highland Colorado is a pretty season, cool and pleasant and colorful. So it was in the little Rio Blanco town of Meeker late in
October of 1896. It was a good time to be alive. It was also a good time
for a holdup, or so thought hard case Jim Shirley. He had his eye on the
busy Meeker bank, which was part of a well-known local emporium called
the J. W. Hugus and Company General Store. The bank was located
inside the store building and was accessible through several different
doors. It looked like a robber's dream.

Shirley was between forty and fifty years old, and he had been
around. He had obviously thought a lot about the details of this raid, and
he had done a good deal of planning and preparation. Shirley wasn't
going in alone, for one thing; he was taking along a couple of fellow outlaws. One was a tough, dense gunner about thirty-five years old, inap-
propriately named George Law—his real name, in fact, was perhaps
George Bain. The other bandit was a youngster, maybe twenty-one years

old. His name was probably Pierce, but he is known to history simply as "the Kid."

Shirley and his two henchmen had acquired three extra horses and cached them outside the town at a place called Three-Mile Gulch. The plan was to race their current horses to the gulch after the robbery, then change to fresh mounts for the rest of the escape. Shirley and his boys had thoughtfully cut the fences along their line of retreat as well, the better to leave the country at the high lope once the deed was done.

Shirley had other ideas up his sleeve as well. In a grim foretaste of twentieth-century viciousness, Shirley planned to surround himself and his hoodlums with hostages on the way out of the bank, using whatever local citizens might be handy at the time. He also decided that he would wear a peculiar pair of blue goggles, apparently something he had acquired to disguise his appearance. There were other steps in his grand plan as well. Not long before, Butch Cassidy had struck the bank at Montpelier, Idaho, and maybe Shirley was trying to emulate the master-planner of bank robbery. In the end, he may have planned too meticulously for his own good.

Shirley and his boys rode in from Brown's Park and set up camp along the White River, just south of Meeker. They had everything arranged, or so it seemed, and it must have been with considerable confidence that the boys started out for unsuspecting Meeker on the morning of October 13, 1896. Nearing Meeker, they crossed the river, entered the town near its lumberyard, and tied their horses to a freight wagon standing in an alley. The alley ran beside the Hugus store, so their all-important transportation was parked just yards from their objective. Shirley marked time in the alley until his confederates had time to spread out. Then all three men went inside at about the same time, entering through three different doors: rear, side, and front.

Business was brisk inside the store. In addition to store manager A. C. Moulton and assistant cashier David Smith, the robbers threw down on customers C. A. Booth, Victor Dykeman, Ed Hall, Joe Rooney, and at least one other citizen. The robbers herded these men into a group, where they stood helpless, their hands in the air. One hostage commented later that the bore of the weapon aimed at him "looked big enough to sleep in." Hall casually picked up a scale weight from the counter, with the fanciful notion of throwing it at Shirley. He abandoned that plan when Shirley turned his revolver on him and told him to forget about it. A local citizen named W. P. Herrick wandered in during the holdup and became part of the group of hostages.

Smith, the assistant cashier, had been in the middle of waiting on Joe Rooney when he felt a "heavy hand on his shoulder," and looked around to see one of the bandits stick the muzzle of his revolver through the bars on the teller's cage. Shirley—or Law, depending on which account you read—demanded money, and told Smith to be quick about it. Looking down the ugly end of the pistol, Smith perceived that he had very little option but to deliver.

So far, things had gone according to plan for Shirley and his cohorts, but big trouble was coming for the bandits, and coming quickly. As Meeker sheriff Ed Wilburn recalled many years later: "Uncle Phil Barnhart, the old stage driver, was on a drunk. He came out of Willis' Saloon and in the glass front [of the store] he could see what was going on and he began to holler: 'Boys, get your guns. They are robbing the bank!'"

And so they were, but for a while Uncle Phil had a tough time getting anybody to believe him. A woman passing in the street assumed Uncle Phil was drunk and ignored his warning to get out of the street. "I guess I know my business," she scoffed. "Go on in, lady," Uncle Phil replied, "and get your butt shot off!"

A youngster called Jerm ran to H. S. "Simp" Harp's livery stable. The terrified Jerm was "about the whitest boy you have ever seen," but he managed to tell Harp, "They are holding up the bank and they have killed Dave Smith!" Charlie Duffy, sitting on a box in front of the stable, decided to go down and investigate this alarming report.

Duffy also briefly ignored Uncle Phil, but then, as the sheriff remembered long after, "Charlie come down to look in the window, and he just turned a back somersault going back up the walk." Simp Harp, the livery stable owner, remembered that Duffy "came running back faster than a race horse could run." "Where's your gun, Simp?" Duffy asked. "When I got down there to the bank I stepped up to the door and a fellow said 'Hands up!' and I said 'I don't have time.'" Tom Shervin of the Meeker Hotel also saw the robbery in progress and ran down Main Street to rally some help. There would be lots of it.

If anybody else doubted Uncle Phil, they didn't for long, for a gunshot from inside the Hugus store alerted everybody within earshot that there was real trouble in town. It so startled a workman that he fell off some scaffolding at the Meeker Hotel. The bandit covering Smith, thinking the cashier was moving a little too slowly—which he probably was—had fired a round close to him, a bullet that tore the bank's cash book to pieces. Then, to compound his foolishness, the outlaw fired again.

Now the fat was in the fire, although amazingly Shirley and his men seem not to have realized that they had stomped on a large nest of hornets. They wasted enough time, in fact, for a citizen to run home twice for guns. Outside, the men of the town were rallying quickly, and the little village began to bristle with weaponry. Simp Harp, Tom Shervin, Jo Hantgen, and Uncle Phil all grabbed weapons and converged on the bank, but nobody fired because of the danger to their fellow citizens, who were herded together inside the Hugus building. "Don't shoot in there," cautioned Harp, "because they'll start shooting and kill the whole works."

Inside, however, the outlaws still proceeded methodically and according to plan, and what the plan called for next was entering the bank office. The inept George Law could not seem to get the door open himself, so Shirley had Law move Smith away from the door and turned on the cashier. "Mr. Cashier," said the outlaw, "we want you." He then forced Moulton to open the office door and asked him the critical question: "Where is your money?" "Here it is," Moulton answered, gesturing to the cash drawer. "Help yourself."

And they did, to the tune of about $1,600, dumping the loot into an old sugar sack. They could not, however, get into the bank's safe. Oblivious to the likelihood that somebody had heard one or the other of Law's ill-advised shots, Shirley tarried in carrying out the next part of his scheme. The outlaws collected all the rifles in the store—general stores often sold weapons in those days. They loaded three of them for their own use, and broke the stocks off the rest, presumably to discourage armed pursuit. One witness and the local paper estimated that the outlaws squandered five precious minutes or so bashing rifles.

Then came the last and vital part of the plan: to herd the hostages together, get out of the building, and put some miles between themselves

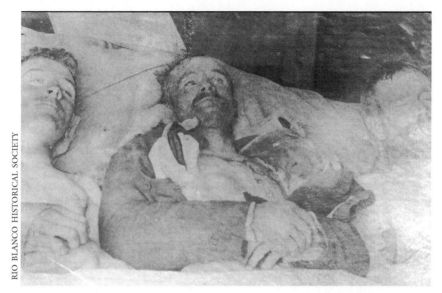

RIO BLANCO HISTORICAL SOCIETY

*The Meeker bandits after their failed robbery attempt*

and Meeker. And so Shirley and his boys herded a selection of citizens out the side door into the alley. Shirley pushed Joe Rooney ahead of him, while the other outlaws sheltered behind Smith, Moulton, W. P. Herrick, Victor Dykeman, and others. Dykeman remembered that Rooney was in front, Law and the Kid were somewhere in the middle of the line, and Shirley was in the rear. The outlaws herded their captives some 25 or 30 feet down the alley toward their tethered horses, and started to untie their mounts.

The street was deserted, or so it seemed. Just for a moment, the robbers might have congratulated themselves on a plan well made and well executed. Then Shirley saw game warden N. H. Clark watching him from behind the Hugus grain warehouse. Shirley snapped off a shot at Clark and hit him in the chest, and then catastrophe struck. The hostages ran for it.

The Kid opened fire on the fleeing hostages and hit several of them: Dykeman was wounded in the right arm and had a "streak" cut in his scalp by a slug that tore through the brim of his hat; Herrick was nicked on one finger; another hostage, C. A. Booth, was shot in the arm, as well. But nobody stopped running, and so in no time flat the outlaws found themselves alone and unprotected. They mounted their horses, but then they ran out of luck.

Bullets poured in from all directions, and Shirley and his men were hit repeatedly. Simp Harp and Jo Hantgen fired from behind a board fence and nailed the Kid no fewer than seven times. He finished his short life in the dirt, face to the sky. The Kid had carried a small brand book in one pocket, and the sheriff recalled that he took "two holes through that brand book and plumb through him."

The probabilities are that Harp and Jo Hantgen hit Shirley as well, for the bandit leader didn't live any longer than his young henchman. Shirley was hit in the left lung, but kept on shooting until he sank down near the Kid. He dropped his rifle when the bullet slammed into his chest, but managed to pull out his revolver as he fell. He lay on the ground, spasmodically emptying the weapon, hitting nothing but his own hat-brim. Law made a run for the river and reached it, but there was no safety for him there or anyplace else. He took a bullet in the right lung—probably from Ben Nichols—and still another in the left leg. Law wasn't even going to make it across the river, much less survive to face a Colorado jury. He lasted about an hour. The citizens carried him up from the riverbank, took him over to a cabin, and laid him down. Law would not tell them who he and his dead comrades were. Reportedly, all he gave them was a collection of innocuous aliases. He said his own name was George Harris, and he identified Shirley as Charles Jones. The Kid, he said, was named Billy Smith.

But Law did ask the townsmen to take off his boots. Like so many western hard cases who came to a bitter end, he did not want to die with his boots on. His last words, according to the local paper, were "oh, mother."

Dykeman was probably the most badly injured of the citizens, and he would recover handily. Though both the town's doctors were away, Dykeman received some basic medical treatment from the bartender at the Meeker Hotel: a full glass of whiskey. "Drink this," the barkeep told the wounded man, "and you will feel better."

"I did," Dykeman wrote many years later, "and it put me to sleep." While he was sleeping, as the *Meeker Herald* reported, "Link

RIO BLANCO HISTORICAL SOCIETY

*George Law, as he lay dying of gunshot wounds*

Taggert made a record-breaking ride after Doctor French, and the latter responded in about as quick time."

Herrick was apparently less perturbed about his minor wound than about the damage to his new suit of clothes—an outlaw bullet had ripped his vest across the front. Curiously, he blamed Moulton, and demanded of him—or the county—the price of a new suit.

As it turned out, Jim Shirley, the would-be master outlaw, had worked for Sheriff Wilburn for three weeks or so not long before the robbery. Simp Harp recognized Shirley too, and called him "one of the most pleasant men you've ever seen . . . also the nicest cook . . . he worked for me two years." And the Kid was tentatively identified as one of two men who robbed the Meeker-Rifle Stage about a year before. Beyond that scanty information, they remained ciphers.

That night, as Dykeman later remembered, "the saloons were open all night and the drinks were free to everyone. The outlaws [Dykeman thought] were part of the famous Butch Cassidy gang from the Brown's Park area and the people expected more of the gang to come later, and they were ready for them."

Not everybody was overcome with joy after the town's defeat of Shirley and his men. Some of the ladies, at least, "fluttered" in the words of one historian, and one of them, viewing the outlaws' bodies laid out in a cabin, passed out altogether. "Loosen her corset and she can breathe better," somebody advised.

At first, there was considerable doubt about the actual identity of the dead outlaws. Some people even guessed that Shirley was the notorious Tom "McCarthy" (they meant McCarty), leader of the bank raids on Delta and Telluride. And an article in the *Denver Post* opined that the bandit leader—whom it also identified as Charles Jones—might be "Dunham, the California murderer."

The *Rocky Mountain News* confidently identified the robbers as Charles Jones (Shirley), George Harris (Law), and William Smith (the Kid). The *News* based the identities on the strength of Law's dying mutterings. The paper also reported that somebody had summoned the bandits to surrender, but was answered with "a fusillade." The citizens' response, said the article, was overwhelming: Jones, as the paper called him, would have died of "any one of a dozen shots," something of an exaggeration to be sure. More accurately, it said that Harris, "mortally wounded, held a revolver, and still staggering, continued to do battle until he fell."

A coroner's jury was convened, and lost no time in deciding that "the deceased came to their death by gun-shot wounds inflicted by the citizens in the defense of life and property, and that the killing was justifiable."

A local photographer took the usual grisly pictures of the dead outlaws, and what remained of Shirley and his boys was planted in Potter's Field by the local undertaker. The bandits' only memorial was a set of wooden crosses. And there they remained, forgotten and unmourned, for almost seventy years.

Then, in 1965, the commissioners of Rio Blanco County decided that the area in which the bandits were buried, now something of a slum, wanted sprucing up. So, the county funded three small stone slabs, and the local historical society added a plaque reciting the history of the raid. Not everybody in town was happy about the new stones, there being some sentiment that the cemetery also held citizens of Meeker who were far more worthy of recognition.

A sad postscript to the botched Meeker robbery was the fate of the three getaway horses, stashed, Butch Cassidy–style, near Three-Mile Gulch. Deprived of their riders, the poor animals languished for seventeen days without food or water, until at last they were found. It was too late for one of the horses, which had tried to lie down, slid down a slope, and strangled in its harness. The remaining pair lived out what remained of their lives with a Rio Blanco rancher.

And so passed the short-lived Shirley gang, victims of a town full of people who didn't take kindly to being pushed around. The *Meeker Herald* produced a long story of what it called this "red letter day in Meeker's history," also reminding its readers, tongue-in-cheek, that a copy of the paper was available for "ten cents a copy. No need to borrow, beg or steal it—or sneak into the barber shop and read it."

So ended, the paper said:

> *the first attempt to rob a bank in this part of the state . . . and a very creditable showing for the citizens of Meeker. . . . The cool display of judgment and bravery exhibited under trying conditions establishes for the men of Meeker a reputation to be proud of, and will give this town a creditable name throughout the length and breath [*sic*] of the land.*

The outlaws' performance, said the paper, "showed evidence of amateurishness in many particulars, but the lightning-like promptness by which they were disposed of showed that the citizens of Meeker knew how to act and shoot."

They did indeed.

## MURDER!

### *The Rifleman of Delta*

"MURDER!" SCREAMED the headline of the *Delta* (Colorado) *Independent*. "Three Robbers Commit a Horrible Deed." The small weekly paper devoted the whole front page and two columns of the other three pages to the excitement. On the floor of Delta's Farmers and Merchants Bank, an unarmed bank cashier, father of a large family, lay dead, a bullet through his skull. Two more men, both bandits, were sprawled in their own blood in the dirt of a Delta street, and a grim posse was in hot pursuit of one surviving outlaw.

In the autumn of 1893, Delta was a quiet little town, like hundreds of other young communities across the West. It had been called Uncompahgre not long before, but it was platted in the spring of 1882 as Delta, named for its nearness to the delta of the Gunnison and Uncompahgre Rivers. It was a growing town in 1893, a settlement with a future: Delta already boasted two saloons, three hardware stores, three lawyers, a couple dozen other commercial enterprises, and two banks.

The seventh of September was a miserably hot day. A Delta resident of the time called it "stifling," the sort of day on which people moved slowly and stayed in the shade if they had no pressing business. Like the surprising heat on that autumn day, another unwelcome guest was about to pay a visit to the town of Delta. Veteran outlaw Tom McCarty had his eye on the citizens' hard-earned savings at the Farmers and Merchants Bank, and with him were his brother Bill and Bill's seventeen-year-old son, Fred. The three had been watching the little town and its bank for several days, and they were at last ready to move.

Tom McCarty was a professional hoodlum. His father brought his large family west to Montana and Utah, where they settled for a while close to Circleville, home of one Leroy Parker, better known as Butch Cassidy. The family moved on to Nevada, then back to Utah in 1877. The McCarty brothers became ranchers on their own, but they weren't very good at it, at least not for the long haul, or maybe they were just not very interested. In time, whatever the reason, taking other people's money began to seem a good deal more attractive than working. For a while, at least, it was.

Tom rode with Butch Cassidy and Matt Warner, among others, and had been part of the famous 1893 robbery of the San Miguel Bank in Telluride, Colorado. That raid, which netted more than $20,000, was reputed to be Cassidy's first venture into bank robbery. Tom McCarty was also the central figure in the celebrated robbery of the First National Bank of Denver in the spring of 1889.

When McCarty and Warner robbed a gambling hall in Butte, Montana, they sought shelter at a hardscrabble "ranch" in Baker, Oregon, owned by McCarty's brother, Bill. Things were tough in the ranching business for Bill and his son Fred, and both joined Tom to follow the apparently easy money of the owlhoot trail. It would prove to be an exceedingly poor decision in the long run, however short the grass was at Baker.

For a while, though, the outlaw business went fairly smoothly. The four men robbed a placer camp called Sparta, Oregon, coming away with a haul of currency and gold nuggets. They rode into Moscow, Idaho, to rob, of all things, a circus, and then returned to Enterprise, Oregon, to rob a bank. More holdups followed, including a bank in Roslyn, Washington. The Roslyn job went bad: One of the gang shot a man in the stomach and the robbers had to run for it, with a posse hot on their heels. Warner was eventually captured and spent some time in jail, awaiting trial. Acquitted and released, he was smart enough to quit once he got out of jail. McCarty wasn't that bright.

Now without the redoubtable Warner, the McCarty brothers and young Fred were determined to empty the coffers of the Farmers and Merchants Bank, one of Delta's two banks. The story of what happened when they tried to do so varies, depending on whose account you read. A couple of stories of the raid don't even agree on the date: While it is clear that the holdup took place on September 7, some accounts have it happening on the 3rd or the 27th.

The three outlaws apparently arrived at Delta about the first of the month, and spent some time casing the town. They seem to have spent considerable time in the Steve Bailey Saloon, otherwise known as the Palace Sampling Rooms, which were right across the street from the bank. They camped outside the town prior to the raid, perhaps in nearby Escalante Canyon—at least they are thought to have stopped there for a meal at the John Musser cattle ranch. They brought with them a string of spare mounts, and they took their time sizing up the bank and the town.

When in town, the outlaws stabled their horses at Fadley's Corral on the north side of Delta and spent some time yarning with one George Smith, keeper of the steam engine that drove the municipal water pump. The three hoodlums were chatty types, asking what were later called innocent-sounding questions over a friendly drink in the town's watering holes. In the afternoons they rode out of town, letting it be known that they were shopping for a ranch site. One source says young Fred was used as a scout for the gang, and even played a bit in a marble game with some of the Delta boys. The outlaws ate a meal at Bricktop's restaurant on Main Street, and at least two more at Central House. In between a drink or two and some card playing at the Steve Bailey Saloon, they shopped for shoes and a bottle of whiskey.

On the seventh of September, they were ready. Tom probably performed his usual role: He liked to be the outside man, watching the street and holding the horses for the other two robbers. Local citizen H. H. Smith watched Tom down at least one slug of liquid courage just before the raid began. Tom then entered the alley behind the bank with all three men's horses. At about 10:15 A.M., Bill and his son walked into the bank. It probably did not occur to any of the outlaws that this broiling day was the anniversary of the James–Younger Gang's disaster at Northfield in 1876.

*Ray Simpson*

Inside the bank were two men: A. T. Blachley, a cashier, and H. H. Wolbert, teller and assistant cashier. One book on the Wild Bunch puts a third employee in the bank, a bookkeeper called John Trew, but no other authority does. At the back of the bank, in a sort of lean-to used as an office, sat attorney W. R. Robinson. Across the street, in Simpson and Corbin's Hardware Store—or Simpson and Son's, depending on the source—sat William Ray Simpson.

Simpson was Kentucky-born and raised and had moved west with his parents for his health. He settled in Delta, but took time out to return to Kentucky for his light of love, Mary Ann Hays. The pair eloped, the story goes, since Mary Ann's father insisted that his family was superior

*The Farmers and Merchants Bank in Delta, Colorado*

to any other. Apparently the attraction between the two young people was of some years' standing, for Simpson reportedly had seen young Mary Ann jumping horses at the county fair back in Kentucky. "There's a pair of thoroughbreds if I've ever seen one," he said, "and I'm going to marry that girl when she grows up."

It's a nice story, maybe even true, and it is certain that Simpson and the lady married, probably in Decatur, Texas, on the way west. They settled in Delta, and produced three daughters. Simpson was a solid citizen, a respected merchant. He was about to become the town's hero.

To this day there is no certainty about everything that happened inside the bank. Blachley, one of the bank's founders, was typing; Wolbert was working nearby, and the bank's safe stood wide open. Two men walked into the bank and Blachley rose to wait on them. He found himself looking into the business end of two guns. The bandits demanded the bank's assets forthwith, and one of the robbers, probably young Fred, jumped up on the bank's counter.

14

Wolbert made a motion toward a pistol, but gave it up when one of the bandits warned him against such a rash move. Cashier Blachley, with more courage than discretion, seems to have shouted for help, and one of the outlaws told him to shut up or get his head blown off. Nothing daunted, the gutsy cashier shouted again. This time he got two bullets at close range: The slugs entered his neck and tore out through the top of his head. Or maybe, as other versions tell it, he was killed by a single round through the top of the skull, the second round slamming harmlessly into the boards of the bank's floor. In either case, Blachley's gallant defiance had cost him his life. The *Grand Junction News* also reported, probably erroneously, that the robbers had shot at Wolbert, but missed him.

Tom McCarty's autobiography simply says that two men entered the bank and a third waited outside with the horses, without naming who did what. He also says that the cashier "reached for a pistol" and was shot down. This version is unsupported by any other version of the raid, and sounds very like an attempt to justify cold-blooded murder.

The inside men, probably Bill and Fred McCarty, grabbed a bag of gold coins, snatched between $700 and $1,000 of bills and stuffed them inside their shirts, and then ran out through the lawyer's lean-to at the back of the bank. One version of the story says Tom McCarty "covered the lawyer at his desk," while the other two bandits were busy in the bank, although this seems at odds with Tom's usual job as outside man. Still another account has Tom killing Blachley, after which "Fred rushed to the horses, quickly followed by the other two."

In *Desperate Men*, James D. Horan names Tom as Blachley's killer, but he also has Matt Warner, who wasn't there, holding the gang's horses. In still another account, "Bill McCarty began scooping money in a bag, Tom leaped over the railing and pushed a six-gun into Blachey's [*sic*] ribs." Fred, in this version, is the man who covered the attorney at the rear of the bank. Who shot Blachley is not made clear, and the account loses some force by claiming erroneously that Blachley's "assistant," presumably Wolbert, was wounded. Still another version says flatly that young Fred murdered Blachley.

Whatever had happened inside, the robbers dashed into the alley, herding Wolbert along with them, one of them calling to his confederates,

"Get on your horses quick, for God's sake." It was good advice, for citizens were already moving toward the front of the bank. One account of the raid says the two inside men arrived in the alley to find their horses waiting, "but Tom had jumped on his horse and was long gone."

Leaving behind their loot, the outlaws mounted in haste and fled, leaving loose currency strewn up and down the alley. While Blachley's shouts had apparently not been heard outside the bank because of a high wind, the shots that killed him certainly had been. Among those who heard them was Ray Simpson, and he reacted immediately.

According to one version of the Delta raid, Simpson was cleaning his rifle—most accounts call it a .44 Sharps—in the back room of the hardware store, right across Main Street from the bank. Or maybe, according to another version, he just grabbed a repeating rifle from the rack in the store: That rifle would probably have been new stock, and therefore might not have been a Sharps, since the Sharps company had failed in 1881. Other accounts refer to Simpson's "trusty Winchester." The Delta County Historical Society reports, however, that it has the very rifle in its museum: a single-shot .40-caliber Sharps.

Simpson himself told a fascinating story about being prepared to take on the robbers. He said later that he had dreamed a local bad man had vandalized his shop and he, Simpson, had to shoot the intruder. The vision so stuck in Simpson's mind that the next morning, he cleaned his rifle and set it with the cartridges where he could get it quickly. In fact, he was telling his father and the town night watchman of his strange dream when two shots rang out in the bank across the street.

Although angry citizens were gathering in front of the bank, Simpson noticed that there were no horses tethered there and guessed that the gang had stashed their mounts in the alley behind the bank. He ran out on the street, hearing somebody yell, "Get your gun; it's a holdup." He sprinted to the corner of Third Street and Main, loading the single-shot Sharps as he went. At the corner Simpson turned toward the alley as the three outlaws galloped past him. Simpson raised the Sharps and pulled down on the nearest one. He hit Bill in the back of the head— "in the hatband," according to one source—and the bullet tore off the top of Bill's head complete with his hat. One account says Bill's brains ended up 20 feet away from the rest of him. Fred hesitated, and author

DELTA COUNTY HISTORICAL SOCIETY

*Bill McCarty*

Horan even says Fred returned to kneel over his father, but this sounds a bit like journalistic embroidery, since a glance would have told Fred that the top of Bill's head had been blown away.

There's a good deal of dubious prose about Simpson's fine shooting, making it maybe even better than the remarkable performance it really was. One writer said Simpson took off the crown of Bill McCarty's head at "240 feet," an astonishing shot with iron sights at that distance, fired offhand at a man on a galloping horse. Even more phenomenal is the same author's description of what happened next. Simpson, he wrote, then ran north on Main Street, reloading on the move.

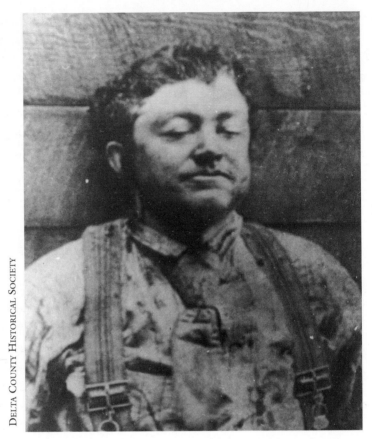

DELTA COUNTY HISTORICAL SOCIETY

*Fred McCarty*

Now, says this version, Simpson halted near Bill's corpse and took aim at Fred, nailing him at a range of 385 feet. Simpson was a superb rifleman, and it's a great story, but the math is a little hard to follow. Simpson had to have run 240 feet, reloading the heavy Sharps, then halted, aimed, and fired at the fleeing outlaws. During the time it took him to run 240 feet, their galloping horses would have only taken the remaining robbers 385 feet. Of such calculations is born the mythology of the West.

These distances are at odds with Tom McCarty's own version of what had happened in Delta. However, Simpson did say afterward that Fred fired three times at him and paused long enough to glance at his father, quickly perceiving that the older man was dead. A later article in the local paper has Fred galloping back to his fallen father, "coming to a skidding halt," and leaning over to look at the lifeless body on the ground. Maybe Fred's hesitation accounts for him still being within 385 feet when Simpson took his second shot.

Whatever Fred did, it was the last thing he did, for Ray Simpson put the next round into the base of Fred's skull (Horan says Fred died when Simpson's bullet "split his heart"). A citizen named John Travis reportedly fired several shots at the bandits with a revolver. He doesn't seem to have hit any of the outlaws, but it may have been one of his bullets that in fact killed Bill's unfortunate horse.

Simpson had done some truly fine shooting, whether the actual distances at which he fired are exaggerated or not. For by the time he fired at Fred, Simpson may have been as much as a block away from the fleeing bandits. Fred's corpse stayed in the saddle for a block, his horse galloping on, and there the second McCarty bit the dust. Asked about his marksmanship later, Simpson commented that where he came from in Kentucky, "boys are taught to shoot squirrels in the head to keep from spoiling the meat."

The usual moonshine surrounds the Delta robbery. Along with the "trusty Winchester" references, there is an account that has Simpson shooting Bill McCarty from the hip, and refers to Fred as Bill's nephew. The reference to Fred and the marble game also seems a little hard to swallow, for kids grew up fast in those days, and it's hard to imagine an experienced outlaw hunkered down in the dust with a couple of local urchins.

Along the way Simpson, or somebody, shot one of the outlaws' horses, an animal that a local citizen saw sprawled in the alley against the doorsill of a store. It was probably Bill's horse, which may have galloped back toward the bank after its rider was killed. The horse may have been mortally wounded by the same bullet that killed its rider, or so Simpson believed. Or maybe, according to another account of the raid, some unidentified "smart aleck" shot the animal. In any case, this horse trotted on down to the post office hitching rack, and stood among other horses until it bled to death. Fred's mount, dripping with its rider's blood, was caught by a local woman.

Tom, veteran outlaw, wanted nothing more to do with Simpson's deadly rifle, even if he did leave two kinsmen dead in the street behind him. As *Where the West Stayed Young* put it, Tom himself "let it be known later, however, that the two or three bullets Simpson sent in his direction came uncomfortably close." He realized that he and his gang had been well and truly whipped by a single man, and he did not stay upon the order of his going. He changed horses in the gang's camp outside town and lit out at the high lope for southwestern Colorado. He left behind several horses and a mule, and, as it turned out, he also left the bank-robbing business for good.

A manuscript, purporting to be McCarty's autobiography, was sent to his father-in-law, and was supposedly published by a newspaper in Manti, Utah. It is now in the possession of the Utah State Historical Society. Charles Kelly, who wrote of the Wild Bunch, believed the manuscript to be genuine. In it, McCarty tells his own story of the fight at Delta. Here he tells the story of the gang's flight:

> As we passed the first street I heard the sharp crack of a rifle, and looking for my partners, I saw one of them [Bill] fall from his horse; my other companion [Fred] being a little ahead, then partly turned his horse as though he wanted to see where the shot came from. I told him quickly to go on, but as I spoke another shot came which struck his horse and before he could get his animal in motion another shot came which struck him and he fell dead. His horse began to run back toward the place where the shots had come from. . . .
>
> [L]ooking back I saw a man standing by the corner of a building, having what I supposed was a Winchester and shooting as fast as possible at me. . . . The first man he killed could not have been more than twenty-five yards from him . . . the other about one hundred and fifty feet. . . . Several bullets passed so near me that I felt the force of the balls as they passed; one of his bullets struck my horse . . . near the heel, which crippled him. . . .
>
> [A]fter I had traveled about seventy-five miles I found some friends who told me that both of my relatives had been shot dead, both having received the bullets through the head.

After the raid there was some debate, dutifully reported by the Colorado papers, about the real identify of the dead outlaws. Some said they were obviously McCartys; others disagreed. At first it was thought that the older of the two dead bandits was Tom McCarty, not Bill. It did not take long to resolve the puzzle, once men who actually knew the family saw the corpses.

Delta sheriff W. S. Giradet raised a posse, which included the redoubtable Simpson, and gave chase, but could not come up with fleeing Tom McCarty. They recovered his horse, which was cut up, saddlesore, and exhausted, but McCarty had changed horses. The posse at last returned on September 12, the only reward a couple of McCarty's other horses and an abandoned pack. They had come close enough to the outlaw to find a campfire still burning, but they never saw the man himself.

One story of the raid relates a rumor that circulated in Delta, to the effect that the outlaws "had escaped attention by dressing up as women," a somewhat fanciful notion in view of Bill McCarty's prominent mustache and generally ugly visage. Nevertheless, a woman in Delta "suddenly found herself being followed by a crowd of fearless, gun-toting men who wanted to make sure she was indeed female and not a cleverly disguised bandit."

The remains of Tom McCarty's confederates were hauled off to Gale Brothers Undertaking Parlor. There, after they had set a while, both corpses were propped up to have their picture taken, after the fashion of the times. The photographer's son, young Ben Laycock, who was ten years old according to the Delta Historical Society, had been "bathing prints" in front of his father's shop when the fireworks began.

Ben helped out with the arrangements to photograph the bodies. Undertaker Gale, who also dealt in lumber and furniture, helped to prop up the remains. Fred was stiff enough to stand up on his own, but Bill kept sagging inconveniently. So Gale borrowed some boards from the lumberyard and propped Bill into a suitable upright position. They put Bill's hat on him to cover the spot where Simpson's bullet had shortened his head, and he stayed upright long enough for Ben's brother to take his photo. Bill promptly sagged and collapsed again after the picture was taken, but by then he was superfluous, and nobody cared.

In later years, Ben may have embellished a little on the tale of the photos. "The old man," he wrote, meaning Bill, was "limp as a wet sack," so Ben and Gale had to hold him up for his last picture. The rest of Ben's story is worth quoting:

> *Finally we put boards under his arms, and Gale and I held him until just as Henry was ready to take the picture. He looked like hell with the whole top of his head shot off, so Gale rustled around and got a hat to set on his head. We let go of him, jumped back out of the way, Henry snapped the picture, and we grabbed him before he toppled over on the ground.*

Well, maybe, but considering the length of time it took to make a decent exposure in those days, it may be that Ben is exaggerating just a mite. It's a good story, anyway.

Having done their duty for the camera, Bill and Fred were carted off to Potter's Field and planted in a single box, apparently without ceremony. The *Delta Independent* says they were dug up the following Sunday, twice, to be identified, then re-interred. In the miserable heat of the time, no doubt some haste in burial, and re-burial, was deemed appropriate. Another account tells us that Bill's uncle-by-marriage came from Moab, Utah, and a police officer arrived from Denver to identify the remains of the two bandits.

A vest found on one of the horses yielded an interesting insight into outlaw bookkeeping. The *Delta Independent* reported discovery of a notebook listing various purchases, "largely whiskey," the prices added together and divided by three: "my part," read a notation next to the result. Other notes listed the writer's gambling losses, presumably to his companions, showing the "grand total I owe: $493."

Blachley's funeral was attended by several hundred people, the largest crowd ever to turn out for a burial in Delta. The paper carried a eulogy by a local woman, which concluded,

> *And all who mourn their dead today*
> *Look on the bright and changing earth*
> *And see in shelter of decay,*
> *The symbol of immortal birth.*

DELTA COUNTY HISTORICAL SOCIETY

*A. T. Blachley*

The widow was left with nine sons, whom she raised on a "poor, barren, little ranch." The gallant lady was an Oberlin College graduate—quite a rarity on the frontier in those days—and supported her family by teaching music. It is pleasant to note that her boys went on to become prominent, educated men.

After the Delta disaster Tom McCarty dropped out of sight. One tale of the raid has him hiding out in Moab, Utah, sheltered by his brother-in-law, until a mysterious stranger came to town asking questions. McCarty then moved north to the Green River area, where he was supplied with food by his son Lew, a local saloonkeeper. The inquisitive stranger showed up in Green River as well, and McCarty moved on, meeting Harvey Logan and a defrocked priest called Cleophas Dowd.

The stranger trailed McCarty yet again, and Logan ambushed the man and shot him down. He was, in Tom's opinion, the "damned Pinkerton what's been on my trail for two years since the Delta job." The author of this version tells us that he later secured a letter to Dowd from Logan, sent from Kansas City in the spring of 1896, which read in part like this: "I never did explain too good killing that Pinkerton in your back yard but you know he needed killing . . . I now [sic] you was upset about it at the time and I was only thinking about stopping the sneaky bastard before he stopped us."

Some sources report that a shaken McCarty headed back to his hideout in the Blue Mountains to brood upon the repulse of his last raid. Maybe so. After all, he had lost two kinsmen to a single rifleman, and had taken to his heels in flight. His ignominious retreat could not have fit with his own image of himself. In any case, his sulking is supposed to have given rise to one of the most colorful tales in the history of American outlawry. It goes like this:

In the fall of 1896, Tom McCarty sent word to Simpson, by then Delta's postmaster, that he was going to kill him. Just how that message was sent, not every version of the tale recounts. Horan says McCarty came to Delta and sent "an emissary" to tell Simpson he was doomed. Simpson's answer was classic. He sent McCarty—by emissary or otherwise—a small card punched with ten bullet holes, put there by Simpson "at 225 feet," "with his new Winchester." Charles Kelly's *The Outlaw Trail* states that after Simpson received the threat from McCarty, "a government detective was sent to trap the outlaw if possible."

> *To this operative Simpson presented his famous card, with instructions to deliver it to McCarty at the earliest opportunity. It consisted of a small piece of black cardboard perforated with ten holes, all within the circumference of half a dollar.*

At 225 feet? Some shooting, that, extraordinary even with a modern rifle and first-class optical sights. This version of the tale also does not explain how the detective was supposed to make delivery.

Still another account, by a Delta resident, tells that Simpson received threatening letters for years after the raid, and that Mrs. Simpson "suffered a complete nervous breakdown" and died when the couple's youngest daughter was very small. Another version of the raid does not mention the famous card at all, but does repeat the story that in later years Simpson received threatening letters, supposedly from McCarty. This account says Simpson was finally forced to leave Delta and settle in California. He is said to be buried in Glendale.

Considerable uncertainty surrounds Tom McCarty's later years. Variously, it is claimed, he was shot to death in about 1900 up in Montana's Bitterroot country after he picked a fight with the wrong man; he was killed near Green River, Utah; he died in Skagway, Alaska, during the gold rush; or he died in California, where he lived with his son Lew. One account, the most reliable one, has him living peacefully in Wallowa County, Oregon, after the turn of the century, even becoming a justice of the peace and "road supervisor."

One source says that McCarty corresponded for years with a friend in Brown's Park, Colorado. The return address on his letters was Rosebud, Montana, where he is said to have worked herding sheep. Author Kelly surmises that McCarty probably dictated his autobiography at Robber's Roost about 1898, and was killed shortly thereafter.

However Tom McCarty ended his days, he must have been forever haunted by that hot day in Colorado, the day he ran from a single citizen, leaving his kinsmen dead in the dust behind him.

## THE HARD MEN OF CAMPO

### *The Formidable Gaskill Boys*

IN 1875, THE TINY SETTLEMENT called Campo was an important stop on the road from Yuma to the California coast at San Diego. It lay about 50 miles east of San Diego, not far above the Mexican border, in relatively high country that provided some relief from the dreary heat of the flatland to the east. The town was situated along a pleasant creek of clear, cold water, the land studded with sycamores and oaks. The place had been called *Milquetay* at one time, an Indian name meaning "wide, flat fields." But its new name came from an extraordinary pair of settlers, the formidable brothers Gaskill.

Campo was no metropolis, but it offered all that a traveler could want in that desolate country. There was a small hotel, a combination general store and cantina, a blacksmith shop, a post and telegraph office founded by the army, and a number of miscellaneous buildings. There was also a very large house, luxurious by the standards of that time and place. This complex was the home of the brothers Gaskill, the kings of Campo. In addition to operating the store, the hotel, and the forge, they also ran cattle over some 900 acres, raised hogs and sheep, and shipped large quantities of honey from their 400 hives. The Gaskill boys were entrepreneurs.

They were also very tough men indeed. Silas Edward, forty-six, and Lumen (or Luman) Humphrey, thirty-two, came of a fiddle-footed family that arrived in California by ship, by way of the Isthmus of Panama. The family occupation, at least in California, was apparently mining, and the boys had been bear hunters up in northern California before founding their Campo empire. Silas was heard to claim that he had killed 302 bears, and in view of what happened later in Campo, the claim might well have been true.

Lumen was known around Petaluma, California, as something of a healer, a mixer of home remedies for almost anything that ailed you. He also had a somewhat darker side to his reputation. Men said that years earlier, he had killed a man up in San Joaquin County, after which he removed himself to San Jacinto, in the south, and lived there under an alias. The brothers had lost none of their pugnacious manner when they came south to make their fortunes along the Mexican border. It is said that even cattle rustlers stayed clear of the Gaskill boys' herds, in spite of the settlement's isolation and the nearby sanctuary of Mexico.

In an 1889 article, the *San Diego Union* painted a vivid picture of the Gaskill boys' formidable reputation:

> *In those days it was very warm along the border, and a man had to be able to shoot, and shoot quick, or he would stand very little chance of dying of old age. Luman Gaskill and his brother Silas were two of that class who could protect themselves even if their safety was at the price of the lives of their opponents, and that was usually the case.*

Lumen had married Eliza Benson, a Utahan, in 1868. In the same year the brothers settled in the place along the Mexican border called Milquetay by the Indians, and renamed it Campo. They steadily acquired more and more land, until, by 1875, Campo had grown into an important way station. The ten-mule-team freight wagons that served Fort Yuma came through Campo, and the Capron stagecoach line stopped there twice a week.

Down below the border lay the settlement of Tecarte, now called Tecate, which in those days was something of a headquarters for a rich assortment of thieves and murderers. For a while they stayed away from the Gaskill boys and the buildings at Campo, knowing the tough brothers' reputation and aware of the fact that the Campo settlement was, as a San Diego newspaper put it, "always in a condition of defense."

Among the worst of the Mexican marauders were a number of survivors of the gang once led by the infamous Tiburcio Vasquez. Some of them had reportedly also followed the vicious and much-feared Joaquin Murieta, whose head, suitably preserved in a jar of alcohol, had long glowered spitefully at visitors to Dr. Jordan's raree show in San Francisco.

Vasquez was also history. Jumped by lawmen near Los Angeles in the spring of 1874, he had been knocked down by two loads of buckshot and captured. At his trial, according to a newspaper account, he "declared his captors could hang him as soon as they pleased." And they did.

Others were ready to take his place, however. One of these, a bad hat called Colodovio Chavez, died with his boots on the preceding November. He had been planning a ranch robbery when he was accosted by two tough cattlemen named Roberts (or maybe a single rancher named Clark Clotvig). Chavez objected to being arrested and the Roberts boys—or Clotvig—obliged by shooting him dead. The brothers pickled his head in a cask of brandy, the better to preserve it and collect the reward offered from the state capital in Sacramento.

With Chavez dead, one Cruz Lopez, fresh from murdering a shopkeeper in California, had succeeded to the mantle of outlaw leadership, and he was putting the old gang together again. Lopez, who might well be called a homicidal maniac, meant to recruit a large outlaw army to murder, rape, and pillage down in Sonora, and for that he needed arms and supplies. He figured to get them by raiding some of the isolated ranches up across the border in the United States, and he set his sights on the Gaskill spread.

It was not a good idea at all.

Lopez collected a large contingent of hoodlums down in Tecarte and made his plans. He would hit the Gaskill place with overwhelming numbers, and carry off the loot in a couple of wagons, which would wait down the road while Lopez and his boys murdered the Gaskills and anybody else they might meet. The brothers would be caught unsuspecting and unready.

But they were not. Years later, Silas Gaskill described the event:

*I was working at the forge when I learned that the robbers were going to raid us. A Mexican was hanging around the shop and he seemed to be pretty nervous. I was busy and paid no attention to him. He waited until he could talk to me alone. Then he slipped up and whispered in my ear. He said Pancho Lopez and his gang were coming to clean us out. I had been on good terms with the informer and fed him occasionally when he was broke.*

And so the Gaskills prepared. They rounded up six shotguns—all muzzle-loaders—and set them in strategic places: the forge, the stable, the post office, the house, and a spot outside near the post office. And then, being the hard, bold Gaskills and having work to do, they calmly went on with their chores.

The outlaws were on the way, murdering and robbing as they came. Just four days after Chavez was shot down, Cruz Lopez showed up in a town about 40 miles south of Tecarte. From there, it appears, he set up the ambush murder and robbery of an American store clerk named Henry Leclaire, whose buggy was carrying some $600 in gold to San Diego. Leclaire never made it, and with him died a well-known passenger, Don Antonio Sosa, sometime Mexican governor of Baja California.

That was the end of November. On the morning of December 4, Lopez led his men off to raid the Gaskill complex at Campo. His strike force numbered six men, himself included. The poisonous Lopez had an ugly reputation. It seems he made something of a fetish out of murder, and "delighted in killing." As the *San Diego Union* reported, he "fancied he knew just where to send the bullet that would glaze the eyes and speed the soul. With him, to kill poorly argued poor professional skill."

Down the road behind Lopez and his raiders, his two teams and wagons waited, ready to haul away the booty they thought they would find at the Gaskill complex. Standing by with the wagons were no fewer than nine more outlaws, and still another, Raphael Martinez, was already in Campo. Altogether, Lopez should have had more than enough muscle and firepower to overwhelm a peaceful little settlement and two hardworking men.

The six outlaws rode into Campo about 10:00, dismounted, and spread out, apparently according to plan. Jose Alvijo and Alonzo Cota went into the Gaskill store, where Rafael Martinez was already trying to look inconspicuous. Martinez then went outside and met Teodoro Vasquez, a relation of the unmourned Tiburcio Vasquez, and Pancho Alvitro, a murderer wanted in Los Angeles. Lopez, the leader, positioned himself by the doorway to the store, from which he could watch his cohorts both inside and out. The idea seems to have been to attack and murder both Gaskill brothers, by surprise and separately.

The bandits chose a moment when Lumen Gaskill was working in the store and his brother Silas was in or near the blacksmith shop, working on a wagon bed. A pile of rocks made it impossible for one brother to see the other, so the situation should have been perfect for the assassins. As Lopez, Cota, and Alvijo reached for their guns, however, several things happened at once. Into town rode a man described as a tall French sheepherder, come to pick up mail for his boss. Lumen saw the outlaws pulling their guns, shouted "Murder!" and dropped flat on the floor behind the counter, trying to reach his shotgun, some distance away.

Two of the outlaws leaped over the counter and jumped on him before he could reach his weapon. They managed to hold Lumen down until Lopez closed in. He pushed his pistol close to Gaskill's face, aimed at his heart, and fired.

Or maybe Alvijo did the shooting. In any case, the bullet slammed into Lumen's chest and tore through one lung, smashing a rib. Blood poured from Lumen's mouth. One story of the raid says that one of the outlaws urged Lopez to shoot Lumen again, but the bandit leader was sure of his point-blank marksmanship. Certain that Lumen was finished, the outlaws left him alone on the floor behind the counter, in a puddle of blood.

Meanwhile, Silas, hearing his brother's shout, bounded over the wagon bed and grabbed a shotgun leaning inside the door to the forge. As Vasquez charged through the door of the shop, he fired at Silas with a revolver, wounding him in the side. Silas stayed on his feet, however, and his return fire put a load of buckshot in the middle of Vasquez's chest, whereof, in the quaint terminology of the day, Vasquez forthwith expired.

Running outside, Silas met Alvitro and Martinez, and put the second barrel into Martinez. Alvitro, apparently unable to count to two, the number of barrels of the shotgun, ran for cover behind a pile of lumber near the Gaskill mill. Silas sprinted toward the house, handed his empty shotgun to a passing stranger named Livingston, and ran inside to get another shotgun.

In the excitement he could not find one, but that did not stop the redoubtable Silas. Running back, he discovered Alvitro back in the open and pointing a pistol at Livingston. Silas grabbed his empty weapon from Livingston and brandished it at the dense Alvitro, who still had not figured out that two loaded barrels minus two emptied barrels equals nothing left to shoot with. Panicked by the empty weapon, Alvitro again took flight, running for cover behind the blacksmith shop.

The "French sheepherder," seeing this band of desperados trying to murder the Gaskills and take over little Campo, promptly joined the action himself. On foot, firing across his horse's back, he hit Lopez in the neck with a slug that knocked the bandit leader down and drove a chunk of cloth from Lopez's overcoat into the wound. Lopez was still shooting at him, however, and Cota and Alvijo, running out of the store, also opened fire on the Frenchman, who was badly hit in both arms.

About now, bloody and bedraggled, Lumen Gaskill reentered the fight. He crawled to get his shotgun, and then pulled himself to the doorway of the store. There, on his belly, slowly recovering from temporary paralysis of his left arm and leg, Lumen was still full of fight. He rested his weapon across his still-numb left arm and promptly dropped Alvitro with the first barrel of his shotgun. Then, seeing Alvitro retreating from Silas Gaskill's empty weapon, Lumen put the second barrel into him.

His shotgun empty, his vision blurring badly, Lumen now crawled back into the store and slipped through a trapdoor into the swift little creek that ran beneath it, a stream so cold that it was used to preserve perishable items for short periods. Standing in the water, he met the local telegrapher, who just then was taking the best cover he could find. He told Lumen that he had also exchanged fire with the outlaws, although the San Diego newspaper later scoffed that the telegraphist was a "coward," "quaking with fear," who hid instead of helping the beleaguered brothers.

Lumen then worked his way painfully up the creek toward the house, the cold water helping to staunch the blood pouring from his wound. Though his vision was badly blurred, he was still determined to reach his home, find his .45-70 Springfield, and carry on the war. When he arrived home, however, he was so soaked in blood that a terrified Eliza did not at first recognize him.

"Don't you know Lumen?" he said.

"Are you my husband?"

"Yes."

"Are you hurt?"

"No, I guess not, but I may be killed."

Once his wife recognized Lumen and let him in, he picked up his rifle and staggered back to the front porch, undaunted and still full of fight. But now, soaked in gore and spitting great gouts of blood from his lung wound, he was too weak even to raise the weapon.

He did not need to, for by now it had become clear to the embattled outlaws that they had bitten off a lot more than they could chew. Lopez, Alvitro, and Cota, who was the only unwounded hoodlum, galloped out of town, leaving Vasquez dead on the ground and the badly wounded Alvijo crawling off into the brush to hide. Cota carried the only loot from the busted robbery, a sack of useless pistols, all of which needed maintenance and were unserviceable. The bandit reinforcements apparently heard the heavy firing in Campo, drew the correct conclusions, and promptly took flight.

As news of the attack spread across the border country, ranchers began to converge on Campo from all over the surrounding countryside. In the process, Rafael Martinez, wounded, was apprehended. Among the men who answered Campo's cry for help was a San Diego doctor named Millard, who rode 75 miles, much of it through Mexico, arriving at Campo about 11:00 P.M. Dr. Millard immediately went to work on Lumen and concluded that the tough rancher had a "fair chance for recovering under favorable circumstances." The doctor then turned to help Silas, whose wounds were serious but less dangerous than his brother's.

In the afternoon, a posse of ten ranchers rode out on the Yuma road to the east, and parties of Indian trackers fanned out, looking for traces of the fleeing outlaws. One such party found the body of Alvitro, quite dead, near the road about 3 miles west of Campo. There is a very good chance that the wounded outlaw, unable to keep up with his comrades, had been murdered by Lopez, perhaps afraid of what Alvitro might tell the local law.

As for Lopez, the *San Diego Union* told its readers that the battered bandit, fleeing on foot, had stopped on his way to Mexico to build a fire to warm himself. Then, when he got going again, he lost his bearings and walked the wrong way until he was back at Campo. In any case, early the next morning, Lopez, shaking with cold and full of buckshot, tottered up to the Gaskills' door and asked for help. He said he had fallen from a horse, but as he stood by a fire in the room where Lumen Gaskill lay wounded, he was recognized.

Lopez was put under guard along with Martinez, under the eye of Sheriff Hunsaker, of San Diego, and three deputies, who by then had arrived in Campo. But that evening, while the sheriff and two of his officers were elsewhere, a band of local men emerged out of the night and disappeared with the two Sonora outlaws. The jailer, also named Gaskill, facilely explained, with his own somewhat creative spelling, that a "gang of men came into the room . . . tied my hands and took the prisenor out of the room. That is all I no of the prisenors now deceased." And deceased they surely were. They were found the next day, hanging from a tree by a single piece of rope, a curious display of economy.

The hanging seems to have irritated the residents of the outlaw town of Tecarte considerably, and swarms of hostile Mexicans rode in from other parts of Sonora already in a state of chaos. Dozens of campfires gleamed in the valley near the town, and on the American side, the ranchers banded together in Campo, stockpiling supplies and preparing for war. On the fourteenth of December, Silas Gaskill wrote to a friend in San Diego, complaining of the tension around his home:

> We have been told by parties from Ticarte that they intend to try us again; that they are determined to rob us before they give up. They say they will try it next time with a force sufficient to go through us. It seems rather tough that we can't be protected in some way from being robbed and murdered here at home.

A great deal of worry and dither followed. Posses were formed and a small army detachment was stationed at Campo. In the end, nothing came of the threats and posturing of the Tecarte contingent, and the Campo country slowly returned to normal. Tough Lumen Gaskill survived, although at the outset even he supposed he would not recover. Just after the fight, when his worried wife wanted him to lie down on the bed, Lumen answered, "No, I'll lay on the floor. I can't last long. There's no sense in getting the bed all dirty." A tough cookie, this pioneer; although he didn't know it just then, he still had many years left to live.

Not so, however, the valiant Frenchman who had pitched in to help the Gaskill boys. His arm wounds worsened, and he died several days after the fight. He had heard, or been told, of an expert San Francisco doctor who, he hoped, might have the skill to save his life. Trouble was, the Frenchman had to spend several days on a coastal boat to San Francisco, and by the time he arrived, he was so far gone that the doctor could only fill him with morphine and let him die easily.

But the Frenchman had his revenge, for murderous Cruz Lopez would die very hard indeed. He never recovered from the neck wound the Frenchman had given him, which abscessed and grew steadily worse as he ran from the law. About a year after the Campo raid, Lopez was dead, and the ghastly abscess had grown to cover his entire face. That made the box score four very dead bandits, with two more wounded and long gone, not counting the fainthearted reinforcements. There may have been still another bandit involved in the attack, but if there was, he too had disappeared.

Nothing daunted by their close call, the Gaskill boys stayed on in Campo and prospered. They had eyes on the government contract to carry the United States mail between San Diego and Fort Yuma, over on the Arizona border. To move that mail, they built an elaborate steam engine, designed to cross any sort of terrain they might encounter on the long haul. Trouble was, the thing consumed more fuel and water than it would carry, and the boys had to abandon their cherished scheme to win the mail contract. The great engine became the driving power for a Gaskill sawmill.

One thing the Gaskills did not have to worry about in these days was rustling or robbery. According to the *San Diego Union*, the surviving bandits spoke for the criminal fraternity along the border: "Those Gaskills are devils," they said, "and cannot be killed with lead bullets." Silas Gaskill tersely summed up the effects of the brothers' victory: "They left us alone after that."

Even so, all was not beer and skittles for the Gaskill boys; not everything they touched succeeded. There was their attempt to grow sugar cane, for example, a crop that did not prosper for them. And then there were the accusations against Lumen Gaskill. South of the Gaskill spread, in Baja California, lay the ranch of one Captain Jacob B. Hanson. In 1885, Captain Hanson suddenly disappeared, and he had been last seen at Campo on a trip to San Diego. Worse, his buggy was discovered at the Gaskill place, sporting a fresh coat of paint. Beneath the paint were marks that might have been the pockmarks from a load of shot.

In August of that year, three men were arrested by Mexican authorities at Hanson's ranch in Baja California. One of them was Lumen Gaskill. The men were held in jail in Ensenada, and in December of 1896, Lumen and one other man were convicted of changing the brands on Hanson's cattle. The third man, having escaped, was quick to tell the papers that Lumen and his companion had Hanson's papers and billfold, and were "guilty of the murder of Captain Hanson, but it could not be proved."

Lumen never served any time, however. It seems the local authorities lost interest in transporting their prisoner to the territorial prison in La Paz once they discovered the cost. Neither did they have the money to feed him. And so Lumen Gaskill was simply released and told to report to the governor every day. He was apparently kept on a long leash, however, for he was remembered in the border country as the man who spread word of a gold strike at a place called Santa Clara, some 50 miles from Ensenada. He seems to have dabbled in mining in Mexico, and in the fullness of time simply rode away from his Mexican detention and returned to Campo.

Lumen sold out at Campo in 1901. He was fifty-eight, maybe feeling the aches of all the years on the frontier, maybe tired of the hard life of the southern border. In any case, Lumen moved to San Diego and left Campo for good. He is said to have died in Whittier or Los Angeles, California, in May 1914, and one account has him buried in Los Angeles.

Curiously, however, the Waitsburg City Cemetery in Walla Walla County, Washington, lists "Luman H. Gaskill" as one of its permanent residents, records the correct years of birth and death, and shows that Eliza was buried with him. Wherever Lumen rests, he was survived by two sons and three daughters.

Silas passed on in the same year, in San Diego. He had married at some time in the 1870s, but he and his bride soon parted. Silas married a Boston woman named Catherine in 1881. This marriage took, and the two were together until Silas died more than thirty years later. After the raid, Silas seems to have avoided the drama that followed the life of his brother, living quietly and moving to San Diego at some time prior to 1897. He is buried there.

Interviewed by a reporter shortly before his death, he recalled the Campo fight clearly:

> *We had heard of some of the depredations of this gang, . . . and were not going to take any chances. They were the remnant of the old Vasquez gang . . . they made it a practice to murder people and rob ranch houses. We didn't encourage that sort of thing at Campo.*

They sure didn't.

## THE SIXTH RIDER

### *Terminal Arrogance at Coffeyville*

THEY RODE IN FROM the west on a crisp, brilliant October morning in 1892, a little group of five dusty young men. They laughed and bayed at the sheep and goats along the way, enjoying the lovely autumn morning. In a few minutes they would kill some citizens who had never harmed them. And in just a few minutes more, four of these carefree riders were going to die.

These young men planned to rob the First National Bank and the Condon Bank in bustling Coffeyville, Kansas. Three of the men were brothers named Dalton, and they knew the town, or thought they did, for in the past they had lived nearby for several years. Not so long before, Coffeyville had been a raucous railhead town, accustomed to trail herds and wild cowboys and lots of booze and prostitutes and barroom fights and such. But these days it was a prosperous, peaceful place, center of a thriving wheat-farming district, a quiet settlement where the town marshal—a schoolteacher filling in as a lawman—didn't even carry a gun.

The Dalton boys knew the law was already breathing down their necks. Even now, bulldog Deputy U.S. Marshal Heck Thomas was on their trail, and only a day or so behind them. During their last train holdup, the Dalton Gang had shot down a couple of unarmed, inoffensive civilians, and in doing so had committed one of the few mortal sins of the frontier: Both the men they had shot were doctors, an unwritten

37

protected profession in the West. One of the wounded doctors was dead. Now, with every man's hand against them, they were determined to pull off one final job, a robbery that would equip them with enough loot to take them far away from pursuing lawmen.

For Bob Dalton, leader of the pack, there was also a certain outlaw braggadocio attached to the Coffeyville raid. They would do, he boasted, what no outlaws had ever done before. They would rob two banks at once, a feat not even managed by their famous cousins, the Younger boys, now languishing in a Minnesota prison, nor by the Youngers' boon companions, Frank and Jesse James.

Now, more than a century after the raid, much of what really happened that pleasant day in Coffeyville is lost in the chilly, swirling mists of time. Today it's hard to sort out fact from invention, and one of the remaining riddles is this one: How many bandits actually rode up out of the Indian Territory to steal the precious savings of hardworking Kansas citizens? Most historians say there were five raiders, but some argue there was a sixth man, one who fled once the shooting started, leaving his comrades to die under the flaming rifles of Coffeyville's angry citizens.

Coffeyville was wholly unprepared for a raid from the most notorious outlaw gang of the day. In such a peaceful little town, where nobody carried a gun anymore, the gang might have gotten away with stealing the citizens' savings. But Coffeyville was a town with a penchant for civic improvement, and while some of its downtown streets were being paved, the city fathers had moved the very hitching-rack to which the gang had planned to tether their horses. All this came as a complete surprise to the robbers, for they had done no planning worthy of the name.

The outlaws rode around the busy streets until they found a spot in an alley behind the police judge's house. There they tied their mounts to a pipe in that narrow passage, which is today called Death Alley. Some of them attached some unconvincing false hair to their faces and together they walked down the alley, five dusty men carrying Winchesters. They crossed an open plaza where several streets came together, and walked into the two unsuspecting banks. Tall, handsome Bob Dalton was the leader, an intelligent man with a fearsome reputation as a rifle marksman. Grat, the eldest, was a slow-witted thug whose avocations were thumping other

*The Dalton Gang after their last raid*

people, gambling, and sopping up prodigious amounts of liquor. As Harold Preece put it, "Grat had the heft of a bull calf and the disposition of a baby rattlesnake." Emmett, or "Em," was the baby of the lot, only twenty-one on the day of the raid, but already an experienced robber. The boys came from a family of fifteen kids, the offspring of Adeline Younger—aunt to the outlaw Younger boys—and shiftless Lewis Dalton, sometime farmer, saloonkeeper, and horse-fancier.

Backing the Dalton boys were two experienced members of the gang, Dick Broadwell and Bill Powers. Powers was a Texas boy who punched cows down on the Cimarron before he decided that robbing people was easier than working. Broadwell, scion of a good Kansas family, allegedly went wrong after a comely young lady stole both his heart and his bankroll, and left him flat in Fort Worth. Perhaps because he was reluctant to split the expected booty more than five ways, Bob left behind several veteran gang members, journeymen criminals like Bill Doolin, Bitter Creek Newcomb, and Charlie Pierce.

Grat Dalton led Powers and Broadwell into the Condon. Em and Bob went on across the street to the First National. Inside, they threw down on customers and employees and began to direct the bank men to deliver the banks' money and be damn quick about it. What the robbers did not know was that somebody—probably a storekeeper who had known the Dalton family when they lived near Coffeyville before—had recognized one of the brothers as they crossed the plaza. He quickly spread the word that the dreaded Daltons were in town, and the citizens began to search about for weapons.

Next door to the First National was Isham's Hardware, which looked out on the front door of the Condon and into the plaza, and from there down Death Alley, where the gang had left its horses, 300 feet or more away. Isham's and another hardware store started handing out weapons to anybody who wanted them, and more than a dozen public-spirited citizens armed themselves and prepared to ventilate the gang as it left the banks.

Inside the First National, Bob and Emmett had taken a sack full of cash, in spite of the bank men's deliberate foot-dragging. The brothers finished up their looting, collected some hostages, and then pushed out the door into the plaza. That's when all hell broke loose in Coffeyville.

The first shots were fired at Emmett and Bob, who dove back into the First National. Bob shot one citizen through the hand, and then he and his brother ran out the back door. The two kept going, circling around through a side street, out of sight of the waiting citizens, killing a young store clerk along the way. Bob was ready, he told his brother, to do the fighting. Emmett's function was to carry their loot in the grain sack that was standard equipment for robbers of the day.

Inside the Condon Bank, Grat had started out collecting a prodigious pile of silver, so heavy that it would take more than one man to carry it. Then, when he got down to harvesting the portable cash, he had been entirely bamboozled by a courageous young employee, Charley Ball. Ball looked the outlaw square in the eye and blandly announced that the time lock to the vault, which had opened long before, would not unlock for several minutes. "Eight minutes," crowed a later newspaper report, "was the time consumed by Cashier Ball in his one-act skit of 'the Bogus Time Lock.'"

That eight minutes saved the bank treasure and cost the Dalton Gang its existence. While Ball courageously sold credulous Grat Dalton this colossal fib, another employee helpfully rattled the vault doors to complete the illusion. He didn't pull on the doors, of course, because, had he done so, they would have swung open.

Grat, instead of trying those doors himself, stood stupidly and waited for the hands of the clock to move, while outside the townsmen loaded Winchesters and found cover. About the time thickheaded Grat began to suspect that he was being had, somebody outside fired a shot, and the battle of Coffeyville was on. A pair of house painters bailed off their scaffolding and hit the ground running, women shooed their children indoors, and the gathering of defenders over at Isham's opened up. One especially courageous soul even crawled out on a porch roof and began popping away with a pistol.

Bullets began to punch through the windows of the Condon Bank, and one tore into Broadwell's left arm. "I'm hit!" he yelled. "I can't use my arm!" Grat, Broadwell, and Powers could not match the firepower of the citizens, as some 200 projectiles of various sizes slammed into the windows and facade of the Condon. One defender at Isham's was hit in the chest by a rifle round and knocked flat, but all he got from the outlaw bullet was a bruised chest, for the slug had hit an iron spanner he carried in his shirt pocket.

The townsmen's heavy and accurate fire convinced even dull-witted Grat Dalton that it was high time to go. Leaving behind their enormous heap of coins, the three outlaws charged out into the bullet-swept plaza, running hard for their horses, now so very far away down the alley. They ran straight into the line of fire of the rifles at the hardware store. There was no cover for them all the way down the alley, and it must have seemed as if everybody in town was shooting at them. The citizens in the hardware store opened up on them as they ran, and men were also firing at them from the offices upstairs in the Condon.

Here Grat's lack of even rudimentary good sense again showed itself. Grat could have led his men around the corner on which the bank sat. Had he done so, they would have been out of sight of that deadly nest of riflemen at Isham's in just a couple of strides, at least until some of the citizens could leave the store, run across a street, and follow the

*Bob Dalton and an unidentified woman, possibly Eugenia Moore*

outlaws around the corner. Or he could have sought the bank's back door, through which an upstairs tenant had poked his head—and instantly withdrawn it—during the robbery.

Instead, Grat led his men out into the plaza in front of the bank, directly into the killing zone, running hard for the alley and snapping shots at the men inside Isham's Hardware. All three outlaws were hit before they reached their horses. Witnesses saw dust puff from their clothing as rifle bullets tore into them.

Meanwhile, Bob and Emmett ran out of the First National down the alley behind it and around a block, still out of the defenders' sight. They came in behind the townsmen, who were still facing down the street toward the First National and the Condon. Bob shot down a shoemaker armed with a rifle. An older man, a Civil War veteran and also a cobbler, reached for the fallen man's weapon and Bob killed him, too. He then drove a round through the cheek of still another citizen, and then the outlaw brothers fled, trying to get to Grat and the all-important horses.

They kept a block of buildings between them and those deadly rifles, then turned down a little passage and emerged in the alley about the time Grat and the others got there. About the same time, Town Marshal Charles Connelly appeared in the alley from another direction, but miscalculated the position of the fleeing outlaws and came in between them and their horses. Grat, already wounded, shot the lawman down from behind. Liveryman John Kloehr, the town's most expert shot, then put already-wounded Grat down for good with a bullet in the neck.

As Bob and Emmett ran into the alley, somebody—or several somebodies—nailed Bob Dalton, who sat down on a pile of cobblestones, dying. Still game, he kept on working his Winchester and fired several aimless shots, one of which slammed into a box of dynamite over at Isham's. Then tough John Kloehr drove a bullet into Bob's chest and put him down to stay. The outlaw leader slumped over on his side and died in the alley. Powers lay dead in the dust about 10 feet away.

Broadwell, mortally wounded, still managed to get to his horse and ride a half-day. Young Emmett, still carrying the grain sack of loot from the First National, miraculously managed to get mounted. Hit several times in quick succession, he jerked his horse back into the teeth of the citizens' fire, reaching down from the saddle for his dead or dying brother Bob. There's a good deal of mythology about Bob's last words to his brother, "Don't surrender. Die game!" or something similar, but all that dramatic stuff comes in later years from Emmett, never renowned for adherence to the truth. Whatever Bob Dalton may or may not have said, Carey Seaman, the town barber, chose that moment to blow Emmett out of the saddle with both barrels of his shotgun, and the fight was over.

Four citizens were dead. Three more were wounded. The man with a rifle slug through one cheek was hurt very seriously indeed, and at first was expected to die. Four bandits had also died, and Emmett was punched full of holes—more than twenty of them. He was carried up to the second-floor office of Dr. Wells, who set out to try to save the young outlaw's life.

While the doctor was at work, a group of citizens, angry at the death of four of their fellows, appeared in the doctor's office carrying a rope. The idea was to tie one end to a telegraph pole outside the doctor's window, attach the other end to Emmett, and throw him out the window. "No use, boys," said the doctor. "He will die anyway." "Are you sure, doc?" said a voice from the crowd. "Hell, yes," said Doctor Wells, "Did you ever hear of a patient of mine getting well?" That broke the tension, somebody laughed, and at last cooler heads prevailed. Emmett was saved, preserved for trial and a long spell in the Kansas State Penitentiary.

The four expired bandits were propped up to have their pictures taken after the custom of the time, both vertically and horizontally, and people came from far and near to see the corpses and collect souvenirs: bits of bloody cloth, hairs from the dead horses, and so on. Some brought the kids, thinking that the edifying sight of dead bandits was helpful in keeping the young on the straight and narrow path of righteousness. Some of the sightseers indulged in a macabre experiment in hydraulics, for somebody discovered that if you worked Grat Dalton's arm up and down like a pump handle, blood squirted out of the hole in his throat.

The rifles at the hardware store, John Kloehr, and Carey Seaman, had accounted for all the bandits . . . or did they? Emmett always said there were only five bandits involved in the raid. However, four sober, respectable townsfolk, the Hollingsworths and the Seldomridges, said they passed six riders heading into town on the morning of the raid, although nobody else who saw the outlaws thought there were more than five. Two days after the fight, David Stewart Elliott, editor of the *Coffeyville Journal* and the only reliable historian of the raid, had this to say: "It is supposed the sixth man was too well-known to risk coming into the heart of the city, and that he kept off some distance and watched the horses."

Later, in his excellent *Last Raid of the Daltons*, Elliott did not mention a sixth rider, although in his book he used much of the text of his newspaper story about the raid. Maybe he had talked again to the Seldomridges and Hollingsworths, and maybe they told him they could not be certain there were six riders. Maybe, but still another citizen also said more than five bandits had attacked Coffeyville. Many years later, Tom Babb, one of the courageous employees of the Condon Bank, told a reporter that he had seen a sixth man gallop out of Death Alley. According to Babb, the man rode away from that deadly plaza, turned south, and disappeared.

If Tom Babb saw anything, it might have been Bitter Creek Newcomb, one of several nominees for sixth man. He was a veteran gang member, said to have been left out of the raid because he was given to loose talk. However, one story has Bitter Creek riding in from the south "to support the gang from a different angle." If he did, Babb might have seen him from the Condon's windows, which faced south.

The trouble with Babb's story is not the part about seeing a sixth bandit; it's the rest of it. After Grat and his men left the Condon Bank, Babb says, he ran madly through the crossfire between Isham's Hardware and the fleeing bandits, dashed around a block, and arrived in the alley as the sixth man galloped past: "He was lying down flat on his saddle, and that horse of his was going as fast as he could go." Finally, he stood "right next" to Kloehr, the valiant liveryman, as Kloehr cut down two of the gang. Maybe so. Babb was young and eager, and, as he said, "I could run pretty fast in those days."

Still, it's a little hard to imagine anybody sprinting through a storm of gunfire, unarmed, dashing clear around a city block, and fetching up in an alley ravaged by rifle slugs. To stand next to Kloehr, he would probably have had to run directly past the outlaws, still shooting at anything that moved. And nobody else mentioned Babb's extraordinary dash, although at least a dozen townsmen were in position to have seen it if it had happened.

Even so, there is no hard evidence to contradict Babb. Nor is there any reason to think that his memory had faded when he told his story. Maybe he exaggerated, wanting just a little more part in the defense of the town than he had actually taken . . . and maybe he told the literal truth. So, if Babb and the others were right, who was the fabulous sixth man?

Well, the most popular candidate was always Bill Doolin, who in 1896 told several lawmen he rode along on the raid. No further questioning was ever possible, because in 1896 Doolin shot it out with the implacable Heck Thomas and placed second. A whole host of writers supported Doolin's tale. His horse went lame, the story goes, and Doolin turned aside to catch another mount, arriving in town too late to help his comrades. The obvious trouble with this theory is that neither Bob Dalton nor any other bandit leader would have attacked his objective short-handed instead of waiting a few minutes for one of his best guns to steal a new horse.

Nevertheless, the Doolin enthusiasts theorized that Doolin had grabbed his new horse and was on his way to catch up with the gang when he met a citizen riding furiously to warn the countryside. The man stopped to ask Doolin if he had met any bandits. Doolin cleverly said he hadn't, and, ever resourceful, added: "Holy smoke! I'll just wheel around right here and go on ahead of you down this road and carry the news. Mine is a faster horse than yours." According to a quaint little book called *Oklahoma Outlaws* by Richard Graves, Doolin then "started on a ride that has ever since been the admiration of horse-men in the Southwest. . . . Doolin . . . crossed the Territory like a flying wraith . . . a ghostly rider saddled upon the wind."

The "flying wraith" and "ghostly rider" language is much repeated, for the words are certainly evocative. One writer says Doolin "never stopped" until he reached sanctuary "west of Tulsa," which is a distance of at least 100 miles. What a horse.

But before anybody dismisses Doolin as the sixth bandit, there's another piece of evidence, and it comes from a solid source. Fred Dodge, an experienced Wells Fargo agent, stuck to the Daltons like a burr on a dogie. He was with Heck Thomas, only about a day behind the gang, on the day of the raid.

Dodge wrote later that during the chase, an informant told him that Doolin rode with the other five bandits on the way north to Coffeyville, but that on the day of the raid he was ill with dengue fever. Although Heck Thomas remembered they received information that there were *five* men in the gang, Dodge had no reason to invent the informant. If the information was accurate, Doolin's dengue fever would explain his dropping out just before the raid a great deal better than the fable about the lame horse.

Not everybody agreed on Doolin or Bitter Creek as the mystery rider. After the raid some newspapers reported the culprit was one Allee Ogee, variously reported as hunted, wounded, and killed. Ogee, as it turned out, was very much alive, and industriously pursuing his job in a Wichita packinghouse. Understandably irritated, Ogee wrote the *Coffeyville Journal*, announcing both his innocence and his continued existence. A better candidate is yet another Dalton, brother Bill, who had moved from California with wrath in his heart for banks and railroads. This Dalton sibling had few scruples about robbing or shooting people; after Coffeyville, he rode with Doolin's dangerous gang and finally set up as a gang leader on his own.

Before he was shot down trying to escape a tough deputy marshal, he said nothing about being at Coffeyville, and afterward he couldn't comment, being dead. So nothing concrete connects Bill Dalton with the story of the sixth rider, except his perpetually surly disposition, his propensity for the crooked life, and his association with his outlaw brothers.

In later years, Chris Madsen commented on the Coffeyville raid for Frank Latta's *Dalton Gang Days*. If what Madsen said was true, neither Doolin nor Bill Dalton could have been the sixth bandit. Madsen was in Guthrie when the Coffeyville raid came unraveled, was advised of its results by telegram, and forthwith told the press.

Almost immediately, he said, Bill Dalton appeared to ask whether the report was true. Madsen believed that Bill and Doolin both were near

Guthrie, waiting for the rest of the gang with fresh horses. You have to respect anything Madsen said, although some writers have suggested that he was not above making a fine story even better. We'll never know.

Other men have also been nominated as the one who got away, among them a mysterious outlaw called Buckskin Ike, rumored to have ridden with the Dalton Gang in happier times. And there was one Padgett, a yarn-spinner of the "I bin everwhar" persuasion. Padgett later bragged that he left whiskey-running in the Cherokee Nation to ride with the Daltons. At Coffeyville he was the appointed horse-holder, he said, and rode for his life when things began to come unstuck in that deadly alley.

Some have suggested that the sixth rider might even have been a woman, an unlikely, but intriguing, theory. Stories abound about the Dalton women, in particular Eugenia Moore, Julia Johnson, and the Rose of the Cimarron. The Rose was said to be an Ingalls, Oklahoma, girl, who loved Bitter Creek Newcomb. According to legend, in the middle of a firefight with lawmen, she defied death to shinny down the wall of a building on a rope of sheets, carrying rifle and ammunition to her beleaguered bandit boyfriend. The story appears to be pure romantic moonshine, but it's a nice tale.

And then there was Julia Johnson, whom Emmett married in 1907. Emmett wrote that he was smitten by Julia long before the raid, when he stopped to investigate celestial organ music coming from a country church. Entering the building, he discovered Julia in the bloom of young womanhood, playing the organ. It was, of course, love at first sight for both of them. Well, maybe so, although Julia's granddaughter later said that Julia couldn't play a lick, let alone generate angelic chords from the church organ.

Julia, Emmett said, was the soul of constancy, and waited patiently for her outlaw lover through all his long years in prison. Never mind that Julia married two other people, who both departed this life due to terminal lead poisoning. Never mind that she married her second husband while Emmett was in the pen. Julia has been proposed as the sixth rider more than once, on the flimsiest theorizing. However, aside from the fact that Julia probably never laid eyes on Emmett until he left prison—that's what her granddaughter said, anyway—there's no evidence Julia rode on

Rose of the Cimarron, member of
the famous Doolin gang.

*Rose of the Cimarron*

any Dalton raid, let alone into Coffeyville. The myth of maidenly devotion is too well entrenched to die.

Eugenia Moore was said to be Bob's inamorata and spy. Eugenia, we are told, rode boldly up and down the railroad between Texas and Kansas, seducing freight agents and eavesdropping on the telegraph for news of money shipments. Eugenia might have been Flo Quick, a real-life horse thief and sexual athlete, something of a legend in her own time. When she rode out to steal, she dressed as a man and called herself "Tom

King." The *Wichita Daily Eagle* rhapsodized: "She is an elegant rider, very daring. She has a fine suit of hair as black as a raven's wing and eyes like sloes that would tempt a Knight of St. John . . . her figure is faultless."

Even if the reporter overdid the description a little, Flo was no doubt a real looker by the standards of the day. She could be charming, too, so maybe she was indeed Bob Dalton's mistress. If so, she might have been along on the raid, although there is no evidence whatever to place her there.

And so, if there was a sixth bandit, who was he? He could have been some relative unknown, of course—Padgett or somebody like him—but that is unlikely. This was to be a big raid, the pot of gold at the end of Bob Dalton's rainbow. He would not take along anybody but a proven hard case, even to hold horses.

Doolin is the popular candidate, with substantial supporting evidence. Bill Dalton emerges with persuasive evidence, in spite of Chris Madsen's story. Granted, there is no direct evidence to link him with the raid. However, he may well have gathered intelligence for the gang before they rode north to Kansas, and he certainly turned to the owlhoot trail in a hurry after Coffeyville. He repeatedly proved himself to be violent and without scruples, and he loathed what he considered "the Establishment": banks and railroads.

For those who scoff at the idea of a sixth bandit, there's one more bit of information, a haunting reference that was apparently never followed up. In 1973, an elderly Coffeyville woman reminisced about the bloody end of the raid: "Finally *they* got on their horses . . . *those* that were left. Several of 'em of course, were killed there, as well as several of the town's people. And *they* got on their horses and left" [emphasis supplied].

So passed the Daltons, in one of the most famous and badly executed holdups in the history of crime. Bob and Grat are still in Coffeyville, up in the cemetery. They have a headstone these days, but planted alongside it is a piece of ordinary pipe. For many years it was their only monument, and it is surely the most enduring one.

It's the pipe to which they tied their horses in that deadly Coffeyville alley.

## BAD DAY AT SOUTHWEST CITY

### *The Passing of Bill Doolin*

BILL DOOLIN WAS A SMART outlaw, by most accounts. Born in Johnson County, Arkansas, in 1858, he had been a cowboy once, and a top hand. It seems that he started out on the wrong side of the law with the shooting of two local lawmen up around Coffeyville, Kansas. The story goes that a pair of constables objected to Doolin and some cronies celebrating the Glorious Fourth with a keg of beer, Kansas being a dry state in those days. One thing led to another, and finally to shooting, and Doolin was on the run.

After that, like some other tough young cowpunchers of his day, Doolin decided that stealing other people's money beat working for a living. He had been a member of the notorious Dalton Gang in the days before they were shot to pieces by the tough citizens of Coffeyville, Kansas, in 1892.

A lot of print has been spent on the question of whether Doolin might have been part of the Daltons' Coffeyville raid. There is a persistent tale that he was included in the raiding party, but dropped behind the rest of the bandits when his horse went lame. By the time he found another mount, so the legend runs, the gang had been destroyed. And so he turned away, riding "like a ghostly rider saddled upon the wind" until he reached safety far to the south in Indian Territory.

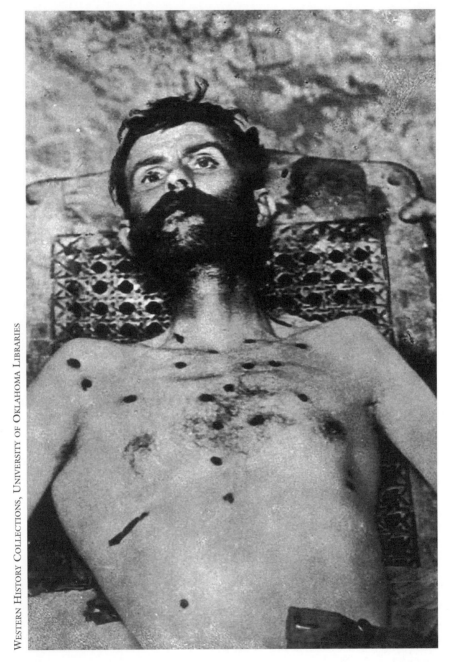

*Bill Doolin*

Whether or not Doolin was anyplace close to Coffeyville on that bloody day, he did not learn much from the fate of the Dalton boys and their two accomplices. Instead, he lost no time in getting back on the owlhoot trail, and with him rode many of the old Dalton boys, eager for easy money. A string of robberies and gunfights followed. After the 1892 stickup of the Ford County Bank in Spearville, Kansas, lawmen tracked down and killed one Doolin gang member, the eager, but inept, Ol Yantis. That should have been a warning to Doolin and his steadily growing gang, but they paid no heed.

After a train robbery west of Cimarron, Kansas, which may have netted the gang as much as $13,000, lawmen intercepted the Doolin bunch on their way back south into Oklahoma. In a running fight on the Cimarron River near Ashland, Kansas, Deputy Marshal Chris Madsen got a rifle round into Doolin's foot. The gang escaped, but the wound would trouble Doolin all his days.

In September of 1893, a murderous gun battle between the gang and federal deputy marshals erupted in the outlaw town of Ingalls, Oklahoma. In that fight, three lawmen died, a young bystander was killed, and still another citizen was seriously wounded. Two saloon owners were also shot as they cowered in a bar where the gang had taken refuge. Roy Daugherty, known as Arkansas Tom Jones, was captured after he shot down three deputy marshals from his room upstairs in the town's hostelry, a primitive hostel called the OK Hotel. Of the others, Bitter Creek Newcomb and Dan "Dynamite Dick" Clifton were wounded, but both men escaped with the rest of the gang.

At least one account says Doolin himself was badly wounded by a rifle bullet that "lodged at the base of Doolin's skull," causing him headaches and occasional seizures for the rest of his life, which in any case would not last all that much longer. In fact, the outlaw who took a round in the neck was Dynamite Dick. He carried the scar with him for the rest of his short, disgraceful life; it helped marshals identify him when he was arrested on a minor whiskey-running charge and tried to claim he was somebody else.

After the bloody fight at Ingalls, every peace officer was gunning for the Doolin Gang, who were in turn threatening to kill the two lawmen who had set up the marshals' raid. The *Guthrie* (Oklahoma) *Leader* spoke for decent men everywhere. "Nothing will do . . . but the killing of the scoundrels as one kills a wild beast." Running them down would not be easy, however, and it would not be quick. Doolin's followers were professional hoodlums, rough men used to rough ways, as outlaw Cole Younger had once said about himself and his own companions.

After this series of crimes, in March of 1894 Doolin and Dalton awakened the Santa Fe station agent at Woodward in the middle of the night, took him to the depot, and forced him to open the safe, which yielded a little more than $6,500. They then forced the agent and a boy they encountered on the street to carry another, smaller safe to the edge of town, where they broke it open. Just outside town they rendezvoused with six other horsemen, presumably the rest of the gang. All the riders then fled, but they did not stay together.

The gang split up, perhaps the result of a falling-out between Doolin and the ever arrogant and overbearing Bill Dalton, who may have challenged Doolin for leadership of the gang. Bitter Creek Newcomb rode off with Dalton, but left him after the two tried to rob a small store at Sacred Heart, a Catholic mission settlement. It should have been an easy score, but it turned out to be big trouble. The store owner was one W. H. Carr, an older man, but also a retired deputy marshal and a very tough cookie indeed.

Carr recognized at least one of his visitors, pulled his gun, and tried to arrest both men. Newcomb drew his own weapon, and in a short-range gunfight, Carr sent a bullet into Newcomb's left shoulder. A wound in the right arm forced Carr to drop his gun, and he took a second round in the belly, but the gutsy storekeeper scooped up his pistol and went on shooting, left-handed. The two robbers fled. That was the first of April of 1894.

A month later the gang had set their sights on the Southwest City Bank in McDonald County, Missouri. McDonald County is down in the far southwest corner of the state, a farming and mining country, and in those days it was bordered by Indian Territory to the west and Arkansas just to the south. The town lay on the banks of Honey Creek, a small, pleasant community of about 1,000 hardworking people, without the slightest suspicion of the peril in which they lay.

Doolin had with him some of the veterans of midwestern out-lawry: vicious Red Buck Waightman (or Weightman) was there, and so were Little Bill Raidler and Tulsa Jack Blake. Dynamite Dick Clifton, Little Dick West, and Charlie Pierce rounded out the gang, as unsavory a cadre of career hoodlums as the West ever produced. Some accounts also place both Bitter Creek Newcomb and Bill Dalton at Southwest City, but the best evidence is that neither man was there. Newcomb, painfully shot up at Sacred Heart, had not yet rejoined the gang, and Dalton was far away with other criminal escapades in mind.

There is also a story that Doolin had brought along an equally unpleasant confederate, one Charles Wynn, a doctor who called himself a "cancer specialist." Wynn, says this tale, had a lucrative sideline in treating sick or wounded criminals, and he also picked up extra cash by casing new criminal jobs for an assortment of criminals.

The story goes that Wynn did exactly this for Doolin in Southwest City, just as he had done for Henry Starr before Starr's successful robbery in Bentonville, Arkansas. In fact, one account says that Doolin and his gang spent the night of May 9 at the doctor's Fairland, Missouri, home. This version says that the crooked physician rode with the outlaws to Southwest City and then went on ahead to scout the quiet town. Dr. Wynn went home after he reported to Doolin the results of his reconnaissance, and the outlaw leader and his followers trotted in toward the bank.

It was about 3:00 on a fine spring afternoon, May 20, 1895. Doolin's men had their assignments. One source says that two of them set up in the yard of a doctor named Nichols, and two more went into a poolroom across the street from the post office. Both pairs then began to hoorah the quiet town in the time-honored style, firing their pistols and yelling at the citizens to get inside you thus-and-such, intending to clear the streets of any possible opposition. The town newspaper reported a total of seven outlaws, and had two robbers remaining with the horses, two more outside the bank, and three inside.

Doolin and at least one other outlaw went into the bank and threw down on the cashier, a man named Snyder, and Mr. Ault, the bank's owner. At first the robbery went without a hitch. One outlaw covered the bank men and the other crawled through a teller's window to clean out anything he could find in the cashier's drawer and the vault. They took almost $4,000, stuffing the loot into a feed sack. In the street, the four outside men kept yelling and banging away until Doolin and his companion dashed out of the bank and ran for their horses.

This is when the whole operation began to come unglued. Doolin would have been better advised to try to quietly purloin the hard-earned savings of Southwest City's people with as little fuss and noise as possible. The firing and yelling outside the bank quickly turned out to be a bad idea, for it left no doubt in anybody's mind that there was trouble downtown.

Now, the citizens of Southwest City were no shrinking violets to be bullied by a bunch of transient trash. But, as the *Cherokee Advocate* told its readers, "the people rushed out unprepared, and five of the citizens were shot." However, some of the local folks, at least, turned out with a variety of weaponry and began shooting back, and for unprepared defenders they laid down quite a healthy barrage. According to the *Oklahoma Press-Gazette*'s inflated account of the raid, there were "One Hundred Shots Fired." Early reports from Southwest City stressed that the outlaws were heavily armed, carrying both "Winchesters and revolvers."

Laying down a barrage of gunfire, the robbers made it to their horses and started out of town. On the way, however, fire from the citizens killed one of the gang's horses, and somebody opened a window and blasted away with a shotgun at the fleeing bandits.

One buckshot struck Doolin in the left temple, up near the hairline, and blood poured down the outlaw leader's face. He swayed in the saddle, but did not go down. Another buckshot lodged in the neck of his horse, Old Dick; the animal courageously carried Doolin out of town to safety, but the horse would never be the same again. The bandit who had his mount shot out from under him quickly robbed a passing farmer of his horse and galloped off with the rest of the gang.

As the bandits left Southwest City, Little Dick West opened fire on some citizens in front of Dustin's Hardware Store. None of these men seem to have been shooting at the fleeing bandits. There is no evidence that they were even armed, but that didn't stop West. "Screaming maniacally," according to one dubious account, West took a shot at them, and two men went down.

His pistol bullet hit Oscar Seaborn in the belly, tore on through, and bored into the lower abdomen of his brother, J. C. Seaborn. Both men had simply stepped out of the hardware store to see what all the fuss was about. Oscar would survive, but J. C., a former state auditor and prominent citizen, would not. He died of his wound several days later.

Another noncombatant, Mart Pembree, a shoemaker, was struck by an outlaw bullet that ripped through the wall of the Baker Saloon and fractured his foot. Deputy Marshal Simpson Melton took a slug in the thigh, but would survive. Nobody knows what injuries the bandits sustained, but it does seem reasonably certain that somebody fired a missile—probably buckshot—into the back of Doolin's head. The round remained there for the rest of the outlaw's brief life.

Whatever hurt the citizens inflicted on the raiders, the outlaws stood not upon the order of their going, but galloped out of town, and, as the *Daily Oklahoma State Capitol* put it, "started for the Nation at full speed." A posse followed the fleeing bandits, but lost the trail near Grand River, up in the Cherokee Nation. After all the shooting, hurt, and death, the gang's take was something between $3,000 and $4,000, although one account puts the booty as high as $13,000.

Tough federal judge, Frank Dale, in spite of threats against his life, had recently sent Arkansas Tom Jones off for fifty years for his part in the Ingalls fight. The judge was sick and tired of Doolin and his bullies, and so he called in U.S. Marshal Evett. Dumas Nix and gave him some plain and probably welcome guidance:

> *Marshal . . . I have reached the conclusion that the only good outlaw is a dead one. I hope you will instruct your deputies to bring in dead outlaws in the future.*

It was straightforward advice, clear and concise. The lawmen hunting Doolin and his men would do precisely what the judge had told them to do. After Ingalls, they had little compassion for the outlaw.

In May of 1895, Doolin and his men struck the Rock Island Railroad at a tiny hamlet called Dover, near Kingfisher in Payne County. The express car and the pockets of the passengers yielded several thousand dollars, but this time the federal law received speedy notification by telegraph. Deputy Marshal Chris Madsen, five posse men, and two Indian scouts charged down the line from El Reno on a special train, complete with a car carrying the posse's horses. Disembarking at Dover, they quickly picked up the trail and came up with their quarry about nightfall. In the firefight that followed, a lawman's bullet hit Tulsa Jack Blake in the cartridge belt, exploding a shell. Blake fell dead, and the rest of the gang fled.

In 1895, near Elgin, Kansas, Bill Raidler was shot full of holes by Bill Tilghman and two other officers. Raidler was captured and sent to prison. Shattered in body, he was later released with Tilghman's help, but Raidler was never again a whole man. In the same year, Bill Dalton was killed by federal officer Loss Hart not far from Ardmore, Oklahoma. Also in 1895, Charley Pierce was ambushed—along with Bitter Creek Newcomb—and shot down by bounty hunters at a ranch in the neighborhood of the outlaw town of Ingalls.

Red Buck Waightman came in second in a gunfight with officers in 1896, near Arapaho, Oklahoma. In April of 1898, Little Dick West died of lawmen's bullets on Cottonwood Creek, not far from Guthrie, Oklahoma. Dynamite Dick Clifton, West's cohort at Southwest City, had been run down and killed by peace officers in the fall of the year before.

And in 1896, even smart, experienced Bill Doolin came to the same dead end. Walking down a dark country road at night, he was challenged to surrender by Deputy Marshal Heck Thomas, who was backed by a small posse. Even though he was not certain where the lawman was in the gloom, Doolin chose to fight and blazed away at the sound of Thomas's voice. The posse returned the fire, and somebody—probably Heck himself—filled Doolin full of a fatal load of buckshot. In September of 1896, Thomas wrote to Bill Tilghman that Doolin

> shot at me and the bullet passed between me and B. Dunn.
> Had let one of the boys have my Winchester and had an old
> No. 8 shotgun. It was too long in the breach and I couldn't
> handle it quick so he got in another shot with his Winchester
> and as he dropped his Winchester from glancing shot, he
> jerked his pistol. Some of the boys thought he shot once and the

*others twice. At about that time I got the shotgun to work and the fight was over.*

Nevertheless, at least one other writer, Bailey Hanes, asserted in *Bill Doolin, Outlaw O.T.* that one of the Dunn brothers, who were posse members, actually killed Doolin. Thomas, he wrote, had a rifle, and could not have fired the fatal round. Ramon Adams, writing an introduction for Hanes's book, took the same unlikely view. Whoever perforated the veteran outlaw, the elusive Doolin was at last, as the *Guthrie Leader* commented, "*non est.*" His body, so the paper said, showed the marks of twenty buckshot, plus a wound in the arm from a rifle bullet.

There followed a ludicrous wrangle over just how Doolin had actually died. A rumor, apparently fostered by a local man with a grudge against Heck Thomas, spread that Doolin had died a "natural death." Then, the story went, the posse had propped the corpse up and shot it full of holes, in order to "claim the reward." An even more preposterous variant on this tale had Doolin dying of "galloping consumption," and being shot up after death with the connivance of his widow, to whom a share of the reward was promised.

At least there was no dispute that the body *was* Doolin, no reprise of the farcical allegations that had followed Bill Dalton's death. At the inquest following the killing of Doolin, the chief clerk of the Guthrie marshal's office testified, as others had, that the corpse was Doolin, and added this:

> *We were informed that a bullet had lodged in his head during the fight over at a Southwest City, Missouri, bank robbery some years ago. . . . I . . . found there was a bullet embedded in his skull which had lodged there. I told Dr. Smith to make an operation and watched him perform the same during which he removed the bullet in the skull at the above location.*

Another witness testified that Doolin had told him he was part of the Southwest City robbery, and had been wounded in the head there, where it "seemed like it struck the front of the temple at about the edge of the hair and then glanced up and lodged over his eye." The same witness testified that Doolin had been badly crippled by a shot in the heel during his flight after the robbery at Cimarron, Kansas.

Doolin was buried in Guthrie on August 28, with only a few onlookers. His monument, which would endure for the next sixty-three years, was an old buggy axle, an eerie echo of the length of pipe that was the only marker on the graves of the Dalton boys in Coffeyville, Kansas.

# AT ALL COSTS

### *The End of George Birdwell*

*It is evident now to everybody that Boley was the
wrong location for a successful bank robbery.*
                    —Daily Oklahoman, *November 25, 1932*

THE 1930s WERE TOUGH years for most Americans. Nowhere were
they tougher than in Oklahoma, where hard times were made even
harder by the drought that produced the Dust Bowl and the westward
migration that followed.

Times were hard in Boley, Oklahoma, as well, although the
drought had not hit Boley as hard as it had many other places. Boley was
different in another way, too: It was an all-black community, one of about
two dozen such towns in Oklahoma. Just why Boley was settled as an all-
black town back in 1903 is not entirely clear. Booker T. Washington
wrote that it was the result of a bet between two white men on whether
black people could govern themselves. The truth seems to be much more
prosaic: The town's origins rested mostly on a purely commercial venture, a Creek Indian father's desire to see his daughter's 160-acre land
allotment put to profitable use as the basis for a town.

In 1932 Boley's principal commercial street, Main Street, boasted
forty stores along its five blocks, including Hazel's two-story department

store and the Farmers and Merchants Bank. Across the street from the bank stood the Masonic Temple, an impressive three-story structure. The bank, the town's centerpiece, was the creation of its president, D. J. Turner, a shrewd, hardworking businessman who nevertheless loved his town and was reluctant to foreclose on any struggling family.

But Turner worried, as did other citizens in Boley and hundreds of small towns across Oklahoma. For this was the time of the bank robbers, notably a homegrown hoodlum named Charles Arthur Floyd, called "Choc" by his friends, but known to the world at large as Pretty Boy. In the first three months of 1932, Floyd and other bandits had hit Oklahoma banks for some $62,000, a lot of money to small depositors in struggling towns. People who referred to Floyd as a latter-day Robin Hood never thought about the little people whose savings were wiped out by his raids.

The ordinary Oklahoman was alarmed, for unless the bank had some sort of insurance, the depositors were out of luck. For the citizens of Boley, there was a good deal of reason to worry about bank robbery: Floyd and his gang had already struck the banks at Paden and Prague, not far away, and had done so on the same day. And just the last January, a gang had robbed the bank in Castle, a mere 6 miles down the road.

Boley's citizens were determined that it wouldn't happen to their town. Bank president Turner, according to one source, had said flatly that he would "defend the town's savings at all costs." When Turner said something, he meant it, and he had done some preparing. His bank had installed a brand-new electric alarm system. It triggered automatically when the very last dollar bills were removed from the teller's drawer, whether snatched out by a robber or removed under duress by a bank employee. The alarm not only made a noise like the last trumpet, but was tied into four nearby businesses: Hazel's Department Store, Shorty Bragg's Barber Shop, Aldridge's Pool Hall, and a meat market run by John Owen.

There were other preparations, too. Butcher John Owen was a formidable figure, a retired lawman who always wore a big, black Stetson with a bullet hole in the crown, a memento of a gunfight with the Haskell gang of bank robbers in Prague, just 14 miles away. He and other citizens of Boley kept their shotguns and rifles close at hand, and more weapons

WESTERN HISTORY COLLECTIONS, UNIVERSITY OF OKLAHOMA LIBRARIES

*David J. Turner*

were apparently stashed in the Masonic Temple for easy access.

And then there was the Boley sheriff, Langston McCormick. Any criminal who tried to hold up the Boley bank would have to come through Lank McCormick, all six foot seven of him, very tough and very capable. Whoever wanted the hard-earned money of Boley's citizens would have his work cut out for him.

Enter George Birdwell, companion and supposed chief of staff to Pretty Boy Floyd himself. Birdwell was an interesting man, a cowboy and oil-field roustabout turned robber, a veteran criminal with a volatile temper. He nevertheless had the reputation of being a devoted father who took care not only of his wife and four children, but also of his two nephews. He was later described by a lawman as "the man who planned these activities and handled the machine gun in their raids."

Birdwell and Floyd had held up the American State Bank in Henryetta, Oklahoma, early in November of 1932. They had taken more than $11,000, a very sizeable haul for those impoverished days. Birdwell was almost immediately ready for further adventures, and he settled his sights on Boley.

Birdwell recruited some help for his Boley expedition. One of his thugs was C. C. "Champ" Patterson, an experienced outlaw. Birdwell also added a brand-new bank robber, a black gambler from Boley named Pete Glass. It may have been Glass who actually suggested the raid to Birdwell, for Glass boasted that he was going to "show the gang how to rob a colored bank."

There is a story that Ruby Floyd, Pretty Boy's ex-wife, was about to be released from the hospital after surgery and needed money to pay her hospital bills. In later years, Birdwell's son, Jack, related his memory of the occasion: "My dad heard that Ruby needed to pay the medical bills before she could get released from the hospital. Choc [Floyd] was in Kansas City, so Dad went out to rob a bank and get some money for Ruby." Which may be exactly the case, or maybe it's what the youngster was told after his father went off to Boley and never came back.

In another version of the story, at a meeting in their Cookson Hills hideout, Birdwell tried to interest Floyd in the Boley bank. At first Floyd agreed to do the job, but on second thought the famous robber decided that he wasn't having any. It was a wise decision.

Maybe Floyd was becoming just a little suspicious of Birdwell's reliability. There is some reason to believe that Birdwell had begun to hit the bottle harder than Floyd liked. Or maybe, and more probably, Pretty Boy knew much better than Birdwell did, the temper of Boley's citizenry. Whatever the reason, Floyd had grave misgivings about taking on Boley. "Somebody's liable to get killed in that Nigra town," he said. While his refusal to join in the venture may have disappointed Birdwell, it certainly didn't stop him. He would take on the Farmers and Merchants Bank with the two men he had, Patterson and Glass.

Two days before Thanksgiving, Birdwell and his cohorts drove their big, black Buick down to Boley to reconnoiter the town and its bank. They spent some time casually hanging out at Aldridge's Pool Hall, shooting a few games and watching the bank across the street. Birdwell may have visited the bank some days earlier, on the excuse of cashing a personal check.

Neither he nor the rest of the bandits seem to have aroused any suspicion until, just as they drove out of town, they said something ungentlemanly to Bennie Dolphin, a pretty secretary who worked for Dr. W. A. Paxton, across the street from the bank. The words they used were, in Bennie's opinion, "flirting remarks." She didn't like them at all, so much so that she told Sheriff McCormick that the car looked suspicious.

That night the three robbers got drunk together at Glass's sister's home near Earlsboro. The next morning they moved on to eat breakfast at Dock Hearn's home. Hearn was a sort of outlaw groupie, a great admirer of Floyd. He boasted that Floyd had given him a silver dollar for every bank he robbed in Oklahoma. After breakfast, allowing time enough for the Boley bank to open, the three climbed into their Buick and started for their objective.

Patterson, who usually drove on holdups, took the wheel, but somewhere just short of Boley, he moved over for Glass to drive. Apparently the idea was that a black man waiting outside the bank, behind the wheel of a car, might appear to be a chauffeur, or at least would arouse little suspicion. The outlaws' plan, as far as there was one, seems to have been to drive up Main Street and stop just short of the bank. Out of sight of anybody inside the bank, they would park on the wrong side of the street, pointed north, away from the highway. And that is what Glass did.

Once Patterson and Birdwell had the cash and returned to the Buick, Glass would back up the car a short distance, making a U-turn as he did, and then drive hard to the south, to the highway and safety. You have to wonder why the gang did not make their U-turn as they entered the town, and park facing south toward the highway. It would have saved them a few precious seconds in fleeing Boley, leaving the right side of the car facing the bank, thus opening two of the car doors to receive the running bandits instead of one. But then, proficiency in bullying bank employees and shooting peace officers is no guarantee of common sense.

It was the day before Thanksgiving, and many farmers were in town to buy supplies. Some were also buying shotgun ammunition since quail season was to open the following day. Inside the bank, Turner was working at his desk. He seemed to have a premonition of trouble or danger that morning, even before he left home. He said to his wife, "Well, I'm kind of glad tomorrow is a holiday . . . I won't have to go down to that trap." Mrs. Turner, concerned, asked what he meant by "that trap," but Turner would say no more. He put on his coat, said good-bye, and began his walk to the bank through a very cold morning.

Also working in the bank on that morning was bookkeeper Herbert C. McCormick, the brother of Sheriff McCormick. Herb would turn out to be made of the same hard rock as his brother. The sheriff had advised him to keep a rifle in the vault, a perfect spot from which to fight if robbers struck the bank. Herb's Winchester was in place that morning, ready to hand. Nearer the door, Treasurer Wesley W. Riley was talking to Horace Aldridge, a customer. Out on the street, big Sheriff McCormick was making his rounds. He was dressed in high boots with his trousers stuffed into them, a plaid shirt under a sheepskin coat, and a big cowboy hat.

The sheriff was checking the stores to which the bank's alarm was wired. He stopped to chat with Hazel and told him about his concerns over a bank robbery. But "once I hear that alarm," Hazel said, "I'll be at 'em like a duck on a June bug. Git me a Pretty Boy for breakfast." The sheriff agreed that Hazel had the perfect spot from which to be "at 'em," for a long veranda ran halfway around the second floor of the department store, overlooking the street in front of the Farmers and Merchants Bank.

The outlaws drove into Boley and turned up Main Street. Glass stopped the Buick as planned, pointing north just south of the bank. Birdwell and Patterson climbed out of the car; Birdwell carried a .45 1911 Colt semiautomatic pistol and Patterson had a sawed-off shotgun concealed beneath his overcoat. As they entered the bank, Riley looked up from his conversation with Aldridge, but suspected nothing. Turner, the president, arose from his desk and moved up behind the bars on the teller's window to serve Birdwell. He found himself looking into the bad end of the Colt pistol.

*Boley Town Council members*

"We're robbing this bank," Birdwell said. "Hand over the dough! Don't pull no alarm!"

Turner said nothing, but began to pull bills out of the cash drawer, sliding them under the bars toward the waiting bandit. Meanwhile, Herb McCormick heard and saw what was going on at the teller's window and slid softly to the floor, crawling back toward the vault. As Turner pulled out the last bills in the drawer, the alarm sounded with a deafening din, both inside the bank and outside, in the four other stores wired into the system.

"You pulled that alarm," yelled Birdwell. "I'll kill you for that!"

And the doughty Turner looked the bandit right in the eye: "You bet I pulled it!"

Riley, standing helplessly in front of Patterson's shotgun, saw what was coming. "Don't hurt nobody, please!" he pleaded, but he was answered only with obscenities. Infuriated by Turner's defiance, Birdwell's mercurial temper tore loose and he drove four .45 slugs into Turner at point-blank range. Turner staggered and went down, clutching the desk for support as he fell.

Herb McCormick reached the vault and his rifle, and as the bank president fell, McCormick drove a Winchester bullet into Birdwell's neck. Blood spurting from the wound, the outlaw dropped his pistol and the sack full of about $700 in loot. "I'm shot," he cried, no longer bold and arrogant. "Hold me! I'm . . ." And down he went.

Patterson then ordered Riley and Aldridge to pull the fallen Birdwell to the door of the bank and outside. Under the ugly, unblinking stare of the shotgun, they did. Glass, hearing the gunfire, came running into the bank, pistol in hand. As he fired random shots toward the back of the bank, he and Patterson moved toward the door, both men still trying to scoop up the bills that were scattered across the counter and floor.

Outside, the outlaws saw several citizens headed their way, running toward the bank from all directions, carrying rifles and shotguns. The hostages took advantage of their captors' consternation and dropped Birdwell on the sidewalk in front of the bank. They took off running and disappeared out of sight down a side street. His forced labor and human shields now fled, Patterson himself bent over to pick up Birdwell. About this time a citizen named Zeigler, firing from behind Turner's Hardware Store, slammed a load of shot into the bandit's hip and leg.

Glass crawled toward Birdwell's body. At the same time, Patterson saw Hazel out on his store's veranda and fired at him. Realizing that Birdwell was quite dead, Glass looked up to see the giant form of Sheriff McCormick heading for him, followed by more citizens who had armed themselves at the Masonic Temple. Glass, realizing the fat was in the fire, abandoned what remained of Birdwell and ran to the Buick. The wounded Patterson, stubborn or stupid or both, still tugged at Birdwell's corpse, and Zeigler put another load of shot into him.

Bullets flew all over the street, and it must have seemed to Patterson and Glass that everybody in town had a gun and was using it, which was substantially true. The fire was so heavy that Herb McCormick, inside the bank, could not raise his head at the window to get a shot at the robbers just outside. Hazel fired at Patterson with his shotgun, but missed him. Patterson, raising his own shotgun to reply, took a volley from Sheriff McCormick and Boley High football star Ray Parker. Their rounds knocked Patterson's weapon from his hands and put a hole in his right shoulder and neck. He was also shot in the hip, legs, and a knee, "tattooed with buckshot," as the *Daily Oklahoman* put it.

Glass climbed into the Buick, miraculously untouched by the hailstorm of lead flying around the main street of Boley. He started the car, slammed it into reverse, and began backing up to turn around and make tracks for the highway. At this point, retired sheriff John Owens entered the scene, rifle in hand. Kneeling in the center of Main Street, some 50 yards from the Buick, Owens coolly put a bullet into Glass. Roaring backward, now unguided, the car crashed into a parking lot wall, where it stopped. As it sat there, everybody within range poured bullets into it.

The car was junk; Glass was a corpse.

The sheriff shouted for a cease-fire, and the firing died away. Dr. Paxton ran across Main Street toward the bank, shotgun in one hand and medical bag in the other. Inside, he found Turner on the floor, only semiconscious and soaked in blood. Herb McCormick was kneeling beside him. The bandits' hard-won loot was strewn on the bank floor.

Outside, angry townsmen gathered around Patterson's bloody form. He was riddled with birdshot—according to one source, as many as 450 shot. As the citizens learned what had happened to Turner, there was no mercy in them, and they began to shout about finishing the job. The sheriff, however, had other plans. "Now, I don't stand for no different treatment. He's my prisoner. Now y'all back off." McCormick meant business, and the crowd pulled away. As they did, somebody asked, "Which one's Pretty Boy?"

"Neither one, I don't reckon," the sheriff answered, to the intense disappointment of the citizens.

Turner, still clinging to life, was loaded into Dr. Paxton's car for the trip to the hospital at Okemah. Before the doctor could start, however,

*David J. Turner in front of bank*

Turner's wife drove up and jumped into Paxton's vehicle to join her husband on the trip. Sadly, neither her love nor the doctor's ministrations could save the gallant bank president. He died on the road.

Patterson survived his multiple wounds to reach Okemah's hospital. Already out on bail awaiting trial for assault on a Shawnee police officer, he faced a dreary future. Next day, according to the *Daily Oklahoman*, Patterson, unable to talk because of his neck wound, confirmed by nodding his head that the dead bandit was the infamous Birdwell. Birdwell was also identified by a Seminole police chief and an oil company employee, both of whom had known the outlaw for years. Glass's sister also identified both men, and added: "He and Pete got drunk last night and Pete told him he would show him how a Negro robbed a bank."

More than 5,000 people turned out for Turner's funeral on November 28. Among other eulogies was one delivered by a man representing the Oklahoma Bankers' Association. The town of Boley won the general thanks of the rest of Oklahoma for ridding the earth of a major pest. The Muskogee *Daily Phoenix* put it pretty well:

> *The state of Oklahoma owes a debt of sincere gratitude to the little town of Boley which made possible the permanent removal from its sordid bank robbery picture of one of the state's most active criminal menaces. . . . Boley has accomplished at least in part something that the law enforcement agencies have been attempting to do with no success whatever—break up the "Pretty Boy" Floyd bank robbing ring.*

And the *Daily Oklahoman* spoke in like manner:

> *All Oklahoma should pay to the people of Boley the tribute of unstinted praise. . . . They have set an example of law enforcement, which if generally followed, would make Oklahoma the most dangerous state for thieves in all this broad republic. Incidentally, they have set an example of strict economy, for there will be no costly court trial, no hung jury, no trivial penitentiary sentence, and no speedy executive pardon. A generous quantity of Negro buckshot has settled the whole business and settled it for keeps.*

Lawmen tried to use the citizens' success at Boley to lay hands on Pretty Boy Floyd. They watched the morgue where Birdwell's body lay, and then the funeral itself, in hopes that Floyd would show up to pay his last respects to his extinct lieutenant. The officers were disappointed. They listened to Reverend Robert Hedrick preach about "As ye sow, so shall ye reap," which surely seemed a theme appropriate to the occasion, and they heard "Just as I Am" and "Rock of Ages" sung as Birdwell was planted. They saw Mrs. Floyd, too, "stylishly dressed," as the paper put it, standing among the fifty or so mourners.

The paper did the best it could with this mundane funeral news. Floyd's wife, it said, "was mysteriously spirited from a Tulsa hospital Wednesday, the day Birdwell and a Negro companion, Charles Glass, were killed in an attempted robbery of a bank at Boley." Why her departure from the hospital was somehow mysterious was not explained, but the sentence at least raised the story a notch above a standard obituary.

The peace officers' failure to find Floyd anywhere near Birdwell's funeral was due at least in part to an acute case of over enthusiasm on the part of the *Daily Oklahoman*. On page one of its issue of the day before, November 25, the paper trumpeted, "Officers Hope to Get Floyd at Pal's Bier," and then went on to explain the law's plan for all, including Floyd, to see:

> *Recalling that Birdwell defied the law two years ago to pay his respects at the bier of his dead father, officers . . . looked to sentiment to bait their traps as reports came that Floyd intended to view the body of Birdwell at a Seminole funeral home.*

Pretty Boy Floyd didn't show.

When Birdwell went down, however, it was as if Floyd had lost his right arm. As one detective put it, "Without him, Floyd's days will be few in the land." And so it was to be. Whether or not it had anything to do with the Boley debacle or with Birdwell's death, Floyd himself would leave the state before the year was out, never to return except to get himself buried at the biggest funeral ever seen in Oklahoma. Within two years, he would be cut down by lawmen in the dirt of an Ohio cornfield.

Herb McCormick received all kinds of hate mail afterward, most of it berating him for ridding the world of the worthless Birdwell. One such letter was sent to a Memphis paper. It denied all responsibility for a robbery in Tupelo, Mississippi, and was signed by Floyd, or somebody using his name. It also mentioned the Boley shoot-out, and said,

> *The man who killed my pal Birdwell will never live to see Christmas. . . . I have five men with me and will be over in Oklahoma, my home state, to spend Christmas with my folks.*

Floyd did not carry out his death threat, if he ever made it at all. Herb McCormick would live past Christmas and for many years thereafter.

Some of McCormick's friends mounted a twenty-four-hour guard over him for a time. McCormick went on with his life, although for a while he did carry the .45 that Birdwell had used to shoot Turner. He received a $500 reward from the Oklahoma Bankers' Association for killing Birdwell, and Boley's "vigilance committee" received another $500 for exterminating Glass. Governor "Alfalfa" Bill Murray invited McCormick to Oklahoma City, where the governor conferred on him the honorary title of "Major." So he was known for the rest of his life.

Alfalfa Bill took advantage of the occasion to expatiate on the great social value of bounties for outlaws. He would offer $500 for any bank robber "killed in the act," he said, and went on:

> *I will pay $250 for every accomplice killed in a bank holdup. I mean the fellow who is holding the horses—maybe I should say waiting in the automobile—while others rob the bank. . . . The way to stop these robberies is to get at the source. The county isn't going to be out lots of money for a trial and we'll know we have the right man.*

The governor's logic seemed impeccable. The writers of the threatening letters were also wiser than Birdwell had been.

They were smart enough not to come to Boley.

## THOSE MEN WILL BEAR WATCHING

### *The James–Younger Gang's Disaster at Northfield*

*Jesse James was a lad who killed many a man*
*He robbed the Glendale train;*
*He robbed from the rich and he gave to the poor,*
*He had a hand, a heart, and a brain.*
*Poor Jesse had a wife, to mourn for his life,*
*Two children they were brave;*
*And the dirty little coward, who shot Mr. Howard,*
*Had laid poor Jesse in his grave.*

MAYBE THAT ANONYMOUS songwriter believed all that stuff about his hero. Lots of other people believed the Jesse James myth, too. A lot of these were ordinary people who confused this Missouri hoodlum with Robin Hood. Others idolized Jesse and other Missouri outlaws as paragons of southern manhood, still living the lost dream of the Confederacy, driven from their homes and into a life of crime by damn Yankee persecutors. Among these was their chief apologist, Missouri newspaper editor John Newman Edwards.

Edwards could never admit that his outlaw idols did anything really wrong, and he celebrated Jesse and Frank and their hoodlum friends with lots of treacly lines like "We call him outlaw, but fate made him so."

It was true that both of the brothers had ridden with the bush-whackers, the Missouri guerillas, Frank with Quantrill and Jesse with Bloody Bill Anderson. They had seen a lot of fighting at its worst, the bloody internecine war of ambush, murder, arson, torture, and treachery that marked the vicious guerrilla conflict in Missouri. No doubt the war had left its mark on both men, as it did on hundreds of thousands of other men on both sides.

Still, most of their fellow Missouri guerrillas—including most of Quantrill's and Anderson's men—went home after the war and settled down, but Jesse and his brother Frank found it easier to take what other people earned rather than work. And if these other people objected, the brothers simply shot them down. Along the way, the James brothers collected some kindred spirits, including ex-bushwhackers like Cole Younger, and went off to rob banks and trains and stagecoaches. In the miasma of bitterness and poverty and anger that was the legacy of guerrilla war, there grew in the minds of some the fantasy that the outlaws were indeed Robin Hood and his Merry Men come again, or something very like it; they were seen as decent, openhanded southern boys driven to crime.

The reality was that if Jesse James robbed from the rich, it was because they had more money than the poor. And he robbed the poor as well, train and stagecoach passengers, and anybody who had a few hard-earned dollars saved up in the local bank. When outlaws knocked off a bank in those far-off days, there was no FDIC around to help out the depositors. That helpful agency didn't appear until 1933, all of seventy years later. The small farmer, the teamster, the laborer, the school-teacher, the drugstore clerk could lose all or part of their hard-earned savings, sometimes all there was keeping them from destitution.

With his brother Frank, the three Younger boys (Cole, Jim, and Bob), and a changing cast of other outlaws, Jesse committed a number of robberies and train holdups across Missouri, Iowa, Kentucky, and Alabama, with some murdering thrown in for good measure. There is no telling now just how many crimes they committed. In popular fiction and in the movies, Jesse has been cast again and again as the leader of the gang, but the chances are very good that the more commanding voice was that of his elder brother Frank, or maybe that of Cole Younger. Both

On left is the bank held up by Frank and Jesse James, Cole, Jim and Bob Younger and others, in Northfield, Minn., Sept. 7, 1876, for which the Youngers served time in Stillwater pen.

*This bank in Northfield, Minnesota, proved a match for the James–Younger Gang.*

Cole and Frank were older men, veterans of substantially longer Civil War service than Jesse could boast.

Likewise, there is no substantial evidence that Jesse or other outlaws "gave to the poor." Sometimes they paid handsomely for meals at a farmhouse, but it wasn't difficult to pay handsomely when you were using somebody else's money. A bit of largesse was good for the ego and the reputation, and it might encourage a discreet silence in the beneficiaries. Ego and the desire for money drove Jesse and Frank to broaden their robbing range.

Nobody knows for sure why the James–Younger Gang decided to leave their favorite stomping grounds and venture up to far-off Minnesota to rob a small-town bank. It may have been a built-in scorn for Yankee sodbusters, as some writers have suggested. Or maybe the one Minnesota man in the gang suggested the raid. Cole later said that they picked the Northfield bank because ex-Yankee officers had money in it, but that is probably a justification created after the fact.

What is sure, however, is that this collection of eight veteran outlaws set out for Minnesota in the early autumn of 1876. In addition to the two James brothers and the three Younger boys, the supporting cast included Clel (or Clell) Miller and Charlie Pitts, old Missouri associates of the brothers, and ex-jailbird Bill Chadwell—in fact one Bill Stiles, probably born in Monticello, Minnesota.

The gang went north by train, equipping themselves with horses and horse furniture once they arrived. Then, after a sort of leisurely grand tour of the Minneapolis area, including trips to gambling halls, houses of prostitution, and even a baseball game, the gang searched around rural Minnesota for a suitable target. One tale tells that they passed up a bank in one town because there was a crowd around the bank, and people in the crowd pointed at them. They did not realize that these people were simply sidewalk superintendents interested in nearby construction, and the pointing was to call attention to their fine saddle horses.

In any case, they finally settled on little Northfield. A prosperous mill town with a single bank, Northfield was a peaceful village in which nobody carried a gun. Its industrious citizens spent their time and energy on business, family, church, and culture, and did not dream that their quiet home was about to be invaded by the most famous outlaw gang of the day.

One entertaining story has a veritable army of hoodlums invading peaceful Northfield: "fourteen white men, three Negroes, and an Indian guide." In fact, the raiders were eight hardcase outlaws, long experienced in hoorahing little towns, shooting down their residents, and taking their money. There should have been more than enough of them to terrorize peaceful citizens, and robbing Northfield's little bank should have been a lead-pipe cinch.

But it wasn't.

As with most famous outlaw dramas, exactly who did what and in what order is largely unknown, but what probably happened is this: In the early afternoon of September 7, 1876, three outlaws—probably Frank James, Charlie Pitts, and Bob Younger—rode in across the Cannon River Bridge and into Bridge Square, just across the river. They dismounted on the corner of Bridge Square and Division, the town's main street. And there, in front of the sturdy stone Scriver Building, which housed the town's only bank and some other businesses, they sat down on some boxes and tried to look like innocent loafers.

Not far behind them Clel Miller and Cole Younger rode in together, stopping on Division Street outside the bank and trying to look equally innocent. Miller was casually smoking his pipe, while Cole pretended to tighten the already-tight saddle girth on his horse. The remaining three outlaws remained behind in reserve, riding in across the Cannon River and stopping on the square. Their mission was to gallop onto Division Street yelling and shooting if things went sour at the bank.

The gang had already aroused suspicion. "Those men will bear watching," said one citizen, like other residents intrigued by the strangers' long dusters and fine saddle horses, something of a rarity in a settled region where most people traveled by wagon or buggy. Hardware merchant Sim Allen jumped to the correct conclusion. "I don't like the look of them," he said. "I believe they are here to rob the bank." Nevertheless, the town remained quiet while the first three bandits rose from their boxes and pushed into the bank. Allen, however, increasingly distrustful of these strangers, tried to follow them inside. He made it no farther than the door, where Miller shoved a pistol against his gullet and told him "not to holler, for if he did, he'd blow his damned head off."

Undaunted by either threat or revolver, Allen promptly ran for it, and he did quite a lot of hollering: "Get your guns, boys," he shouted. "They're robbing the bank!" Then somebody, probably Miller, fired a shot, and the bandits' reserves galloped out of Bridge Square onto Division Street. Everything broke loose in peaceful Northfield. Five robbers were now riding up and down Division Street, firing their pistols and yelling, "Get in, you sons of bitches!" at any citizen who appeared in the street or in a doorway.

Inside the bank the first three bandits forced two employees, Frank Wilcox and Alonzo Bunker, to their knees behind the counter, the bores of the outlaws' pistols looking to Bunker to be "about the size of a hat." As one robber, probably Bob Younger, pulled open drawers looking in vain for the ready cash, the other two outlaws pistol-whipped and threatened acting cashier J. L. Heywood, demanding that he open the safe. "I can't," said Heywood. "It's on a time lock." The bandits, however, would not believe him. Their answer was a smashing blow with a pistol barrel to Heywood's head.

To his everlasting credit, Heywood would not help them, even when they threatened to slash his throat and actually inflicted a shallow cut. Not one of these three veteran outlaws thought to try the door of the safe. It was open. Bob Younger could not even find the ready-cash drawer, which contained several thousand dollars. Meanwhile, outside, the roar of firing in the street grew louder and louder, and Cole Younger yelled repeatedly for the inside men to come out in a hurry. "We're getting all cut up here!" he shouted, but still the men inside the bank did not appear.

While the bandits were busy brutalizing Heywood, Alonzo Bunker made a break for freedom, leaping up and sprinting toward the back door, which was covered only by a screen in the warm September weather. Pitts took a shot at the running man at point-blank range, but missed him, and Bunker smashed through the screen at the dead run, bursting out into the sunlight of the alley behind the bank. Pitts ran after him as far as the door and fired again at the unarmed man. This time the pistol ball tore through Bunker's shoulder. He staggered, but stayed on his feet and ran across a vacant lot, in search of a doctor.

Back inside, the outlaws finally gave up their fruitless search for money and at last heeded Cole Younger's desperate shouts. And then, in an ugly parting gesture of anger and frustration, one of them turned and viciously shot down the semiconscious Heywood. The slug tore into Heywood's brain and he collapsed on the floor of the bank.

Outside, chaos reigned along Division Street. Every bell in town was ringing, and all of Northfield's dogs barked and howled. Citizens ran for shelter, shooed their children and animals off the street, and searched for whatever weapons they could find. Up at Carleton College, a professor's wife organized the female students: "Every girl was to take an axe and we went all of us to the third floor, determined to make a good resistance."

Up and down Division Street rode five violent strangers, cursing, shouting, and firing in all directions. But the town quickly began to fight back.

Elias Stacy's shotgun was loaded only with "chickenshot," but he pulled down on Clel Miller anyway, splattering the load into the bandit's face. At least two other citizens also banged away with shotguns loaded with light shot. In an astonishing display of raw courage, the postmaster and three other citizens, including Ben Richardson, got into the fight with rocks. "Stone 'em, stone 'em!" one of them yelled, hurling, according to a contemporary account, "big and formidable missiles, more fit for the hand of Goliath than for the sling of David."

A. R. Manning was in his hardware store around the corner from the bank. Hearing the commotion and Sim Allen's warning shouts, he grabbed a rifle and ran to the corner, from which he could see down Division Street toward the front door of the bank. With him was his clerk, a man named Phillips, who had helped himself to a pair of pistols. Both men took shelter at the corner, not far from an exterior stairway leading to the second story of the Scriver Block, and began to blaze away.

Although it is not recorded that Phillips hit anybody, Manning did bloody work with his rifle. His first round killed one of the bandits' horses. His second ricocheted from a wooden post to tear into Cole Younger's thigh, and his third slammed into Bill Chadwell's heart. Chadwell fell from his horse into the dust of Division Street. A Northfield lady named Kingman saw him go down:

> I saw him reel in his saddle and nearly fall off. He threw his
> left arm around the horse's neck, and that turned the horse up
> the street again and he came as far as my door, where he fell
> off and died, after a period of intense suffering.

Young Henry Wheeler, a University of Michigan medical student home on vacation, had been relaxing in a chair outside his father's drugstore, across the street from the bank. Driven indoors by the robbers' shots and threats, Wheeler scrounged an old Civil War carbine and four paper cartridges and ran upstairs to a second-floor room in the Dampier Hotel. Here he had a fine view of the street in front of the bank, and he got the carbine into action at once. Wheeler's first round, fired at Jim

*Henry Wheeler*

Younger, went high. His second tore into the shoulder of Clel Miller, already reeling from Stacy's chickenshot. The bullet ripped through the big subclavian artery and Miller too went down, quickly bleeding to death in the street.

Bob Younger, whose horse Manning had killed, advanced on Manning, shooting at the storekeeper from the shelter of the outside stairway. As he exchanged fire with Manning, Bob exposed himself to Wheeler, across the street, and the young student nailed Bob in the right elbow. About the same time, a citizen named J. B. Hyde joined the action with a shotgun—he was using buckshot—and he may also have hit Bob

*The Youngers*

Younger. Bob stayed on his feet, however. He shifted his revolver to his left hand and went on trying to kill Manning.

Unable to get a clean shot at Bob behind the stairway, Manning left his corner to run down the alley at the rear of the bank and come in behind the outlaw. At the same time, Wheeler dropped his last cartridge on the floor, breaking it, and ran to find more ammunition. This was the time the gang chose to make a run for it, for they had had a great belly-ful of peaceful little Northfield. Jim Younger put Bob on Miller's horse, and Pitts, whose horse had sensibly sought safety in a local livery stable, rode double with Cole.

Thoroughly whipped, the most famous outlaw gang in history turned tail and fled, galloping south down Division Street for safety. They had made off with just $26 and some change. The yell-and-shoot hoorah tactics that had worked so well for them in the past had been a dismal fail-ure. The pistols-on-horseback style of the bushwhackers had not been equal to the rifles and shotguns of Northfield's defenders, nor to their amazing determination.

Back at the bank, horrified townspeople picked up dying Heywood and took him home. His wife was made of the same fine mettle as her hus-band: When told how he had staunchly resisted the robbers and protected the money in the bank, she commented simply, "I would not have had him do otherwise." Down the street from the bank, the townspeople dis-covered another wounded citizen, a Swedish immigrant named Gustafson. The man spoke little English, and he probably could not have understood the bandits' shouted commands. He may have been shot down simply for his lack of understanding. Like Heywood, he too was unarmed. Gustafson would linger for a few days, but his wound was mortal.

As Northfield mourned, the gang plodded on to the southwest. The outlaws were not only far from home, but were in bad shape as well. In addition to Cole's painful thigh wound and Bob's shattered elbow, Jim Younger had been hit in the shoulder. Some sources say either Jesse or Frank James, or both, had also been wounded, probably in the leg or thigh. If this is so, however, the wounds were not crippling.

The gang now faced the daunting task of getting clear of Minnesota, where every man was their enemy. There was no refuge here, no hiding place, no friendly kinfolk, and no Confederate sympathizers to shelter and protect them. They were alone and hurt, and hunted by lawmen and volunteer posses that soon numbered 1,000 men or more. To make matters worse, it began to rain and it went on raining, day after dismal day. The outlaws, soaked to the skin, hungry, and in pain, pushed on through an inhospitable land of lakes and swamps and forest.

Bob Younger's elbow was in very bad shape, and Cole's thigh wound was not much better. Even so, at one point they almost shook pursuit, abandoning their horses on the somewhat unconvincing thesis that because the pursuers were looking for mounted men, traveling on foot would be safer. Maybe so, but it was agonizing for the worst-hurt members of the gang.

At last the James boys struck off on their own, stealing a series of horses and in time riding clear into the Dakotas and finally back to Missouri. Their parting from the rest of the gang has been the stuff of all manner of purple prose, several writers asserting that the James boys simply abandoned their weary and wounded companions. A denial by Cole Younger didn't stop the flow of claptrap, like this fanciful passage from a Minnesota newspaper, asserting that Jesse wanted to kill Jim Younger, whose wounds were supposed to be slowing everybody down. Cole Younger is speaking in defense of his brother: "Jesse, we will separate now and here. If Frank shares your sentiment, and if Charley Pitts thinks the same way, you can take them with you, you curs!"

Or this highly suspect exchange from writer Homer Croy, in which Jesse speaks to Cole:

"We'll have to do something about Jim."

"What do you mean?"

"You know what I mean. He's holding us up . . ."

"He's doing the best he can."

"It's either him or us. I'm going to shoot him."

"If you shoot him, I'll kill you."

Or maybe this silliness from author Carl Breihan, famous for dubious dialogue:

"Damn you, Jesse James," hissed Cole. "You are a cold-hearted devil."

It is highly improbable that anything remotely like this ever happened, especially since Cole and Frank James were close friends and remained so long after Northfield. Cole claimed to his dying day that the parting was peaceful.

However the James brothers took leave of their comrades, the battered Youngers and faithful Charlie Pitts were left on their own. Hungry, painfully wounded, exhausted, on foot, they made their fatal mistake. They stopped at a farmhouse to ask for food. The credulous farmer was willing to believe they were ordinary people, but his young son was not. The boy, Oscar Sorbel, pestered his father until he permitted him to take a horse and ride into Madelia. There he found a resident to believe him, a hotel owner who remembered a conversation with Cole Younger when the outlaws passed through town prior to the raid. This man formed a posse and rode off to see whether Oscar had guessed right.

On the shore of Lake Hanska, the posse caught sight of their quarry and pursued them until Pitts and the Youngers were forced to go to ground in heavy brush on the edge of the Watonwan River. The posse surrounded the area, and then came the hard part. Everybody could see that once darkness fell, the outlaws might slip away in the gloom. On the other hand, it was hard to relish the notion of pushing into five acres of heavy undergrowth after four armed and desperate outlaws with nothing to lose. The men turned to their leader, Captain W. W. Murphy, veteran of a Pennsylvania regiment in the Civil War.

"I think we ought to go in after them," said Murphy, and called for volunteers. He had six. One, the Madelia hotel man who had listened to Oscar Sorbel, was also a Civil War veteran. Another volunteer was the local sheriff, a small but feisty man with a well-earned reputation as a fist-fighter. The other four volunteers were ordinary citizens who worked at ordinary occupations, but they were hardy and willing. The men shook themselves out into a skirmish line and walked into the thick brush with their weapons at the ready.

Inside the thicket one of the outlaws, probably Pitts, opened fire on the citizens, and a wild firefight broke out at point-blank range. Once more the professional outlaws came in a bad second. Murphy was jolted by a slug that broke his pipe and lodged in his pistol belt, and two other posse men were grazed by near misses. Nevertheless, all of them kept pouring lead into the outlaws. Pitts was hit by five bullets, one of which tore through his heart and put him down forever. The Younger brothers, already hurt, were hit repeatedly, and their fire quickly slackened and then died. "Surrender!" shouted Murphy, but only Bob Younger answered. "They're all down but me," he said. "I surrender."

It was over.

The outlaws had taken another terrible beating. Pitts was dead, Jim Younger had been shot five times, and Cole had eleven holes in his body. The prisoners were taken into Madelia, and later moved to the county jail in Faribault. In both places they were the center of great crowds of curious citizens. Cole Younger, ever ready to charm an audience, talked almost ceaselessly, while compassionate citizens made the shot-up outlaws as comfortable as possible. It was as well the Youngers were not returned to Northfield, where the citizens' grief and anger over the wanton murder of Heywood ran very deep indeed.

In Faribault, trial was held in November. On the twentieth day of that month, all three pleaded guilty to first-degree murder. Under the Minnesota law of the time, that plea restricted the maximum penalty to no more than life in prison, and that is the sentence the brothers received.

Reams of paper have been expended over the years on the question of who actually murdered Heywood. Charlie Pitts has always been a favorite suspect. Cole Younger said Pitts did the foul deed, but then, accusing Pitts was convenient, for dead men can't defend themselves.

Jesse James has also been repeatedly named as the killer, and the wanton deed is surely consistent with Jesse's nasty personality. One highly suspect account, in Columbus Vaughn's *This Was Frank James,* even reported this colorful and highly improbable dialogue, supposed to have happened when Jesse demanded that Heywood open the safe:

"I will do no such thing," said the brave cashier.

"Open," said Jesse, "or you die like a dog."

"I will do my duty," said the cashier.

"Then die," said Jesse James.

Apologists for the gang have Heywood "springing up" and reaching for a pistol. But Heywood, battered and bleeding, was in no condition to spring anyplace; as teller Wilcox said, "Anyone would know he was not reaching for a pistol and could not have used one had he held it in his hand."

The chances are that the killer was probably Frank James, and that the killing was simply cold-blooded murder. Bunker said flatly that Frank was the killer, although Bunker had fled the scene by the time Heywood was murdered. Although Cole Younger was vague about who shot the cashier at the time, and at one point nominated Pitts, in later years he is supposed to have told a friend that Frank fired the fatal round.

Bob Younger died in Minnesota's Stillwater Prison in 1889. Jim, who had never fully recovered from his wounds, was paroled with Cole in 1901. In declining health, despondent over failure in business, and denied permission to marry (due to his parolee status), he committed suicide in a St. Paul hotel the next year. Cole received the governor's permission to return to Missouri, where he spent some time in a sort of wild west show with old buddy Frank James, made a lot of "what my life has taught me" speeches, and finally died in Lee's Summit, Missouri, in 1916. In 1882, as every moviegoer knows, Jesse was murdered by fellow outlaw Bob Ford in St. Joseph, Missouri. Ford, a thoroughly worthless punk, ended up running a saloon in wild and woolly Creede, Colorado, and there he was shot down by an equally unpleasant character called Ed Kelly. Kelly later tried to murder a tough Oklahoma City policeman and ended up eating his own bullet. Frank James surrendered in October of the same year and spent some time in various jails before he was acquitted. He died at the old James farm at Kearney, Missouri, in 1915.

Chadwell and Miller had failed as outlaws, but both found second careers as cadavers in the dissecting rooms of the University of Michigan Medical School at Ann Arbor. Young Henry Wheeler could see no use in wasting good corpses—after all, he had some claim to the remains since he had killed one of them. And so, with the aid of another Michigan medical student, he had both men dug up and shipped safely to Ann Arbor, disguised as barrels of paint. Once their usefulness there was exhausted, Chadwell became the resident skeleton in now-doctor Wheeler's office. Miller, reduced to bones, in time was claimed by relatives.

Pitts also managed to be useful to society, also as suitable dissection material. He was displayed in Northfield for a time and then was shipped off to St. Paul. There he went on public display on a table in the state capitol. And there he remained until, as author Marv Balousek put it in *Murder In Minnesota,* he became an "unpleasant and disgusting spectacle," which he no doubt was. The surgeon general of Minnesota then claimed the remains and shipped Charlie off to be dissected, this time at a medical school in Chicago. In time, Charlie, too, put in years of service as the obligatory skeleton in a doctor's office.

Charlie, like his compatriots, was more use to society dead than he'd ever been alive.

# DIE GAME, BOYS!

## *A Death in Sonora*

MORE THAN ONE OUTLAW gang has been called "The Wild Bunch," including Bill Doolin's infamous collection of journeyman outlaws. But in the popular lore and legend of the West, that dubious appellation belongs first and foremost to the robber band led by Butch Cassidy.

When you talk about the hard core of the gang, the same names keep cropping up. Both before and after Cassidy and Harry Longabaugh (a.k.a. the Sundance Kid) went off to South America and got themselves killed by the Bolivian Army in 1908, other members of the Wild Bunch kept on plying their nefarious trade. In the fullness of time, most of them were overtaken by the same fate that caught up, man by man, with most professional hoodlums of the other famous outlaw gangs: prison or the grave, sometimes both. But mostly the grave.

Tom McCarty seems to have abandoned the outlaw business after a single tough citizen killed his brother and his nephew and drove Tom ingloriously out of Delta, Colorado, in October of 1896. Always pugnacious, there is a story that McCarty may have died by the gun in the end. One version of his finish says he was killed in a gunfight somewhere in the Bitterroot country of Montana in about 1900. The truth seems to be, however, that he died peacefully, having seen the error—or at least the futility—of his ways, and achieved both respectability and public office in Wallowa County, Oregon.

In 1904, Harvey Logan, after being wounded in a fight with a posse near Glenwood Springs, Colorado, apparently shot himself to avoid capture. His brother Lonnie, fleeing the law, was killed by a Pinkerton agent in Missouri in 1900. His other brother, Johnny, died of buckshot in 1896, in a failed attempt to murder a rancher who had given information to the law about the outlaw Logans. The Logans' cousin, Bob Lee—also known as Bob Curry—was run down by Pinkerton men up in Cripple Creek and went off to prison for ten years. Ed Bullion, a lesser light, was killed by an alert Wells Fargo express messenger near Stein's Pass, New Mexico.

George Curry, veteran of a number of train and bank holdups, was back at his original calling, rustling, in 1899. Called "Flat Nose" or "Big Nose" for reasons obvious when you looked at him, he was killed by a posse in 1900 near Castle Gate, Utah. Ben Kilpatrick, also known as the Tall Texan, lasted a little longer, mostly because he was out of circulation in prison for almost ten years between 1901 and 1911. However, Kilpatrick was eventually bludgeoned to death during a train robbery.

Unlike Kilpatrick, William—Elzy or Elza—Lay and Matt Warner were exceptions to the general rule. Lay died with his boots off, but only after serving time in the New Mexico Territorial Prison. Warner also did some time, but in the end turned a new leaf and actually ended his days at seventy-four, a respected lawman and justice of the peace.

Which brings us to Will—or Bill—Carver and the Tall Texan's brother, George Kilpatrick. Carver was once a well-liked Texas cowboy, well known around Sonora, Uvalde, and Bandera. He had a good many friends, and the respect of everybody who knew him. He was a first-class hand, and famous as a breaker of even the meanest horses.

Just why he went bad is not known. One tale says he turned outlaw after his wife's death, although several years elapsed between her passing and his first known involvement in crime. Or maybe he just grew tired of a lot of hard work for very little pay. Maybe, as a Texas author put it, he was sick of digging postholes in solid rock with hand tools. In any case, Carver is widely quoted as telling acquaintances, "The next time you see me I will be wearing diamonds or in a six-foot box." Nobody can say with certainty where and when he said this, or even if he said it at all, but it has the ring of truth.

HOLE IN THE WALL GANG or WILD BUNCH. Left to right, standing: Bill Carver and Harvy Logan. Sitting: Harry Longabaugh, Ben Kilpatrick and Geo. Parker, alias Butch Cassidy. (Photo by John Schwartz, at Ft.Worth, Dec.1900)

*The Wild Bunch,*
*aka The Hole in the Wall Gang*

SUTTON COUNTY HISTORICAL SOCIETY,
SONORA, TX

Once many of the members were together, they moved on to stay on Ben Kilpatrick's family ranch near Eden in Concho County, Texas. The band included Carver, Harvey Logan, and probably George Kilpatrick. There may have been at least one more outlaw present, a mysterious man generally referred to simply as "Walker," or maybe that was just an alias for Harvey Logan. The men loafed and played croquet, and probably talked about future robberies, but they did not hang around the ranch for long.

Either Carver, legend tells us, or maybe Harvey Logan, killed a young man—one O. G. Thornton—on the Kilpatrick place, perhaps because he thought Thornton recognized them. Thornton may have been unarmed, or maybe, as the *San Angelo Standard* reported, he "came to Kilpatrick's house—complained of Kilpatrick's hogs damaging [his employer's] farm—threw a Winchester on them—was shot by Walker—ran and Walker shot him again." Or maybe Thornton was simply spotted near the Kilpatrick hog pens and one of the outlaws shot him down as a possible spy for law enforcement.

Depending on the version of the incident you read, Thornton may have been killed by a single shot to the chest, or perhaps he had been shot twice. In any case, he was dead, and the local law was understandably interested in talking to people who might have shot him. Whatever happened, Carver rode on with the Tall Texan, and probably George Kilpatrick and Harvey Logan. Carver is often named as the killer of Thornton, but a case can be made for Harvey Logan as Thornton's murderer, rather than Carver, for Logan was a journeyman killer, described by the Pinkerton Agency as lacking "one single good point."

Extracurricular activities aside, the gang focused on Sonora, in Sutton County, down in south Texas. In those far-off days, the town had about 500 citizens, a couple of good-sized general stores and some other businesses, a newspaper, a school, and a hotel. It also had the usual complement of whorehouses, saloons, and gambling houses, for cowboys and goatherds took their fun where they found it. In April 1901, Sonora was still a tough town, out on the edge of nowhere.

The country around it tended to be somewhat dry and the grass was sparse, but the land supported some cattle, herds of Angora goats, and a race of very hardy people . . . as the outlaws were about to discover. In particular, this bunch of experienced bandits was about to run head-on into one Elijah Briant (sometimes Brient), who turned out to be every outlaw's worst nightmare.

Briant, called "Lige" by the many folks who knew him, was the local law. Like Henry V's gallant men of Agincourt, Lige was a warrior for the working day, for he was not a full-time lawman. Like a lot of other small-town sheriffs, he could not live on his job's miserable pay of a few hundred dollars a year. In fact, Lige was a druggist by trade, who prac-

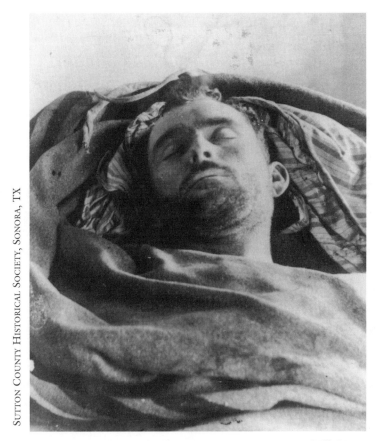

*Will Carver*

ticed his profession in Sonora with a partner called Cusenberry. He would later manage the Sonora Mercantile Company and serve as judge, postmaster, and county treasurer. Just now, however, he was about to face as difficult a challenge as he would ever know.

Though Lige was only a part-time county sheriff, he was a first-class lawman, a formidable cop who remained quiet and courteous to the citizens he protected. What he may have lacked in size, Sheriff Briant made up for in intelligence, determination, and a fighting heart. The *Frontier Times* described him thus:

*When train robbers and bank thieves found refuge in a thinly populated country, to be driven to other points by the coura-geous band of Lige Briant . . . he was absolutely fearless in the face of danger.*

Another source tells that when he was first elected sheriff, Briant was threatened by a "lawless element" with assassination after dark, which seems to have bothered Briant not at all. "Nothing to fear," he said. "Any coward shooting from night ambush will be too nervous to hit me." He had been wounded by a robbery suspect about a year before Carver came to town, but that memory would not hold him back.

Briant was not the sort of man to back away from anybody, Wild Bunch or not. He had a copy of the famous Fort Worth photograph of the Wild Bunch, so he had a pretty accurate idea about the direction from which his town's major trouble might come. He would soon find out.

Carver and George Kilpatrick rode into Sonora looking for horse feed—or maybe, according to one tale of the fight, chewing tobacco—perhaps still unaware that their happy faces had been circulated all over Texas. Their mission in town may have been more than just buying horse feed or a chaw. You have to wonder whether they had something else in mind as well—like maybe an unsecured loan from the bank. One witness said later that Ben Kilpatrick and Harvey Logan were also in town that day.

One reliable account of the incident states that all four men camped outside Sonora. One of them rode into town "to deposit $100 at the bank, in order to check it out." And then, on the evening of April 2, Carver and Logan rode deeper into town, riding up an alley behind the bank, "in order to check for a possible escape route." The same source puts Logan and Ben Kilpatrick waiting in a "draw just outside of town to await [Carver's] signal."

Whatever the two were searching for, they moved deeper into the town and stopped off at the Red Front Livery Stable. By then it was 8:00 P.M. and getting dark. The stable, run by a man named Beckett, was, per-haps significantly, across from the First National Bank, and local tradition in Sonora states that the outlaws took a somewhat circuitous route to the stable, a route that took them close to the bank.

SUTTON COUNTY HISTORICAL SOCIETY, SONORA, TX

*Lige Briant, sheriff of Sonora, with his wife*

It is permissible to suppose that the two were casing the bank and getting the lay of the land before calling in the other two outlaws waiting outside the town. Indeed, Carver was somewhat over armed for a peaceful trip to the feed store. He is said to have been carrying, in addition to his saddle gun, three pistols: a .45 Colt, a .38 Remington, and some sort of derringer tucked away inside his coat.

Whether the two outlaws were really looking for grain or tobacco, or were doing a recon of the area, they then pushed on to Jack Owens's bakery and store, which fronted the same street as the bank, across the way and a little farther down. While the two outlaws headed toward the bakery, they ran into real trouble in the shape of citizen Boosie (or Bossie) Sharp, who tended bar over at the Maud S., a watering hole named for a well-known racehorse.

Sharp thought the outlaws resembled the men wanted for questioning in the killing of Thornton. He correctly identified them, as the paper put it, as the "rubber tire buggy men," because they had been seen driving such a rig and pretending to be stock buyers. Sharp promptly sent word to his brother, Henry, who worked as a deputy for Sheriff Briant. The brother forthwith told his boss, and Briant marshaled his forces: Sharp, another deputy named J. L. Davis, and town constable W. H. Thomason. On the way into the bakery, one of the lawmen, maybe Briant, struck a match, probably to examine the brand on one of the outlaws' horses. Although George Kilpatrick saw the flare of the match outside, and mentioned it to Carver, Carver either didn't hear him or didn't pay attention.

According to the *Devil's River News*, Sheriff Briant, "having the least man further identified and the tallest suiting the description of one of the Kilpatricks, acted promptly."

Here's how the *San Angelo Standard* told the rest of the story:

> *He told his men to get ready and the four officers stepped into the store. Sheriff Briant covered the men and required that they hold up their hands. The tall man, Kilpatrick, who was nearest the door, made a surprised or fumbling motion with his hands, but the other went for his gun at once. Sheriff Briant saw the movement and shot instantly, and the man fell to the floor before he could cock his pistol.*

Or maybe, as local tradition in Sonora has it, it was Davis who put Carver down. Davis, says local lore, was a crack shot, and Sheriff Briant was the first to admit he was a lousy marksman. Davis is reputed to have later told the *Devil's River News* that Thomason was trying to take all the

Sutton County Historical Society, Sonora, TX

*Deputy J. L. Davis*

credit. But, he added, "write whatever Thomason tells you . . . I don't want to be known as the man who killed anyone."

Constable Thomason sent a bullet into Kilpatrick, and then all the lawmen blazed away at both outlaws, thoroughly ventilating both men. Carver went down hard, unable to fire off a single shot. According to the San Angelo paper, one of the lawmen's first bullets smashed Carver's shooting hand, but he stayed on his feet and tried the "border switch," tossing his pistol from the injured hand to the other. It didn't work. Swamped by a torrent of lawmen's bullets, neither outlaw managed to fire a shot, and the officers took what was left of them into custody without further trouble.

Logan and Ben Kilpatrick, if they were in town at all, did not appear to support their colleagues in crime. One report said they had galloped into the street in front of the bakery with their guns drawn, but then thought better of it and clattered off into the night.

Carver would survive another three hours, in spite of an astonishing assortment of wounds. The *Devil's River News,* which should have done the most accurate reporting, being local, said:

> *Carver was shot through the right lung and the ball passed through the body and lodged under the skin near the spine; twice in the right arm and twice in the right leg and once in the temple. Both his right arm and right leg were broken in two places.*

Or maybe, as the *San Angelo Standard* had it, he was hit only four times. In any case, Carver was doomed, although he lasted a surprising three hours. At first he gave the officers an alias, saying he was one of the "Off boys." But then an old friend, a cowboy called Ben Binyon, leaned down to him and asked, "Don't you know me, Bill?" And Carver acknowledged that he did.

Toward the end, just before his world ended, under the spell of an opiate given by the local doctor, he became delirious and raved to invisible companions, "Will you stay with me? Will you sweat it out? Die game, boys!" Or maybe it was, "You'll stand by me, boys, won't you?" The attending doctor replied, "Yes. What shall we do?" "Shell 'em!" yelled the dying outlaw, drifting deeper into delirium, "Shell 'em!"

By midnight, Will Carver had ceased shouting and had passed to his reward, whatever that uncertain fortune might be. He had been identified by a number of Sonora residents who knew him well, and there was no longer any doubt of who he was. The editor of the *Devil's River News* sent photographer J. P. Beard to snap photos of the sheriff's famous catch. Such grim photos were, after all, the custom of the times, and were widely sought after by ordinary citizens.

*Bar in Sonora, Texas —*
*Boosie Sharp second from right*

SUTTON COUNTY HISTORICAL SOCIETY, SONORA, TX

A *pro forma* inquest by a local justice of the peace found, not surprisingly, that Carver had been killed by officers of the law "while in the proper and legal discharge of their duties . . . and after having duly demanded the surrender of the man." There were a few who grumbled that the killing was little short of murder, but Sheriff Briant was well respected, and any reasonable man had to conclude that for lawmen to walk into a room inhabited by two hardcase gunmen without having their weapons drawn and cocked would be tantamount to suicide. If example were wanted, back in 1878 a pair of lawmen had tried just that down in Round Rock, Texas, and were shot down by Sam Bass and two cohorts.

On the fourth of April, Carver was buried under the auspices of the local Methodist preacher. And then, early in July, Carver's personal possessions were auctioned off: four horses, a couple of pistols, a watch, a compass, a diamond ring, and some horse furniture. Once the expenses of his funeral were paid, what was left was sent off to Carver's mother, who lived still in Bandera County.

Kilpatrick, amazingly, was still alive, though punctured an astonishing fourteen times—or maybe it was five, or twelve, depending on which version of the fight you want to believe. The *Devil's River News* said he'd been hit five times, and that's close enough. Even more amazingly, he actually recovered from his shattering injuries. Three weeks after the shooting, Concho County Sheriff Howze rode into town, collected Kilpatrick, and took him off for trial.

Even then, Kilpatrick remained close-mouthed. He was asked who had killed young Thornton, according to the *Devil's River News.* The wounded man denied that he had been present during the shooting, but said he'd been told that "McDonald" did the killing. "Was that Carver?" somebody asked. No, said Kilpatrick, forgoing a perfect chance to lay all the blame on a man already dead.

Kilpatrick was ultimately released since there were no charges pending against him.

After the smoke had blown away, people came to view the body, and the usual mythology began. One observer is said to have declared that Carver's corpse had a "glass eye," and another reported that the body's trigger finger was "still twitching."

After Carver was buried in the local cemetery, there appeared the usual story that the corpse was not that of Will Carver, and that old friends had conspired to misidentify the body so that their old friend might ride free. There were too many other people who had seen the body, however—too many people who knew Carver well for that to be so. And the photo of the outlaw in death is a dead—no pun intended—ringer for the debonair outlaw in the famous Fort Worth group photo of the Wild Bunch.

There remains the tale of the "no-name grave." For many years, Carver rested under a stone that gave no more than the date of his death and omitted his name altogether. It is certainly possible, though there are other stories, that his name was omitted out of respect for the dead, on the thesis that if nobody but local folk knew who was buried there, the grave would not be disturbed. Carver's date of birth may have been omitted because nobody knew what it was.

The best story of this odd marker, though, is the local tale, passed on in Sonora by a woman who said her mother had told her of a "heavily veiled woman," who ordered and paid for the headstone, then disappeared and was not seen again. The mystery lady is said to have been the dead man's sister, Frances. One would expect Carver's sister to have known her brother's date of birth.

But then, it's a nice story.

## FIASCO IN NOGALES

### *The Scaredy-Cat Bandits*

THE CHRISTIAN BOYS, BROTHERS Bill and Bob, started their hoodlum career in Oklahoma Territory. Their family lived down in the wide-open land north of the Canadian River, in what would one day be Pottawatomie County. This wild and woolly area was studded with "saloon towns" in those days, wide spots in the road like Young's Crossing, Keokuk Falls, and Violet Springs. Then there was The Corner, a tiny patch of land on the South Canadian, whose low-life saloons attracted the trash of the territory.

Violence was endemic in this part of the world. The booze parlors in Keokuk Falls were aptly known as the "seven deadly saloons." For example, somebody shot a saloonkeeper named Haning in the head and left him on the floor of his bar. Then, apparently having second thoughts, the killer came back "between daybreak and sunrise," to finish the process by driving a rusty nail into Haning's ear. When trains of the Choctaw, Oklahoma, and Gulf Railroad stopped in the hamlet of Shawnee, the conductor comfortingly announced: "Shawnee! Twenty minutes for lunch and to see a man killed."

These towns were hell on wheels while they lasted—until all of Oklahoma went dry in 1907. Even in the larger settlements like Shawnee, booze flowed like water. At the turn of the century, the Pottawatomie country boasted more than sixty saloons and two distilleries, and

Shawnee town's *daily* booze intake in 1903 was said to be 25 gallons of whiskey and 700 gallons of beer.

The area was a ready-made haven for career outlaws like the Daltons, Bill Doolin, Zip Wyatt, and the Casey boys. It also gave sanctuary to a horde of small-time punks. With Indian Territory on two sides, the country was an ideal base for bootleggers who ran prohibited hooch into Indian lands. It was here that the venerable term "bootlegger" may have had its genesis, describing those smugglers who rode into Indian country with pint bottles of John Barleycorn stuffed into their boot tops.

There were lots of good people in the Pottawatomie country too, and the Christian family was numbered among them. The brothers proved to be black sheep, however, and won an unenviable reputation as whiskey runners and horse thieves by the time they were in their twenties. In those days the boys headquartered in Andy Morrison's saloon in Violet Springs. Andy was eventually murdered while sleeping in his own back room, and in 1895 the brothers graduated from small-time crime to killing.

In April 1895, it came to pass that the brothers and a drinking buddy, one John Mackey, walked out of Doug Barnes's saloon and found the law waiting for them. Deputy Will Turner had warrants for the brothers' arrest, and he was tough enough—or unwise enough—to try to bring them in single-handed. Turner didn't count on the brothers and Mackey all drawing on him at once. He died in the dusty street.

Tough Sheriff Billy Trousdale ran down Mackey, and the Christian boys turned themselves in, which turned out to be a bad idea. The court reporter at their trial remembered that the judge gave the brothers twenty-five and twenty-two years for the killing. The *Oklahoma City Oklahoman*, however, told its readers that the Christians had been sentenced to eight and ten years.

Whatever their terms actually were, the pair was transferred to the Oklahoma County Jail in Oklahoma City, which was, at the time, a two-story building fitted out with interior steel cages and thought to be a solid, secure lockup. Confined at the same time, in the same cell, was a nineteen-year-old bad hat called Casey, who, with his brother, had murdered a deputy marshal, Sam Ferris, over in Canadian County in the latter part of May.

One of the Casey brothers—either Jim or Vic, depending on what account you read—had been shot up in the fight with the deputy and later died. But the surviving brother—the *Daily Oklahoman* said it was Vic—was going to stand trial for murder. He was due to be released on bond, but apparently did not care to wait.

Neither did Bob Christian. He prevailed upon Jessie Finlay, his girl-friend, to smuggle in several guns, which he stashed in the stovepipe inside his cell. The outlaws chose Sunday, June 30, 1895, to make their break, for on Sundays the jailer, J. H. Garver, allowed his prisoners to move about in the corridor outside their cells. Garver was either an easygoing sort or just plain negligent; the Pottawatomie law had wired him only the day before, warning about the jailbreak, but he paid no attention.

At first the break went well. Casey and the Christians pistol-whipped the jailer and ran into an alley behind the jail. There, one of the Christians stole a horse belonging to Police Chief Milt Jones and gal-loped out of town. The other brother, probably Bob, fled with Casey on foot. They stopped a couple in a buggy and shoved their pistols into the driver's face. Carpenter Gus White, the driver, would not let loose of the reins, and managed to pull the horses to a halt. Although the fugitives shot White in the leg and the stomach, he would survive.

Chief Jones was closing in on the fugitives, however, and as he came within 8 or 10 feet of the buggy, one of the outlaws turned and shot Jones down. Some observers thought Christian killed the lawman, but the coroner's jury decided Casey was the murderer. Whoever fired the fatal shot, the officer staggered onto the sidewalk and sank down against a building. He was dead in five minutes.

A wild gun battle then broke out on Grand Avenue, the fugitives on one side and officers Stafford and Jackson and several armed citizens on the other. The lawmen drilled Casey through the neck and head, and the desperado died in White's riddled buggy.

Bob Christian was also hit, but managed to run off down Grand Avenue until he met blacksmith Frank Berg, driving a cart. Christian robbed Berg of his cart, whipped up the horse, and clattered off, at least until he stuck up another driver and highjacked a faster team.

With Chief Jones dead in the street and both of the Christian brothers vanished, a posse of angry citizens rode hard after the outlaws.

*Bill Christian*

The *Daily Oklahoman* opined that there was "little doubt" the fugitives would be captured. "Should they be caught," the paper editorialized, "a double lynching will surely follow."

That might well have happened, for the citizenry of Oklahoma City were furious. One journalist accurately described the Christians as "noted thugs and desperadoes," and another, having viewed Casey at the undertaker's emporium, somewhat spitefully commented that Casey "looked much better in death than in life." But to do the abrupt justice everybody wanted, somebody had to catch the Christians. That would prove very tough to do, though posses searched high and low.

Closer to home, the authorities sought out those who had been part of the planning for the break. Jessie, the loyal girlfriend, spent fourteen months in jail for her part. Jailer Garver discovered that he should have paid attention to the warning wire: His negligence earned him ten years in prison, and he served two before he was pardoned.

The Christian brothers were very much in evidence across Indian Territory for the next couple of months. Even as lawmen beat the bushes for them, the bandits embarked on a string of small-time raids on country post offices and general stores, perhaps as many as twenty or thirty of them.

Deputy Marshal F. J. (or F. C.) Stockton killed one gang member, a man named Fessenden, and another Christian cohort, Foster Holbrook, was captured. On the twenty-first of August, outlaw John Reeves, who had helped furnish weaponry for the jailbreak, was arrested near the town of Paoli. Later tried as a conspirator in Chief Jones's murder, he was sentenced to life.

On August twenty-third the Christians shot their way past lawmen west of Purcell; although Deputy Marshall W. E. Hocker was wounded in the fight, the posse believed Hocker had sent a bullet into Bob Christian.

The gang reappeared in Oklahoma County in early September, breaking into the railroad agent's quarters in Edmond. On the sixth of October, they held up a St. Louis and San Francisco train east of Wilburton, but rode off with only another measly haul. In the small hours of September 30, Louis Miller, another of the jailbreak conspirators, was jumped by lawmen near Violet Springs. Miller decided to fight and came in second.

Their last hurrah came in December, when they robbed a mining company store at Coalgate, down in Choctaw country. This raid was another failure: a little over $200 in money, and about $200 in merchandise.

It was enough to travel on, however, and Oklahoma was getting far too hot for the gang. And so, a month or so later, the Christian boys turned up in Seven Rivers, New Mexico. They eventually ended up in Arizona's Sulphur Springs Valley. By this time Bill was calling himself Ed Williams and brother Bob told people he was Tom Anderson.

Bill went to work breaking horses for the 4-Bar Ranch, and soon acquired the handles of "202," apparently from his weight, and "Black Jack," from his dark hair and mustache (not to be confused with Black Jack Ketchum, for whom Christian is sometimes mistaken). His partner, an honest cowboy named Ed Wilson, said of Christian that "a finer partner never lived. Big, strong, fearless, and good natured . . . ever ready to take his part, no matter what the game might be."

Black Jack loved to whoop it up over in the mining town of Bisbee, down on the border, and Wilson recounted that the big puncher "could spend more money than fifteen men could earn." He often said, according to Wilson, that "he had a good idea to get up [an] outfit and go train robbing." He repeatedly urged Wilson to join him, but the honest cowpoke refused.

Others did not, however, and Christian soon raised another gang of hoodlums with a bewildering assortment of nicknames. They included Texan Cole Young, whose real name was probably Harris. Then there was Bob Hayes, who may have been another Texan, or maybe he was an Iowa hoodlum named Sam Hassels. Other gang members were George Musgrave, another Texan, who also called himself Jeff Davis and Jesse Johnson; and Jesse Williams, who may have been just another alias of Musgrave. Finally, add "Tom Anderson," who was probably brother Bob Christian, and you have the gang known in the southwest as the "High Fives."

All of these ne'er-do-wells, according to cowboy Wilson, were "crack shots," who removed the triggers from their pistols and simply thumbed back the hammer "when in a tight place," and fanned the pistol. "The speed," said Wilson, "with which they could shoot in this manner was simply amazing." No doubt, but could they hit anything beyond 10 feet?

With these henchmen and another hard case called Three-Fingered Jack Dunlap, Black Jack rode off to rob the International Bank at Nogales, right on the border. There are half a dozen versions of what happened there on the sixth of August, 1896.

The most reliable accounts generally agree that Black Jack Christian and some of his band, probably Musgrave and Dunlap, stayed outside with the horses. Others—probably three, including Jesse Williams and Bob Hayes—went into the bank. They had excellent luck at first; their mouths must have watered at the sight of at least, according to the local paper, $10,000 in real money. One version made it $30,000, which had been counted out and was waiting for Ed Roberts, a San Pedro valley rancher bringing in a big herd from Mexico.

Very quickly, however, things began to fall apart. In one tale, the bank's directors were meeting upstairs. Hearing the commotion beneath, they threw open windows and opened fire on the astonished robbers. That tale turns out to be pure fantasy. In fact, the major problem for the bandits was a pair of tough bank men, president John Dessart and cashier Frank Herrera, both of whom were all wool and a yard wide.

Herrera was sitting in a chair inside the bank's counter, while Dessart stood at one end of the counter counting bills. Herrera glanced up to find himself looking into the unpleasant end of two pairs of "cocked navy revolvers." "Stick 'em up," the bandits ordered, and Herrera complied, but at the same time he moved closer to the counter and the revolver that lay on a shelf beneath it. He was only a step or so away from the weapon when the bandits told him to stop or they'd kill him. Herrera stopped, but he didn't give up the thought of defending his bank.

Dessart moved toward the front door, hoping, as the *Nogales Oasis* said, "to give an alarm and get a gun." He almost made it around the third bandit, but as he passed, the outlaw slammed a Winchester barrel across his head. Dessart was staggered, but he ran on through the door and up the street, blood streaming down his face. The bandit was right behind him. As Dessart passed the next-door store, he shouted to clerk Harry Lewis. "Call for help," he yelled. "Tell them the bank is being robbed."

The bandit chasing Dessart now stopped and threw down on Lewis. "Touch that phone and I'll kill you," he said, and, as the *Oasis* tastefully put it, "Harry concluded that it was no 'hello' today for him," and stayed away from the telephone.

Inside the bank, Herrera stood helplessly with his hands raised while one of the outlaws moved down the side of the counter toward the door leading inside. There was, according to the *Oasis,* some $10,000 "on the paying desk," just waiting to be collected.

When the bandit reached the door, however, he found himself looking into the bank's "parlor," in which five gentlemen from Nogales and Washington, D.C., were at work putting together a water company. "Put up your hands," said the outlaw, brandishing those two navy colts, and the water planners did so. The bandit shut the door on them, and all five, as the *Oasis* put it, "sought the fresh air through the back door."

About now nature took a hand, in the form of a very strong gust of wind. One story says the rout of the bandits was the work of a passing whirlwind, which slammed the bank's back door and scared the gang's inside men out of a year's growth. According to the newspaper account of the raid, however, the wind's effect was to create a diversion. The crash of the doors and the rattle of bolt chains startled and distracted the robbers, who looked toward the doors. Herrera seized his opportunity. He grabbed the pistol under the counter and began to blaze away.

The bandit in front of the counter sprinted out the front door, running for his life as Herrera's bullets whizzed past him. His compatriot gave up on getting the money on the counting table and fled through the parlor and out the back door of the building. As he ran, Herrera took a shot at him and probably hit him, for the man, thought to be Musgrave, fell and then rose again, limping and holding his knee.

The wounded robber made it back to the main street by running through a store, and his companions helped him to mount. Meanwhile, Herrera had run to the front door and was firing on the outlaws as they rode north out of town. Two citizens, Nace Burgoon and Harvey Walker, also shot fruitlessly at them as they galloped for safety, and two more local men, John Mapes and Charley Mehan, ran to the edge of town and blazed away, also without result.

With all these citizens banging away at them, the fleeing robbers stood not upon the order of their going. As they passed the Montezuma Hotel, one B. E. Hambleton ran out, borrowed a horse from a passerby and a Winchester from Burgoon, and gave chase. By now the outlaws had opened the distance between them and pursuit, but Hambleton followed for a couple of miles and exchanged shots with them. Hambleton wasn't sure whether he'd hit anybody, but in late afternoon somebody reported finding a corpse at a nearby place called Buena Vista. The dead man was probably a casualty of natural causes or of some other quarrel, for none of the High Fives seems to have been missing at the end of the day.

To add to the bandits' woes, either just before or just after the bank's resident hero opened fire, a passerby had also pulled his .41 Colt and begun shooting at the confused robbers. This was cowboy-turned-customs-collector Frank King, a very tough cookie indeed. While King, later a newspaperman, was not one to minimize his own role in the repulse of the High Fives, he certainly contributed.

Whatever the sequence of events, it convinced the gang that Nogales was no place to tarry. The inside men tumbled out of the bank in something of a swivet, dropped their loot, and the whole outfit fled, as cowboys put it, at the high lope. The bank man was still banging away behind them, though all he hit was an unfortunate horse parked across the street from the bank.

King pursued, first on a buggy horse, then on a pony requisitioned from a passing cowboy, turning back only when the outlaws began to shoot at him. Nothing daunted, King raised a posse and pursued, to no avail. Sheriff John Roberts also formed a posse and gave chase, taking with him four Mexican customs gendarmes in case the outlaws should double back into Mexico.

Other posses took the field as well, including Bisbee riders led by Burt Alvord, soon to become a bandit in his own right. Sheriff Bob Leatherwood's party, with Alvord and Cochise County Sheriff Camillus Fly along, came very near the outlaws, who littered their back trail with abandoned food and cooking gear, even a loaded mule, in their haste to reach the Mexican border. But as the posse closed in, the gang turned on them. In the ensuing firefight, one of the posse men died.

The *Tucson Daily Citizen* reported that the lawmen were ambushed in Skeleton Canyon, a place of evil reputation, where a "desperate fight" ensued. Deputy Frank Robinson went down "at the first volley," with bullets through his forehead and his temple. The deputy's horse galloped off with him, dead or dying, and the waiting outlaws took the animal, along with Robinson's money, watch, and revolver.

Leatherwood jumped from his horse as the panicked animal bolted. A lawman named Hildreth then killed Black Jack's mount, but the bandit caught the sheriff's horse and managed to switch saddles, only to have the lawman's animal killed before Black Jack could mount.

Hildreth's horse also went down, but Hildreth, wounded, fought on, though the tree behind which he sheltered was filled with lead. Leatherwood, Fly, Alvord, and another posse man named Johnson also fought back as best they could, but they were shooting only at puffs of smoke.

After the firing died away, the battered posse found their quarry vanished. The lawmen followed, reinforced by more posse men, including deadly manhunter Texas John Slaughter ("I say, I say, shoot first and shout 'throw up your hands after'"). According to one version of the tale, Slaughter was not impressed with the posse's actions thus far, and said so. "You're a fine bunch of officers," he commented. "If there was any ambushing to be done, why in the heck didn't *you* do it?"

But on August 18, Leatherwood wrote from a town in Sonora that heavy rains had washed out the gang's trail. Southern Pacific detective Billy Breakenridge reported that the robbers were back in the United States, holed up at the San Simon Cattle Company's horse ranch.

The gang next struck the San Simon railroad station, then the post office and Wickersham's Store at Bowie. In between, they "liberated" horses whenever they needed new mounts, although in most cases they were careful to let the owners know where their stock was ultimately left. It paid to keep good relations with ordinary people when you were on the run—like paying for breakfast at the little Joe Schaefer ranch with a couple of Bull Durham sacks of change from the post office robbery. That sort of largesse made people feel better about you. After all, it's not much of a burden to be generous if you're using somebody else's money.

The pursuing officers now included Jeff Milton, the bulldog Wells Fargo man. Along the way he and a deputy stayed a night at Brandt's Store in San Simon. Brandt welcomed them with delight since he had already been held up once by the High Fives and feared the outlaws would visit him again. While Milton was at the store, a cowboy came in bragging about how Christian was making fools of the officers, and how he himself "could run the officers out of the country with a smoking corn cob."

That was not a wise thing to say around Jeff Milton. "Go up there," he told the deputy, "and box his jaws. I'll be a-watchin' him, and if he beats you to the draw I'll kill him."

"Sure," said the deputy, "it'll be a pleasure." He whopped the cowboy smartly under Milton's watchful eye. "I didn't see no smoking corn cobs," said Milton afterward.

On a moonless night in October, the High Fives hit the eastbound A&P train at Rio Puerco trestle in New Mexico. The robbery should have been easy, for the train obligingly stopped while the engineer inspected a faulty piston rod. The gang threw down on the train crew, shooting the brakeman in the hand when he came forward to see what the trouble was. But now bad luck appeared again, in the form of a train passenger, Deputy United States Marshal Horace Loomis.

Loomis suspected something was wrong up front, and so he thoughtfully loaded his shotgun and stepped quietly out into the night. He saw the engineer uncoupling the express car as Cole Young shouted orders at him. There was neither obligation nor inclination to shout, "Halt, police!" in those simpler days. And so, without ceremony, the officer dropped Young. The outlaw regained his feet and snapped off a couple of rounds from his pistol before the marshal gave him the second barrel. *Exit* Young. The rest of the gang, uncertain what had happened to Young, at last realized that something was very wrong and galloped off into the night without their loot.

The gang went on with their small-time robberies, holding up a couple of stages and a series of isolated stores. As usual, their labors produced very little money, plus bits and pieces of liquor and tobacco. There was a good deal of casual brutality connected with these robberies. Bob Hayes pistol-whipped one elderly country postmaster, for example, because the old man objected to losing about five dollars, all the money he had.

There wasn't much profit in robbing isolated stores, even for bush-league punks like the High Fives, and it kept the lawmen constantly after them. After robbing a store in tiny Separ, between Deming and Lordsburg, New Mexico, they tangled with a posse at the Diamond A Horse Camp. The story goes that sympathetic cowboys were to display a white cloth on the corral when it was safe for the outlaws to visit the ranch. They hadn't counted on the law moving in and detaining every-body at the camp, spoiling the signal system.

And so, when Black Jack and Bob Hayes rode into camp, unsuspect-ing, the officers raised up out of their hiding place in a salt lick and blazed away. Bob Hayes was blown off his horse, probably killed by the rifle of town marshal Fred Higgins of Roswell (although another story says he was venti-lated by a Santa Fe conductor somewhere around Kingman, Arizona).

Black Jack got away from the Diamond A, even though his horse was killed by the lawmen. If the legend is to be believed, he single-handedly heaved the dead animal up far enough to pull his Winchester clear of the corpse, then shot his way out of the ambush. A posse man shot five times at the outlaw leader, at a range at which it seemed he could not miss, but Christian escaped unscathed, largely because of the bucking and twisting of his frantic horse. Jeff Milton and the other hunters could not close with the gang. However, in February 1897, after a train robbery in New Mexico went sour, Black Jack's own paranoia moved him to kill a gang member called Red Sanders, who, he thought, had talked to the law. It was after that stupid and unnecessary murder that Black Jack moved south to hide out east of Clifton in a tangled, wild gorge, to this day called Black Jack Canyon. It was in that desolate place that the tireless law finally caught up with him.

As is common in the mythology of the West, there are a couple of different stories about the end of Black Jack Christian. After the failed attempt on the A&P train at Rio Puerco, the gang hid out at a goat ranch near Clifton. There they planned another job, but an informer tipped off the law. Deputy Marshal Hall, the formidable Fred Higgins, and posse men Bill Hart, Crook-Neck Johnson, and Charlie Paxton set up an ambush in Cole Creek Canyon, down in Graham County.

Ironically, it was a lost hat that put paid to Black Jack's career. Disappointed, the lawmen had already folded up their trailside ambush and were riding toward the ranch to ask for breakfast when Fred Higgins turned back to look for his hat. It was at this moment that the posse saw three men on the trail behind them, already reaching for their weapons. The first shot came from Higgins, however, whom the outlaws had not seen. The three bandits broke for safety in the dense undergrowth, but one staggered before he could find cover.

The officers intelligently decided that they had not lost anything back in that heavy brush. So, rather than try to search for whomever they hit, they prudently withdrew to nearby Clifton. Later in the day, however, a cowboy named Bert Farmer passed down the same trail, driving horses, and stopped when the animals shied at something near the trail.

That something was Black Jack Christian, mortally wounded. The cowboy took him to a nearby ranch, but Black Jack did not last long. Dying, he murmured that it didn't matter "who he was, or what his name might be." A Mormon freighter brought into Clifton all that remained of this two-bit bandit, tossed on top of a load of lumber. A lot of people proceeded to identify the body, and some of them, inspired either by ignorance or friendship for the deceased, said the dead bandit was outlaw Black Jack Ketchum.

According to lawman Billy Breakenridge, an ambush party led by Deputy Sheriff Ben Clark caught Christian's gang about daylight on April 27, 1897, killing both Black Jack and George Musgrave. Another source differs, and writes that only Black Jack went down, riddled with four slugs from the weapon of famous manhunter Jeff Milton. Both accounts are probably partly wrong.

Musgrave certainly survived the ambush in which Black Jack died. And Milton, the very tough Wells Fargo man, was not part of the posse that killed Black Jack. Later, however, he ran down other High Five members, and it was Milton's shotgun that put an end to Three-Fingered Jack Dunlap, veteran of the bungled Nogales raid and a journeyman villain in his own right.

The two bandits who got away were probably Musgrave and Bob Christian. Christian surfaced in Mexico in the autumn of 1897, where he was arrested and escaped, then disappeared forever. Musgrave appeared later in Colorado, then was arrested in North Platte, Nebraska, in December of 1909. In time, he settled in South America, dying in Paraguay in 1947.

One curious postscript remains. Black Jack Ketchum, regularly mistaken for Black Jack Christian, made an intriguing comment in April 1901, the day he was hanged in Clayton, New Mexico. He knew Black Jack Christian, he said, and insisted that Christian was still alive. "Oh yes," said Ketchum, "I have an idea where he is but I won't tell." And he didn't. The secret, if there was one, went to the grave with Ketchum—both parts of him, for the shock of the drop separated his head from the rest of his body, and he was buried in two pieces.

So passed the High Fives. From the debacle at Nogales to their other nickel-and-dime crimes, they were a remarkably unsuccessful gang of bandits. And in the end, most of them were paid off in the usual coin—6 feet of infertile ground.

## END OF THE ROAD FOR THE BEARCAT

### *Henry Starr, King of the Bank Robbers*

HE WAS RELATED BY MARRIAGE to Belle Starr, the "bandit queen," much celebrated in print and celluloid. Though Belle was one of the West's most enduring legends, she was no queen, and she was also one of the all-time overrated criminals. But he himself was the real thing, all wool and a yard wide; the papers called him "The Bearcat." His name was Henry Starr, and he was probably the most prolific American bank robber of all time. When he started taking other people's money, the outlaw's favorite means of escape was the horse; when he finished his crooked career, he and the rest of America's robbers were carrying off their loot in automobiles.

As Starr himself said, "I have robbed more banks than any man in the U.S." And then he added, "It doesn't pay." But that last part was probably an afterthought, for when he said it, Starr was lying in bed in an Arkansas jail cell. He was dying, and he knew he was. By that time he was worried about making his peace with God, as he put it, surely a matter he might profitably have thought about long years before, for he had been a bank robber for an astonishingly long time.

Henry Starr was part Cherokee, born in Fort Gibson, Indian Territory, in December of 1873. His father was George Starr, called "Hop," son of notorious old Tom Starr and brother to Sam Starr, the sometime husband of the celebrated Belle. His mother, Mary Scott, was a much-respected lady. Starr had what he described as a sixth-grade education before entering the hard adult world of work and choices. He made some bad ones early on.

With practice, Starr got pretty good at larceny, and he raised his sights. In December of 1892, he visited Coffeyville, Kansas, the scene of the Dalton Gang's disastrous attempt to rob two banks at once. There he bought wire cutters and gun holsters, presumably in preparation for greater things.

Oppressed by other people, as he said he was, Starr himself apparently saw nothing wrong in jumping bail after one of his early crimes, leaving people who believed in him holding the bag. Nor did conscience seem to bother him when he hid out at the home of a friend, and then stole the friend's "hog money," about $300, a substantial nest egg in those days. If Satan was tugging Henry toward a life of sin, he didn't have to pull very hard. The friends who had put up his bail offered a reward for him, an offer which would lead Starr straight to even deeper trouble.

Wanted for jumping bail in Fort Smith, he was encountered on Wolf Creek, near Lenapah, by ex-deputy marshal Floyd Wilson, who had boasted that he would bring Starr in "alive—or dead." Wilson was riding with a detective named Dickey, who on this day unfortunately had fallen some distance behind. Wilson took his Winchester out of the saddle scabbard and shouted to Starr, "Hold up, I have a warrant for you." Starr, who had dismounted and drawn his own rifle, yelled back, "You hold up!" and both men opened fire at a range of only about thirty yards. Wilson probably fired first, although that shot may have been simply a warning. Starr later asserted that he had "pleaded with [Wilson] not to make me kill him, but he opened fire, the first ball breaking my saddle and two others passing close by."

In fact, the officer's rifle jammed after that single round, and Starr shot him down. Wilson pulled his pistol as he lay on the ground, but Starr shot him again, and then once more, finally driving a third round point-blank into Wilson's chest. The last round pierced Wilson's heart. Starr turned away from the fallen officer, whose clothing still smoldered from the muzzle blast. He swung up on Wilson's horse and rode away.

Later on, in *Thrilling Events*, a sort of penny-dreadful autobiography, Starr admitted that he killed the officer, but then boasted that he had

*Henry Starr in jail*

"made his companion [Dickey] hug the ground so close that he played 'possum." That part, of course, was pure braggadocio, for Dickey did not reach Wolf Creek until after Wilson was killed. Starr added that he had never had "any qualms of conscience over that occurrence. It was simply a case of their lives or mine."

So far as anybody knows, Wilson was the only man Starr ever killed, but that was hardly due to Starr's peaceable nature. The outlaw surely did a lot of pistol waving in his robbing days, and a good deal of indiscriminate shooting as well. Fortunately for the general public, he never hit anybody else, unless he did some quiet murdering that is not recorded.

Much of Starr's early robbing was bush-league: holdups of country stores, and stealing indiscriminately from store tills and individual citizens. For instance, he and one Milo Creekmore stuck up a little country store in Lenepah, looking for a stockman's $700 that was supposed to be held there. They followed that with another store robbery in which they robbed the clerk of some $500, magnanimously "giving back to the fellow $10 of the $500 so that he might have something with which to do business."

Starr and his growing gang certainly were not getting rich. They were, however, beginning to create something of a reputation. One fanciful story had Starr killing a running coyote at 685 yards, a tale about as likely as that of the Easter Bunny. He would, he said, "show the natives just how real outlaws could perform," an ambition that was real, if not laudable. This dubious goal he surely achieved.

In June of 1893 Starr followed up his success on a previous job with an ambitious attempt to rob a bank in Bentonville, Arkansas, scene of a robbery by the James Gang not long after the Civil War. But the Bentonville bank turned out to be one too many. Starr was cautious at the start of this one. He had the gang's rifles brought into town in a hired buggy to escape attention.

But once the robbery began, the citizens of Bentonville quickly learned what was happening and reached for their weapons. Starr ran for his life amid a torrent of gunfire. One of his men, Link Cumplin, was badly shot up, although he managed to stay on his horse and clear the town. Like other Starr accomplices, Cumplin would finish the year quite dead from his wounds. One townsman took a round in the groin and another was wounded in the chin, but the gang was in full retreat, with a posse hot on their heels.

The gang would never ride together again. Starr managed to evade the posse, but was arrested not long afterward in Colorado Springs. He faced a multitude of charges at Fort Smith and was convicted of several robberies. To add insult to injury, the People's Bank of Bentonville sued Starr for $11,000 worth of money looted from the bank. Starr denied the claim, even though he was carrying much of the money when he was arrested in Colorado.

But the big charge, the deadly one, was the murder of Wilson. That trial, too, ended in conviction, and Starr faced famed "Hanging Judge" Isaac Parker for sentencing. Judge Parker was famous for his lectures to condemned criminals, dwelling at length not only on the vileness of their earthly crimes, but also on the imminent danger to their immortal souls.

That should have been the end of Henry Starr, but it wasn't. The United States Supreme Court reversed the conviction, and the matter was remanded and set for a second trial.

On retrial, Starr was again convicted of the Wilson murder, and again sentenced to death. And again the Supreme Court reversed. Judge Parker left the bench not long afterward and was replaced by Judge John Rogers. Judge Rogers entertained a plea of manslaughter, and Starr went off for a stiff prison term of thirteen years and eight months. Starr was good at behaving, when he wanted to, and after his mother appeared before the Cherokee Council, that body appealed for clemency to President Theodore Roosevelt. In 1901, impressed with the story of Starr's cool disarming of desperate outlaw Cherokee Bill, the president telegraphed Starr in the Fort Smith jail and asked, "Will you be good if I set you free?"

Not surprisingly, Starr said he would.

But that was not to last. With Kid Wilson, an old criminal associate now on parole from New York, Starr struck a country bank in Tyro, Kansas, in the spring of 1908. Things got so hot as a result that Starr and Wilson fled all the way to Colorado, where they robbed a tiny bank in Amity. Moving on to Arizona, Starr settled there under an alias. Traced by a letter he sent to Oklahoma, he was arrested in Arizona and returned to Colorado, where an unsympathetic court gave him seven to twenty-five years in the Canon City Penitentiary. In the fall of 1913, after his usual good behavior, Starr was paroled on the condition that he not leave Colorado.

And for a while, he didn't. He opened a small restaurant, but that venture did not prosper, and in due course Starr abandoned the eatery and left Colorado, taking with him the comely wife of a local merchant. There followed a long string of robberies in Oklahoma, none of them bringing big paydays, but alarming nonetheless. Rewards were posted—dead-or-alive this time—but Starr was hard to find, even though he was living in Tulsa. He even had the audacity to write the governor of Oklahoma, denying he had anything to do with any robberies, a profoundly unconvincing tactic reminiscent of Jesse James's regular "I-wasn't-there-and-I-can-prove-it" letters to the press, some forty years before.

But Starr's luck was about to run out. In March of 1915, he decided to replenish his funds by raiding the bank in Stroud, a prosperous town about dead center in Oklahoma. He rode into town on horseback with six hoodlums to help him, a force that should have sufficed to cow the citizens of peaceful Stroud. This gang should have been enough to accomplish the bank robber's ideal, the dream for which the Dalton Gang had been destroyed in Coffeyville, Kansas, twenty-three years before. They were going to rob two banks at once.

On March 27, 1915, at about 9:00 A.M., Starr and his crew rode into Stroud and set to work. At first the robbery went according to plan. Starr divided his force into two parties of three men, and they entered simultaneously the First National and the Stroud State Bank. Starr led the contingent that would raid the State Bank, brandishing a short rifle he had hidden in his pants leg. As his partners covered two bank men and a customer with pistols, Starr took $1,600 in loose cash, then demanded that bookkeeper J. B. Charles open the safe, or, he said simply, "I'll kill you."

"You'll have to kill me, then," said Charles coolly, "because I don't know the combination." Starr then threatened the bank's vice president, Sam Patrick, who just as coolly told the outlaw leader that the safe had already been opened for the day's operating cash, but was then closed and its time lock reset for the next day. Frustrated, Starr snatched

Patrick's diamond stickpin and herded him, Charles, and a customer out into the street.

Over in the First National, Starr's companions found the safe open and swept up more than $4,000. When Starr joined them, they collected four bank employees and five customers to use as human shields. Herding these nine men in front of them, along with the hostages from the State Bank, the whole bandit gang walked deliberately toward their horses. But word of the holdup had spread through the town, and armed citizens were beginning to collect.

Their first shots, at long range, were ineffective, and Starr's gang blazed away up and down the street to keep them at bay. Starr hid behind bank man Patrick and snapped a shot at a citizen called Charley Guild, a shot that drove the shotgun-toting horse-buyer quickly to cover behind a building. Starr laughed, enjoying himself.

It was to be his last laugh for a while, for more of Stroud's angry citizens were opening up on the outlaws. One in particular proved to be an especially deadly marksman. Seventeen-year-old Paul Curry had seen the robbery unfold from the yard of his parents' nearby home. Curry ran into a butcher shop and came out with a sawed-off Winchester rifle, kept in the shop to kill hogs. Taking cover behind some barrels in front of his father's grocery story, young Curry smashed Starr's leg with a round that tore into the outlaw's left thigh. When the bandit raised his weapon to return the fire, Curry yelled, "Throw away that gun or I'll kill you!" Convinced that this cool, tough youngster meant what he said, Starr dropped his weapon and fell back on the ground.

Curry wasn't through. By this time the rest of the gang, abandoning their leader, had run to the stockyards, where they had tethered their all-important horses. They mounted up in haste and began to ride hard for safety, but bandit Lewis Estes was having trouble controlling his horse and seemed to want to return for the fallen Starr. Young Curry fired once more, and the bullet smashed into Estes's shoulder, breaking it and tearing into a lung. Waving a pistol, the outlaw forced two of the hostages to help him climb into the saddle, and all five bandits rode clear of the town.

Estes managed to stay on his horse for about a mile and half, until he fainted from loss of blood and pitched out of the saddle. His companions, as compassionate for him as they had been for Starr, took his horse

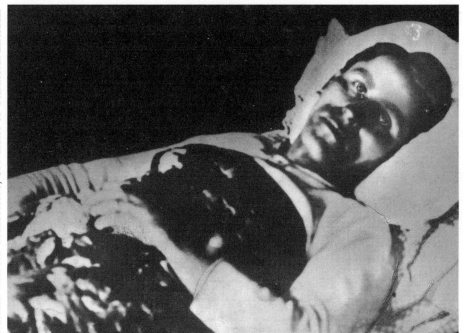

*Henry Starr, wounded*

and left him on the ground. Recovered by a posse, he was returned to town and taken to the office of Doctor John Evans, where Starr already lay. The bandit leader readily admitted his identity, and encouraged the close-mouthed Estes to at least "tell where his parents lived."

As the doctor dug the rifle bullet out of Starr's leg, Starr asked, "What did the kid shoot me with?"

A hog rifle, somebody said, and Starr reacted with embarrassment: "I'll be damned. I don't mind getting shot, knew it had to happen sooner or later. But a kid with a hog gun—that hurts my pride."

Starr did have the good grace to congratulate Curry on his courageous stand. The young man told Starr he would use the $1,000 reward money to get an education, and Starr is reported to have said, "You're all right, boy."

Meanwhile, a posse pursued the fleeing bandits, and the telephone—that new and handy crime-fighting tool—sent lawmen, volunteers, and even state militia chasing after the remains of the gang from all directions. Much of the pursuit was by automobile, and the pursuers came very close. But in the end they were foiled by the mounted bandits' cross-country mobility and their own inability to quickly hire or borrow horses themselves.

As the district attorney prepared for trial, Estes, heretofore playing the strong, silent role, turned state's evidence, and began to talk at length about the rest of the gang. They had, after all, callously abandoned him, so it is surely doubtful that Estes felt any overwhelming loyalty to his recent companions. Three of them were quickly apprehended; the remaining two bandits made tracks into Arkansas and disappeared. Starr entered a plea of guilty, to everybody's surprise, and went off to prison in McAlester with a twenty-five-year sentence. Estes got just five years.

Once more Henry Starr went into his good behavior mode, and he was back on the street again in less than four years. His chief aid and support in this quick return to liberty was Kate Barnard, Oklahoma's first commissioner of "charities and corrections." To her credit, Kate was a holy terror to slothful or uncaring officials, and did much good in improving conditions in state hospitals. She also cordially detested the penal system, which she considered medieval, and considered herself a perceptive judge of character in those confined there. "I have studied men," she said, "until I know from the shape of their hands and head, the gait of their walk and the contour of their faces, much of their mode of life and the character of their thoughts."

She was convinced that Starr would now walk the path of virtue, and thought he had made "one of the sincerest efforts at reformation of all the 20,000 convicts I have known."

Maybe this redoubtable lady did have some powerful insight into the souls of felons, but in Starr's case, she—and others, including the prison chaplain—had been thoroughly bamboozled.

Starr now settled in Tulsa and became involved in that city's burgeoning film industry. He bought an interest in a firm called the "Pan-American Motion Picture Company," and with it produced a silent movie called *Debtor to the Law*. This film, an account of the Stroud debacle, used many of that town's citizens as actors, including young Curry, playing himself. *Debtor to the Law* was very successful, and a series of other films followed.

At that point in his life, after serving prison sentences in Colorado and Oklahoma, Starr had every chance to change his outlaw lifestyle. And for a while it seemed that he would do so. However, not even the bonds of matrimony—he was married twice—could wean Starr away from the excitement and braggadocio of the professional criminal. As always, he would explain his backsliding by blaming others. In this case, he said he had trouble collecting money due him from the film company. He was broke, he said, with a new and very young wife. He even tried to borrow money from Kate Barnard.

Early in February 1921, Starr called on his son from his first marriage, then a senior in high school in Muskogee, and warned him of the dangers of a life of crime. According to the *Osage Journal,* Starr urged his son to "profit by my mistakes . . . and always live your life in a clean, straight manner. Crime cannot succeed." But whatever Starr may have said to his son, he apparently thought crime *could* succeed if you tried it often enough.

Whatever the truth of that was, Starr went back to doing what he did best—stealing other people's money. In spite of the fact that he had not had much luck robbing banks in Arkansas, Starr decided to hit yet another Arkansas town. This time he would try the People's National Bank in the little town of Harrison, not far from Bentonville, where the local authorities had not forgotten him.

And so, on February 18, 1921, Starr and three men drove into Harrison in a Nash automobile and entered the bank. None of them wore a mask, although Starr seems to have worn a pair of cheap glasses, perhaps as a rudimentary disguise. The outlaws had every expectation of a successful haul, for there was indeed some $30,000 in the bank when the outlaws walked in the door.

At first the holdup went just as planned. The robbers pushed up to the cashier's windows and covered bank president Marvin Wagley and cashier Cleve Coffman, pushing out of the way Ruth Wilson, a book-keeper for a grocery firm, who was making a deposit for her boss.

"Hands up!" yelled the bandits, and repeatedly warned Coffman to "keep quiet; don't move." One outlaw then went inside the working area of the bank while a second man began to herd everybody else toward the vault. Starr had thoughtfully brought along a pillowcase, which he now opened. At gunpoint, he told Coffman to do what he was told: "You work with me and I'll work with you." By now the robbers had to watch not only Coffman, Wagley, and Ruth Wilson, but two other female employees and three more customers. Starr and his men also leveled their weapons at William J. Myers, who was a director and onetime president of the bank.

Myers had just entered his office at the rear of the bank, walking right into the middle of the robbery in progress. Having no options, he dutifully raised his hands and followed one robber's orders to walk peacefully into the bank vault. But Myers apparently believed in prior planning, for he had long since arranged for a back door to the vault, specifically for such an occasion as that day's unwelcome visitation.

Myers was just a month short of his sixty-ninth birthday, but he had the heart of a young lion. At the time of building the back door to the vault, which he called his "bandit trap," he had also secreted a loaded 1873 Winchester at the rear of the vault. It had long resided there, and now Myers headed straight for it.

Starr finished sweeping the depositors' money into a sack, and he now ordered Coffman to open the safe. Coffman began to turn the dial, with the outlaw leader looking over his shoulder, and when the door swung open, Starr started to reach inside. At that moment Myers opened up from inside the vault and Starr went down. "Don't shoot," he is supposed to have yelled. "Don't shoot, don't shoot anybody. I am the one that is shot; don't shoot a man who is down." Which, considering Starr's treatment of Kid Wilson so long before, was something less than what one would expect from a bold, boastful bandit.

Myers now advanced out of the vault, his weapon trained on Starr, and the outlaw oddly asked Myers to remove the cheap glasses the outlaw was wearing. Myers did so, then pressed on after Starr's companions, who had not stayed to fight or save their leader. They ran for it, in fact, tearing out of town in their automobile and leaving their boss behind. Myers ran outside and blazed away at the Nash as it raced off down the street, hitting one tire and blowing out the windshield.

Hastily organized posses pursued, but all they found was the Nash, abandoned and set on fire. In the days to come, authorities would arrest three other men for complicity in the crime, but for now all eyes were on desperately wounded Henry Starr. At first, Starr would not reveal who his cohorts were and simply asked to see George Crump, once a U.S. marshal. Crump was not in town, but his son was, and the younger man positively identified Starr.

So once again the celebrated king of the bank robbers was down and hurt, and back in the hands of the law. Once more he had been shot down by an ordinary citizen who objected to Starr's larcenous ways, and this time the hurt would be permanent.

As he lay on a cot in a jail cell, Starr was visited by Coffman, the bank cashier, and on one occasion by an official of a bank in Seligman, Missouri, who identified Starr as one of the men who had robbed his bank the previous year, just before Christmas. Lawmen spent some time with him too, and at last Starr began to give them some information. He also told one physician, Doctor T. P. Fowler, that "I was in debt $20,000 and had to have money, so I turned bank robber again. I am sorry, but the deed is done."

Myers's bullet had lodged in the outlaw's spine, from which it was carefully removed by Dr. J. J. Johnson. The outlaw survived the operation, but the doctor opined that Starr's life was now chiefly in danger from blood poisoning. He also ran the risk of fatal uremic poisoning, the doctor said, because the slug had torn through one kidney on its way to the backbone.

The doctors did all they could for Henry Starr, but it soon became obvious to them, and to Starr, that he was finished. His wife and ex-wives were contacted, along with his mother and his son. Staring death in the face, Starr began to lose some of his outlaw cockiness. "I am going to die," he said, "and I am anxious to make my peace with God." He also said he would give some useful information to the sheriff, which he did.

This time there would be no encore for the Bearcat. He lasted four days, slipped into a coma, and died.

Starr had a sort of posthumous revenge. Kate Barnard, hearing of his death, went into a spasm of impassioned ranting about the perfidy of society. She damned society generally—especially the motion picture industry and the company that owed Starr money—for the return to crime and the death of Henry Starr. "The company . . . is directly responsible for the robbery in which he was shot . . . an example of society at large, which seeks to destroy the man whose foot has slipped," and a whole lot more in similar vein.

He was, she said in a long and convoluted speech, "but striking back at society which had proven itself his enemy." That uncaring society had forced poor Henry back into a life of crime. "It is enough," she mourned, "to make Heaven weep."

While Heaven may have wept, a great many honest depositors and bank employees did not shed a single tear. They would not miss in the slightest, as Kate Barnard did, a boastful professional criminal who lived off the sweat of other people. No amount of weeping and pious lamentation about society's evils would change the fact that Henry Starr was a career thug, a thug by choice, a thug who found it easier to steal what other people earned than work for himself.

Henry Starr was blessed by nature with considerable intelligence and an iron constitution, both of which he chose to squander in robbing other people, running from the law, and wasting his years sitting in prison. Boastful and arrogant, it is the real measure of the man that on the day before his death, sliding toward oblivion, he still bragged to his doctors that he had "robbed more banks than any man in America."

Where he was going, that dubious record would do him precious little good.

## TREACHERY AT ROUND ROCK

### *The Demise of Sam Bass*

*He met his fate at Round Rock, July the twenty-first*
*They pierced poor Sam with rifle balls, and emptied out his purse*
*—from* The Ballad of Sam Bass, *anonymous*

THERE'S NO RECORD that anybody emptied out poor Sam's purse—indeed, there was probably precious little in it—but pierce him with rifle balls they surely did. "They," in this case, were a bunch of tough Texas Rangers and some angry Texas townspeople. When they permanently ventilated Sam, they created a lasting myth, a big, tall, broad-shouldered legend that stood a lot taller and lasted a lot longer than Sam Bass himself. But that was the way of it in the Old West: The quickest way to immortality for a second-rate outlaw was to get yourself killed by the law or irate citizens or a tough express agent. So it was with Sam Bass.

At age eighteen in Denton, not far south of the Red River, he hired on as a teamster and farm worker with W. F. "Dad" Egan, then the sheriff of Denton County. Bass had dark eyes and black hair, and never lost his nasal twang. He was not a prepossessing figure—a stooped young man, about five-eight and around 140 pounds. Still, he was a likeable youngster, if even half of the legends about him are true. And he seems to have been a solid employee for the sheriff, at least until he acquired a fine little sorrel racehorse, famous as the Denton Mare. Jenny the mare brought Sam a measure of independence, and he left Dad Egan's employ for greener pastures, running his swift filly successfully against all comers.

Sam stayed on the right side of the law, at least until he stole a string of horses from an Indian up at Fort Sill—or maybe, depending on what version of the tale you read, he had won the horses fairly and took only what was his. In any case, we next hear of Sam in the summer of 1876, when he and his San Antonio buddy Joel Collins drove a herd of cattle from Nebraska up to boomtown Deadwood, way up in Dakota Territory. The boys apparently liked Deadwood, or maybe it was all the new money there, for they stayed on, first to run a freight line, then to open a saloon and gambling hall. So far, so good, but their excursion into entrepreneurship came to an abrupt end when they bought into a mine. When their digging went belly-up, the boys looked around for other ways to keep their pockets jingling.

The solution seemed easy, especially at first. Surely stealing what other people worked to earn ought to be easier than working for it yourself. All you needed was a gun and a horse, and you could steal the horse, which is precisely what they did. Bass and Collins assembled a collection of similarly minded hard cases to help them: Jack Davis, Missourian Jim Berry, Bill Heffridge, Canadian Tom Nixon, and a bad hat called Robert McKimie, known to Deadwood as Reddy. Equipped with stolen mounts and appropriate firearms, they set off to rob Black Hills stages.

In March of 1877, the gang robbed the Cheyenne stage, an enterprise that went bad from the beginning. Johnny Slaughter, the stage driver, was smart enough not to even try to fight all these robbers and promptly pulled in his team. But then his horses shied, and before he could rein them in, McKimie pulled down on him with a shotgun. The blast killed Slaughter, and his panicked team bolted for home. When the stage rolled into Deadwood, unrobbed, local folks backtracked and found popular Johnny Slaughter's lifeless body lying in the road. The express company nailed Slaughter's bloody vest to its door, a symbol of what it had in mind for the killers.

One story goes that the gang members, angry about the senseless killing, or perhaps upset about losing the loot, told McKimie to leave the gang and be quick about it. He did, says one tale, all the way to tough

*Sam Bass and his gang*

Fort Griffin, Texas, where local vigilantes hanged him for rustling. Nice story, but in fact McKimie was alive enough to be sentenced by an Ohio court in early 1878 for burglary. Bass and the others stayed on to rob more stages, conclusively proving their status as rank amateurs. One of their stickups netted a measly $11; a second garnered them only a dozen peaches. Their disenchantment with stage robbing may have been enhanced by the sudden demise of a robber from another local gang, the Hat Creek outfit. This outlaw, a hoodlum called Towle, came in second in a shoot-out with a stage guard, who thoughtfully brought Towle's head back to Cheyenne in a gunnysack to claim the reward.

And so, hungry and disappointed, the gang decided to switch to robbing trains . . . and they struck the mother lode. After dark on September 18, 1875, they took on a Union Pacific train down at Big Spring, Nebraska. They took a handful of watches and some $13,000— or, according to another source, $1,300—from the well-heeled passengers. Either way, it was the best haul ever, but it was chicken feed compared to what they found up in the baggage car.

There, as they swept up a handful of paper money, one of the hoodlums kicked a wooden crate, and some of its contents spilled out. It was crammed with gold double eagles, something like $60,000 worth of twenty-dollar gold pieces, a small fortune for the time. There is a story that a store clerk, suspicious of Collins, followed him and watched from a hiding spot while the gang split up "sack after sack" of gold. The clerk then rode "night and day" until he reached Ogallala and gave the alarm.

Overjoyed with their haul, the robbers sensibly decided to leave Nebraska at the high lope, but trouble was right behind them. On their way, Collins and Heffridge rode into a desolate Kansas railway depot called Buffalo Station, and there, as the *Kansas City Times* put it, Collins made the mistake of pulling out his handkerchief, clearly labeled "Joel Collins." Since Collins's name had been spread far and wide by telegraph, the station agent notified Sheriff Bardsley, who was nearby with a cavalry patrol. Collins and Heffridge made the very bad decision to shoot it out with the soldiers and lost the ensuing fight, two to nothing.

Berry ended his career down near Mexico, Missouri. The classic *Sam Bass and His Gang* related that he made the exceedingly unwise decision to exchange $9,000 in gold for currency to order "an elegant suit of clothing." When the man he sent to pick up his new suit was followed by officers, Berry elected to fight and was mortally wounded by the posse. Before he died, Berry gasped out the names of the other gang members.

With those three dead, and Nixon gone off to who-knew-where, Sam Bass rode off with Jack Davis. They may have sold off their horses and bought a beat-up buckboard and one or more horses. Driving this unprepossessing rig, and with their shares of the loot stashed in an old pair of pants, they moved south. On horseback, or in a buckboard, or maybe in a carriage, the two made it safely into Texas, where they split up. Sam traveled back to Denton with his saddlebags full of gold.

Before long, though, maybe missing the excitement of living on the wrong side of the law, he was back robbing people. He scraped together a new gang, including Henry Underwood, Frank Jackson (called "Blockey"), and Tom Spotswood, a hoodlum who already had a string of murders to his credit. Jackson, who would be with Bass to the end, came of a solid, God-fearing family, but was orphaned early and grew up left to his own devices, a wild boy. Jackson was nevertheless loyal and courageous.

Sam needed a gang to travel with because he was a wanted man, especially by a particular trio of bulldogs: a Union Pacific detective called Gaines, Grayson County sheriff Bill Everheart, and a tough young Texas Ranger named Lee Hall. They carried a warrant from the governor of Nebraska, and they meant business.

The countryside swarmed with other manhunters as well: peace officers, Pinkertons, bounty hunters, and detectives from as far away as Chicago. Only once did the pursuers catch up to their quarry. The result was a short, ferocious gunfight in Cove Hollow: Sam and his boys shot their way clear, with nobody hurt on either side. By now, Bass had added to the gang a youngster variously called Seaborn Barnes or "Nubbin's Colt." They continued to hold up the long-suffering railroads again and again, at Allen, at Hutchins, and at Eagle Ford, where the gang took a measly $52.

Things were getting distinctly hot for Sam and his comrades. In addition to the posses combing the country for them, the outlaws had to worry about lawmen and express agents who now were constantly on the alert for further attacks on the railroad. There was a lot of reward money around—an extraordinary $1,500 a head—and who could tell when a dirt-poor local man might covet all that gold and turn informer? Clearly a change in tactics was in order.

And so Bass decided to hit a bank, and to do it far away from these swarms of pesky, predatory lawmen. He chose Round Rock, a quiet settlement a long way from his stomping ground close to Denton. He and his men moved south down the stage route from Dallas to Waco, then on through Belton and Georgetown. Along the way they spent the last $20 gold pieces from their 1877 robbery at Big Spring, Nebraska.

Round Rock was named for a huge stone shaped like a table in the center of Brushy Creek, about where the Chisholm Trail crossed the creek. The town had moved a little way to the east since then, drifting over to the tracks of the International and Great Northern, driven through in 1876. By the time Bass led his men toward Round Rock, the center of gravity of the town had shifted over to "new Round Rock," closer to the railroad right-of-way. It was a thriving community of about 1,000 people. "Old" Round Rock was in decline.

For a while, the Rangers had lost track of the Bass gang. On the 16th of July, Junius Peak wrote Major Jones from Denton to report that "nothing has been heard of Bass and party for two or three weeks. It is supposed that they have left this part of the country." Peak also wrote that three promising leads had come to nothing. Reports that Sam had fired on a deputy sheriff and a civilian, that he had "been at old man Collins's," and that he had been seen in Dallas, all had been in error.

And so the raid should have been a piece of cake for an experienced outlaw, an easy hoorahing of a peaceful little town. Instead, it would turn out to be a nightmare. For gang member Jim Murphy had managed to contact the Rangers. Along the way toward Round Rock, he sent at least one or possibly two telegrams or letters, both warning that the gang was going down to Round Rock to rob a bank. On the 17th of July, Ranger Major John B. Jones received one of Murphy's messages, to the effect that the gang was going to Round Rock "to rob a bank or the railroad, and for God's sake to be on hand and prevent it."

Jones quickly made his preparations. His men were scattered, but he sent a messenger galloping to alert Lieutenant N. O. Reynolds at San Saba, more than a hundred miles away. The messenger, Corporal Vernon Wilson, killed his horse on a wild night ride to Lampasas. But he arrived about dawn, in time to catch the stage, hire a horse at the stage stop nearest San Saba, and gallop the last 3 miles to Reynolds's camp. Lieutenant Reynolds immediately mustered eight men with good mounts and set off on the road for Round Rock. Reynolds was ill, too sick to ride, but he had himself loaded into a light wagon drawn by husky mules.

Rangers Dick Ware, George Herold (or Harrell), and Chris Connor rode in from Austin, and Jones recruited Travis County Deputy Sheriff Morris Moore and A. W. "Caige" Grimes, deputy sheriff of Williamson County. Lee Hall and five or six more men came in from Austin and camped outside the town. Hall rode into Round Rock alone to chat with Jones, who issued his orders clearly.

Everybody, said Jones, was to stay under cover. The two deputy sheriffs would watch the street and report anything suspicious. They would be helped in their surveillance by livery stable owner Henry Highsmith, an ex-Ranger, like Grimes. Major Jones also warned the manager of the Williamson County Bank to expect trouble, a kindness that engendered some apprehension at the bank. Two citizens, By Asher and Wayne Graham, prowled about, looking for anything suspicious on the outskirts of town, but reported that they had found nothing.

Unsuspecting, Sam Bass and his gang camped outside Round Rock. Bass and Jackson took a look at the town first and returned confident. On their return, one said to Murphy, "Jim, you were right about coming to this place, for we can take that bank too easy to talk about." The next day Murphy and Barnes also visited Round Rock "to look at the bank and to get shaved," and Barnes was also pleased with what he saw. That evening Bass talked to his henchmen: "Well now, boys, she goes about half-past three o'clock, Saturday evening." The raid on the Williamson County Bank was on.

On that blistering afternoon of the twenty-first of July, the streets of Round Rock must have looked peaceful and quiet, even to a suspicious outlaw. Anybody with any sense who could stay indoors did so, out of that murderous sun. Not much moved on the street. One team was stopped while a man loaded supplies into his wagon; his son stood holding the team's reins. Over at Highsmith's Livery, another boy unloaded fodder. Inside Highsmith's, Rangers Herold and Connor watched the steaming street; over at Burkhardt's Barber Shop, Ranger Dick Ware sat camouflaged behind a face full of lather. Major Jones was down at the telegraph office in search of news, and Hall was at the hotel.

The Rangers did not have long to wait. In the afternoon, Bass, Barnes, Murphy, and Jackson rode into Round Rock through the broiling heat. Murphy left the others at the Livingston and Mays store in Old

Round Rock—to get some horse feed, he may have said. In reality he was wisely getting himself clear of the shooting he feared would erupt in the new town. The other three tethered their horses in an alley behind Highsmith's, walked on down the alley, turned the corner, and sauntered into Koppel's (or Copprel's) general store. They wanted tobacco, they said, and spent some time haggling over the price with Simon Juda, the clerk. Two of the bandits were carrying saddlebags.

But Deputy Grimes had spotted the three men and thought at least one of them was carrying a gun. Maybe, as Murphy later told the story, Bass's coat tails "blew up and exposed his pistol." According to Murphy's account, the other two outlaws still had their sidearms "in their saddle pockets, and if Sam had had his in his saddle-pockets, he might have been living yet." Grimes, instead of alerting Jones or Hall as he had been told to do, turned to Moore and commented that down where he came from, he generally took guns away from men carrying them in town.

"I do the same thing in Williamson County," said Moore, and so the two deputies walked over to Koppel's. Moore waited at the door while Grimes walked up to Sam Bass and the two thugs with him. "I believe you have a pistol," Grimes said, or something like it, which turned out to be a major mistake. Bass, or maybe all three men, said they did, and the outlaws turned on Moore and Grimes and went for their guns.

"Wait, boys," said Grimes, or "hold up," or something similar, but it was far too late to halt what happened next. The store shook with the roar of firing, and a cloud of white powder smoke filled the room.

Grimes reeled back across the store, hit point-blank by bullet after bullet, dying as he fell near the doorway. His revolver was still in its holster when he died, or maybe he fired off a couple of wild shots, again depending on which account you read. In any case, he hit nobody. The outlaws pulled down on Moore as well, but he was shooting back, everybody blazing away through a fog of powder smoke so dense that Moore could not clearly see his opponents. According to Deputy Moore's account of the fight, one of the outlaws fired on him, and the other two shot at Grimes.

As the outlaws rushed past him into the street, Moore took a slug through one lung, but he nailed Bass in his right hand, his gun hand, smashing two fingers. As the outlaw leader passed him, the officer said, he could see Bass bleeding from his side and arm. Moore fired all six rounds in his revolver at Bass and his men, reloaded, grabbed his Winchester from the stable, and started after the outlaws. A town doctor, A. F. Morris, stopped him. "Hold on," he said, "Don't go any further, for if you get overheated your wound may kill you." Moore, feeling "faint and sick," heeded the doctor's words and fell out of the fight.

Today, nobody knows for sure why Moore and Grimes did what they did, but accosting Bass and his henchmen without first drawing their weapons was tantamount to committing suicide. Maybe, as one Ranger later speculated, they recognized the men as Bass and his gang, and wanted the reward money for themselves. That suggestion doesn't make much sense, however, since both Grimes and Moore were experienced lawmen, and surely would have known better than to try to arrest three armed and dangerous men without even drawing their own weapons first.

It's most probable that the two peace officers simply did not recognize Bass and his men and were accordingly careless. Or maybe the officers were only trying to clear obvious gun-carriers off the street before Bass and his gang reached town and the main event really got underway. This was the view of Grimes's cousin, livery stable owner Albert Highsmith, who said that neither lawman had any idea who the three men were.

The hammer of gunfire brought Lee Hall and the rest of the Rangers out on the double, and Major Jones came sprinting back from the telegraph office. The outlaws were running down the alley for their horses, but now they had a gauntlet of fire to run. Dick Ware got into action first, quickly followed by Connor and Herold, who opened up on the bandits as they ran for the alley and their all-important mounts.

Hall arrived on the street in time to see the mortally wounded Grimes drop in the dust, and promptly opened fire on the officer's killers, who kept on running down the alley, firing as they ran. Other citizens now began to join in the action, including a one-armed man named Stubbs, who laid his Winchester across a fence and blazed away (or maybe, in another version, he used Grimes's pistol). Citizens F. L. Jordan and Albert Highsmith also fired on the fleeing bandits. Highsmith blazed away from the backyard of his livery stable, and Jordan fired from the back door of his saloon until his Winchester jammed.

Because of fences lining the alley, however, nobody had a clear field of fire until the bandits arrived at Highsmith's stable. The bandits were firing too, and one of their slugs ripped splinters from a hitching post close to Dick Ware's head. As Bass drew near his horse, Ranger Herold yelled at him to surrender, but the outlaw raised his pistol and pulled the trigger. The hammer fell on an empty chamber, and somebody, probably Herold, got another slug into Sam Bass. It struck a cartridge in Bass's belt and split, and the pieces ripped into Bass near his spinal column, tore through one kidney, and exited near his navel. "Oh, Lord!" Bass gasped.

A bullet from Ranger Ware's weapon slammed into Barnes and put him down for keeps. Shot through the back of the head, Barnes hit the dust in the alley and never moved. Bass, however, managed to get mounted, covered by Jackson. The two clattered out of Round Rock and for the moment left pursuit behind them. Murphy said later that as he sat in "old man Mays' store" in old Round Rock, he watched the two fugitives gallop past. He said he "saw that Sam was wounded in the hand, and he looked like he was sick, and Frank [Jackson] was holding him on his horse." At their old campsite outside town, the two men separated, although legend has it that Jackson wanted to stay with his friend and fight it out, and Bass would not let him stay.

The Rangers followed, but lost the trail and returned to Round Rock for the evening. In the meantime, a crowd had gathered—a crowd that included Murphy, curious about the outcome of the fight and distinctly relieved. He told a reporter, "I wouldn't go through it all again for $50,000 piled down on the floor before me—no sir! With all the anxiety and watching I had to suffer. . . . It's all over now and I am glad of it."

That night the Rangers were joined by Ranger contingents from San Saba and Austin, and the search for Bass and Jackson continued at daybreak. This time the lawmen found Sam Bass, bloody and exhausted, all the fight gone out of him. According to legend, Bass raised one hand and said, "Don't shoot; I am unarmed and helpless; I am the man you're looking for; I am Sam Bass." The lawmen summoned Dr. C. P. Cochran from Round Rock, and after an examination, the doctor told Bass frankly that he was not going to live. His captors then found a wagon and hauled Bass back into town. There, he was lodged on a cot in August Gloeber's tin shop, for the next-door hotel would not take him.

Bass lingered, confident that he would recover, but in fact his young life was finished. To the end he remained close-mouthed about his associates. "Think I will go to hell, anyhow," he said, "and believe a man should die with what he knows in him." If his bullets had killed Grimes, he said, the lawman was the only man he ever killed, which might even have been true. Bass insisted that Frank Jackson had not abandoned him: "He would not leave until I forced him to," Bass said. "He's all sand, that boy."

But on Sunday afternoon, July 21, Bass began to slip away. Writer Harold Preece, ever ready with dubious dialogue, wrote that Bass mumbled "something about 'never stealing a horse' and 'never robbing a widow woman.'" Whether Bass said anything like that or not, by mid-afternoon, after a very hard day, he sank rapidly, and the doctors had to tell him he was dying. "Let me go," he said, and then, a little later, slipping into unconsciousness, "The world is bobbing around." And then, just before 4:00 on that hot afternoon, he was gone. That Sunday was his twenty-seventh birthday.

The Rangers kept alive their formidable reputation. Men would remember that once they got into the fight at Round Rock, the decision quickly went to the forces of the law. The Sunday *San Antonio Express* celebrated the event with a memorably alliterative headline: "Sam Bass and His Gang Captured—The Rollicking Rough Rider Riddled with Bullets—And Is Expected to Pass in His Checks."

One writer attributed the Ranger victory over Bass and his men to "that tombstone quality of the nerves which has always made them about two-fifths of a second quicker with a gun than anybody else." No doubt that "tombstone quality of the nerves" did indeed have something to do with the Rangers' victory, although speed on the draw did not decide the Round Rock fight. Accuracy and aggressiveness did.

There was some later controversy over just who shot whom. Some said that Dick Ware had actually fired the shot that mortally wounded Bass, but the coroner's jury, hearing accounts of the fight at the time, decided that Ware had killed Seaborn Barnes and Herold had mortally wounded Bass.

Deputy Grimes, who left a wife and three children, had a full-fledged Masonic funeral, with a great many mourners to see him off. The people of Round Rock took up a collection for his widow, and the Texas Central Railroad chipped in too.

Bass's burial was perfunctory, although John Ledbetter, a Methodist minister, saw to it that some appropriate words were said. During Bass's planting, however, a curious thing happened. A local woman, who had cooked some meals for the gang before they rode into town for the last time, watched the burial from afar. She said later that she saw a handsome young man ride up on a big bay horse, dismount, and "with an anguished look," toss a clod on the grave and ride away. The lady thought the visitor was Jackson. Barnes was buried in the same cemetery and lies today next to Bass. His inscription is appropriate: "He was right bower to Sam Bass."

In the aftermath of the Round Rock fight, Major Jones tried to obtain reward money for his men who had put an end to Bass and his gang. He was successful in inducing an express company and a railroad to contribute $1,000 each, although another railroad denied it had ever offered a reward. And then, in August 1878, he wrote Captain Peak that he had "procured the reward from the State for the arrest and conviction of [gang members] Pipes and Herndon," by which he meant that he had earned the approval of the governor. There was at the moment no money to pay the rewards, but he suggested, "There is always a market here for claims of this kind against the state . . . [the two men most concerned] thought it best to sell it and have sold it at 71 cents [on the dollar, presumably]."

In the end, in the great Valhalla of outlaw legend, Sam Bass found a place in the pantheon of good ol' boys who weren't really all that bad, never mind the fact that they stole from other people and tried to kill anybody who pursued them or otherwise got in their way.

The inscription on Sam's tombstone may have been somewhat maudlin, but it pretty well summed up the bandit's misspent life: "A brave man reposes here. Why was he not true?" The legend was beginning to take shape, but the folklore picture of Sam—"a kinder-hearted fellow you seldom ever see," as his ballad went—was not shared by everybody, certainly not by the family of Caige Grimes. Nor was it shared by a Denton County man who called Sam "an ignorant, vicious ruffian." Judge Hogg, also of Denton, succinctly summed up Bass's dubious career in a little book he wrote about the outlaw shortly after Round Rock: "Let us capitulate: Sam Bass began his career by horse racing. He went from that to cheating, thence to robbing the express companies and paid the penalty for his crimes—all before he was 27."

While Bass remains something of a folk hero in the annals of the West, the hard words of folklore are, of course, reserved for poor old Jim Murphy, the informer, even though he helped rid the world of men who only avoided being murderers because they couldn't shoot straight. Murphy stayed in the informant business, writing a curious letter to Major Jones on August 27, 1878. Here is a part of it, complete with Murphy's own spellings:

> *Well, Major Jones, I received a message from Frank Jackson this morning—he wants to no of me if thare is anything that he can do to get his self repreved—He says that he will lay the plan to catch Underwod and all the rest of the crowd if it will have him turned loose . . . He ses that he was pursuaded into it and that he is tired of that kind of life and will do anything in the world to get repreved . . . If it hadn of bin for Frank Jackson I would of bin killed shore and that is the reason I want him repreved.*

There is no record that anything came of this letter. Maybe Jones did not trust Murphy, or Jackson didn't; maybe Jones thought his informant could not or would not deliver what he promised. Maybe he categorized Murphy's offer with that of another letter-writer who offered to help bring in the rest of the gang members but needed some front money for expenses.

Not very long after Round Rock, to the satisfaction of the outlaw-lovers, Murphy passed to his reward, whatever that was. Afflicted with a congenital eye disease, he was treated with the drug atropia, a belladonna derivative, by a doctor. There were stories afterward that Murphy deliberately swallowed some of the drug, sick to heart of constant fear and of the contempt heaped on him by people who should have known better.

In fact it appears that during his treatment, Murphy sat up to light a pipe and got some of the drug in his mouth . . . quite accidentally. He died in convulsions.

The Ballad of Sam Bass damned Murphy as a traitor:

*Perhaps he's got to heaven, there's none of us can say; But if I'm right in my surmise, he's gone the other way.*

## THE LAST OF THE DALTON BOYS

### *The Fall of Pompous Bill Dalton*

WHEN SHE WAS SIXTEEN, Adeline Younger married Lewis Dalton, a much older man who was a saloonkeeper in Westport Landing, today a part of Kansas City. Adeline didn't hold with ardent spirits, and so she pestered Lewis until he got out of the business of peddling booze. Thereafter, it appears that Lewis dedicated his life mostly to racehorses, which he followed here and there around the country as tout and bettor. He was away a lot, following the ponies, but he came home often enough for long-suffering Adeline to have fifteen children.

Adeline was a fine woman by all accounts, a good friend and a good mother. After Lewis did the family a favor by dying, Adeline settled on a good piece of land down near Kingfisher, in Oklahoma Territory. She did her best to raise her children on the straight and narrow, and most of the fifteen turned out to be good citizens. One, her eldest son Frank, was a highly regarded U.S. deputy marshal who rode for "Hanging Judge" Isaac Parker out of Fort Smith.

But to Adeline's great sorrow, Frank was murdered by outlaws in the brakes of the Arkansas, and some of the other boys turned out to be good for nothing. First off, Bob, Grat, and Emmett turned bad, forming the nucleus of the famous, and overrated, Dalton Gang. This lawless bunch at various times included in its ranks many of the famous names in Oklahoma outlawry, men like Bitter Creek Newcomb, Bill Doolin, and

Black-Faced Charlie Bryant. When the gang wantonly murdered an inoffensive, unarmed doctor during a train robbery, things got very hot for them. Bob, the gang leader, decided that they had better make just one last raid, a strike big enough to enable them to flee the country.

They chose little Coffeyville, Kansas, near where their family had once lived. They took along a couple of minor-league thugs called Broadwell and Powers, leaving behind the rest of the gang, probably to reduce the number of ways they would have to split the loot.

They would, Bob boasted, rob two banks at once, something that even their cousins, the Younger boys, had never done. That was about the extent of Bob's planning, however, and the Coffeyville raid started to go bad almost at once. In a wild gun battle in the plaza outside the banks, and down the narrow alley where the gang had tied their horses, the aroused citizenry shot the gang all to pieces. When the smoke blew away, Bob and Grat Dalton, and Powers and Broadwell, ended up dead in the dust of Coffeyville's streets, and young Emmett was under arrest with more than twenty holes in his body. The old Dalton Gang was finished.

Enter now brother William Frakes (or maybe William Marion) Dalton, called Bill, an arrogant Californian with a big mouth and an abrasive manner. He came to Coffeyville with his grieving mother, but while poor Adeline was civilized and courteous, and aroused the sympathy of many townspeople, Bill quickly managed to make himself obnoxious to nearly everybody around. "The boys were wrong in trying to rob the banks," he conceded, "but they were right when they shot the men who were trying to kill them." That sort of insulting belligerence did not play well in Coffeyville, particularly when four of its citizens were barely cold, killed by the gang's bullets during the battle in what is today called Death Alley.

But Bill did not hang around Coffeyville long. Whether he had been on the wrong side of the law prior to the Coffeyville fiasco is open to question. But if he wasn't, it is certain that he quickly turned criminal afterward. He now openly became what he may well have been all along, an outlaw like his brothers. At first he joined up with Bill Doolin, veteran Dalton follower, who had rallied a new outlaw gang from survivors of the old one. The Doolin Gang, as the new group was called, promptly became a thorn in the side of honest men. It grew, according to some

WESTERN HISTORY COLLECTIONS, UNIVERSITY OF OKLAHOMA LIBRARIES

*Bill Dalton*

estimates, to as many as twelve or fourteen men, operating near the Cherokee Strip.

In a wild 1893 shoot-out with the Doolin Gang in the outlaw town of Ingalls, Oklahoma Territory, three U.S. deputy marshals were killed. All but one of the gang members galloped to safety and went on with their nefarious doings, although Arkansas Tom Jones (Roy Daugherty) was captured during the Ingalls fight and sent to prison. For the rest, their days of freedom were numbered. Charlie Pierce and Bitter

Creek Newcomb were killed in 1895, and the rest of the gang went down one by one. Doolin himself would survive until 1896, when he departed this earth at the summons of a bullet from the rifle of Deputy Marshal Heck Thomas. Only Little Bill Raidler survived, crippled and imprisoned, and he died not long after his release.

But while the gang lasted, they were a plague to honest citizens throughout Oklahoma Territory. On January 23, 1894, for example, Doolin and Tulsa Jack Blake, backed up by at least one other gang member, Bitter Creek Newcomb, struck the Farmers and Merchants Bank of Pawnee, Oklahoma Territory. They made off with only $300 on this raid because the bank's time lock was still set, but they temporarily kidnapped the cashier, releasing him only when they were well clear of the town.

Less than two months later, Doolin and Dalton, with other gang members waiting outside town, kidnapped the station agent at Woodward in the wee hours, took him to the station, and forced him to open the Santa Fe safe. They got away with some $6,500 on this raid, a considerable sum for the time.

In the aftermath of the Woodward robbery, lawmen circulated a detailed description of Bill Dalton:

*Twenty-five years old, five-feet-ten inches tall, weight 170 pounds, two weeks growth of beard, slouch hat with high crown and crease in top, pants in boots, checkered handkerchief about his neck, dark suit, sack coat, dark complexion.*

The depredations of the Doolin Gang at last inspired Chief Justice Frank Dale of the Territorial Supreme Court to call in Marshal Evett Dumas Nix and issue some instructions, practical if somewhat unjudgelike. "Marshal," said Judge Dale, "I have reached the conclusion that the only good outlaw is a dead one. I hope you will instruct your deputies to bring outlaws in dead in the future." These were the sorts of orders the deputy marshals understood. The gang's days were numbered.

Later, during a robbery of a store at tiny Sacred Heart, Dalton shot down a tough, elderly shopkeeper who strongly objected to being robbed by a couple of hoodlums. The old man had put a bullet into Doolin's confederate. The outlaw, who escaped, was first identified as

George Thorne, but turned out to be none other than veteran Dalton-Doolin outlaw, Bitter Creek Newcomb. It was after Sacred Heart that Doolin and Dalton parted company. The reason they rode their separate ways may have been Dalton's ambition to lead his own gang, or maybe it was the intelligent Doolin's conviction that Dalton was too much of a loose cannon to ride with any longer.

Bill Dalton now struck out on his own. He would, he decided, recruit some guns to help him and try his wings as an independent operator; he would rob a bank. Although Dalton had a world of arrogant self-confidence and an overactive mouth to go with it, it does not appear that he ever amounted to much as an outlaw leader. He was about to demonstrate his lack of leadership.

Still, Bill Dalton's name was well known, and a variety of newspaper stories reported him and his "gang" in a variety of places as far apart as Wagoner, Oklahoma Territory; Kendallville, Indiana; and Washington, D.C. He was variously said to be back in the Ingalls area threatening people, or to be lurking, revenge in his heart, about little Coffeyville, a danger that was taken seriously by the town's citizens. He was accurately identified as a participant in the Woodward affair, but other reports had him killed by lawmen in a couple of different places.

Bill Dalton left his wife and children at a farm owned by a man called Houston Wallace. It was a shabby place near the little town of Elk in southern Indian Territory, down in the neighborhood of the city of Ardmore. Now an independent operator, Dalton turned his attention to Texas, where he had not been reported so far. The target was the First National Bank of Longview, a little town in the eastern part of the state, on the Sabine River out in Gregg County.

To form a gang, Dalton had put together a collection of unimpressive bad men, including one Jim Wallace, brother of Houston Wallace. Jim Wallace took the nom-de-robber of George Bennett. According to one story in the tangled lore of the Daltons, Wallace may have been married to a Longview farmer's daughter, whom he later deserted. If so, Wallace would have provided some knowledge of the layout of the town and the bank, and perhaps he regaled Dalton with tales of the riches awaiting them inside the First National Bank of Longview.

Dalton also added a couple of other eager criminals, usually identified as the two Knight—or Nite—brothers, Jim and Big Asa, a pair of oafs said to have worked for a logging company in the Longview area. Other sources doubt that the Knight boys were part of the gang, reporting the other outlaws to be local sawmill-hand Jim Jones and one Will Jones, presumably a relative. Or maybe the third man was somebody else altogether. A later newspaper story identified Jim Jones as an experienced Missouri bandit and called the hitherto unidentified man Oscar Speight. Speight, the story goes, said he was a doctor and was reputed to have married and murdered several women.

These three amateur hard cases, whoever they really were, would give Dalton his very own gang. This dubious aggregation was a very far cry from the Daltons of other days, or the old, bold James–Younger Gang, but ever-cocky Bill Dalton must have figured his new confederates ought to suffice to knock over a little country bank. He couldn't have been more wrong.

One story of the robbery, repeated in several sources, asserts that Dalton even sent a note to the bank in advance of the raid, a scrawl that said,

> *We take this method of informing you that on or about the 23d day of May, A.D. 1894, we will rob the First National Bank of Longview. So take notice accordingly and withdraw your deposit as this is a straight tip. For further information, see Charles Specklemeyer or the undersigned. Yours for business. B&F.*

According to this tale, "B&F" stands for "Bill and Friends." The bank man who received the note passed it on to his bosses, who understandably decided that it was somebody's bad joke and did nothing.

Well, maybe. But this tale has the ring of fable, that curious mythology of which the Old West has produced more than its share. It belongs with the hoary fantasy of Jesse James saving the poor widow from foreclosure by giving her money to pay off the bank and save the old homestead. Bill Dalton was an arrogant, blustering braggart, to be sure, although he did not lack for courage. He was surely not stupid, which he would have had to have been to advertise his crime in advance and invite lawmen and pugnacious citizens to wait in ambush for him.

In fact, it appears that what really happened was this: Dalton simply did a reconnaissance of the town alone—maybe doing some solitary fishing in the Sabine River, or as other sources say, wetting a line with the rest of his gang, who may have come to town in advance of their leader. In fact, one Frank Fischer, a Gregg County man, said later that he had fished with the gang "several times, and had been introduced to 'Charles Speckelmeyer' after he came to join the three." A Longview woman said much later that as a young girl, she had seen the four outlaws "huddled around a campfire on the Sabine River."

Whatever reconnaissance there was, in midafternoon on May 23, 1894, Dalton led his motley gang into town, headed for the First National Bank of Longview, a stout brick building. A persistent legend tells us that on the way to their objective, the gang passed a local doctor, who reminded Wallace about an overdue bill. "Hey, Jim, how about my money?" Replied the bandit, "I'm going to the bank to get it, Doc."

One of the outlaws, probably Dalton, wore a slicker or duster to cover the Winchester concealed beneath it. Or maybe the bandits hid their Winchesters beneath long, black slickers thrown across their shoulders. Take your choice. One or two gang members stayed with the horses in an alley behind the First National: Dalton and the fourth man went inside. Dalton had ready a curious note, written in pencil on the back of a poster. He handed it to the cashier, Tom Clemmons:

*Home, May 23*

*The First National Bank, Longview*
*This will introduce to you Charles Speckelmeyer, who wants some money and is going to have it. B and F.*

"B and F," according to legend, again stood for "Bill and Friends," or possibly for Brown and Flewellen, owners of the sawmill at which the Knight boys are supposed to have worked prior to the robbery.

Clemmons did not take the note seriously. He thought it was some sort of charity appeal and was ready to donate something. But then he found himself looking down the muzzle of Dalton's Winchester and realized he had big trouble. While Dalton held Clemmons and other bank men at gunpoint, another robber, probably Big Asa, pushed through a door behind the counter area and quickly scooped up whatever money he could find. The haul included, as the *Daily Oklahoman* reported, "$2,000 in ten-dollar bills numbered 9, and nine $20 bills numbered 20, and a quantity of unsigned bank notes." So far, so good.

But now the robbery started to go bad in a hurry. One version of the story tells us that a citizen named Bartholomew walked in off the street, into the middle of the robbery, or maybe it was local businessman John Welborne, who backed quickly out of the bank and ran to spread the alarm. Tom Clemmons called to Jim Knight, "Don't kill anyone," and grabbed a bandit's weapon, variously described as a pistol or a Winchester, belonging to either Knight or Dalton, and hung on to the weapon as the outlaw pulled the trigger.

The hammer fell on Clemmons's hand as the two men struggled for the gun, while the other bandit kept his own weapon trained on J. R. Clemmons, the president's brother. Everybody else in the bank, says this story, intelligently took this opportunity to run out the back door and disappear. The outlaws then herded the Clemmons brothers out of the bank, the outlaw struggling with Tom Clemmons apparently having regained his weapon.

Still another story on the raid tells us that: "Josh Cooke, unnoticed by the bandits, slipped around the vault, climbed over a high board fence, and escaped into an adjoining building, where he gave the alarm."

In fact, it appears that Bill Dalton's plans began to unravel when the local law spotted the gang's outside men and grew suspicious. Or maybe, as the *Longview Morning Journal* later reported, the alarm was given by John Welborne, who ran a business west of the bank. The story goes that he was starting to enter the bank when one of the Knights invited him in; Welborne wasn't having any part of all those guns, however, and ran off down the street shouting, "Bank robbery!"

However the word passed around the town, armed citizens converged from all directions, and a wild firefight broke out in the alley. The outlaws inside the bank cleared out in a hurry. They tried to drive the bank employees with them toward their horses, to use as human shields, but their potential hostages were having none of this and ran away in another direction. Or, according to another, later newspaper account, the outlaws succeeding in getting their hostages mounted double behind them until the bank men either managed to escape or were turned loose.

When the firing broke out, P. T. Boyd, a Longview citizen, was in the courthouse, listening to the trial of a case: "None of us, at first, realized what was happening. . . . But when I saw the city marshal pull his gun and start running for the door, I followed him."

The shooting in the alley rose to a roar as the four outlaws traded shots with an assortment of angry citizens and peace officers. George Buckingham, a bartender, grabbed a pistol and ran to the sound of the guns: he was one of the first citizens on the scene, and his reward was a slug in the face from Wallace's rifle. Buckingham went down before he could fire a shot. As Wallace advanced on the fallen man, a boarding-house owner in the next block, a Mrs. McCullough, courageously shouted from one of her windows, "Don't shoot that man anymore; you have already killed him!" She was wrong—at least a little; Buckingham would hang on to life until the afternoon.

By all accounts, Wallace was shooting a saddle gun from the hip and was, as Boyd said much later, "a dead shot with his Winchester Special." The weapon was afterward found to have sights made of bone. "The story," said a later president of the bank, "—and I don't doubt the truth of it—is that the piece of bone is from a human skull, from the head of one of Bennett's [Wallace's] victims."

Wallace then turned on City Marshal Matt Muckleroy, who was hit in the lower belly. Muckleroy was fortunate, however, for the round caromed off some silver dollars he carried in a pouch in his pocket, split, and did no permanent damage; he would recover from his wound. Boyd said that he "wasn't three feet from Muckleroy when he was hit; it could just as well have been me." More serious was the wound of a saloonkeeper named J. W. McQueen, hit as he ran into the alley at the beginning of the firefight. The shot that slammed into McQueen's body seemed for a while to be a mortal wound, but he too would recover.

Another citizen, Charles Leonard, who was merely walking through the "court house [sic] yard," was hit in the left hand. Other accounts say that mill-hand Charlie Learn—presumably the same man—was "murdered near the courthouse fence."

Wallace seemed to be doing most of the shooting and most of the damage, but he was running out of luck. Muckleroy's deputy, Will Stevens, stood his ground in a shower of outlaw bullets and sent a round into Wallace. Other stories of the raid, however, tell that the fatal round came from a "thirty-one-year-old hardware merchant," who in later years refused to be identified by the press. This worthy man

> *stuck his single-action Colt .45 through an open window of a nearby brick building. He leveled down on Bennett [Wallace] just as the desperado turned to drop City Marshal Muckleroy ... the man with the .45 wouldn't shoot until Bennett turned again to face him. The bandit saw that menacing Colt as he turned and both of the men fired at about the same time.*

The unidentified merchant is quoted as saying, perhaps a trifle pompously, that he

> *could have gotten Bill Dalton and one of the Nite boys from my place in the window ... but they had their backs turned . . . and I wouldn't shoot even a murdering bank robber in the back.*

Well, maybe. But later newspaper accounts of the fight state that Wallace *was* shot in the back, and it's hard to imagine any westerner having such scruples in the middle of a firefight in which his fellow citizens were being shot.

Or maybe the shooter was somebody else altogether. Local attorney Claude Lacy deserved credit for the shooting, according to a retired city judge:

> *Claude was in the saloon next to the bank when the shooting started and he ran to the door. . . . One of Bennett's bullets shattered the glass in the door and forced him to run in the other direction, into a feed store. . . . The windows at the back*

*of the store looked out on the alley and Claude got behind some
sacks of feed and drilled Bennett in the back. . . . At least, he
always got credit for shooting him first but the man was hit
from all directions.*

Whoever fired the fatal round, or rounds, Wallace went down, and
the rest of the gang took to their heels. "Poor Bennett is dead," or "poor
Jim," his comrades commented piously before they ran for their lives. A
newspaper account continued:

*He was identified as George Bennett . . . who was well known
here. He was dressed like a cowboy, with high heeled boots and
spurs, a belt full of cartridges and two double action revolvers.
His horse . . . had 300 rounds of ammunition strapped to the
saddle.*

Wallace was a "reckless fellow," said the *San Francisco Chronicle*,
"who had been here some months ago and married a daughter of a
respectable farmer living near this place, but he left her and went to the
Indian Territory." With Bennett/Wallace down, the surviving outlaws
"dashed away, furiously, firing as they sped."

A large posse soon galloped off on the trail of the fleeing bandits,
but the trail petered out quickly in the pine woods north of the town.
There is also a story that some of the Longview men, infuriated by the
deaths of their fellow citizens, cut up a very dead Wallace's clothing and
hacked off his beard and hair, then dropped a rope around his neck,
dragged the corpse through the street to the train station, and hauled it
up to dangle from the cross-arm of a telegraph pole until the city mayor
ordered it taken down.

That was not, however, the end of the matter. Among other detritus left behind after the fight in the alley was Wallace's hat, which he no
longer needed. Lawmen thoughtfully examined the sweatband of the hat
to discover that it bore the label of a store in Ardmore, Indian Territory
(I.T.). The local law wired ahead to Deputy Marshal Seldon Lindsey,
operating out of the eastern district of Texas at Paris. Lindsey shrewdly
guessed that the fleeing outlaws would head for Indian Territory, and

Lindsey himself took a posse man and rode hard for the Red River crossing at Doaksville, up in the Choctaw Nation.

Lindsey and his deputy were eight hours behind the robbers at the river crossing, but they stayed on the trail, up into Indian Territory. The lawmen recovered the outlaws' horses, exhausted from being pushed too hard. However, Dalton and his two remaining cronies stole more horses near a settlement called Stringtown and turned west toward the Muddy Boggy, riding into the Chickasaw Nation. And there, on May 29, the trail apparently ended.

But the officers did not stop looking. They were as sick of arrogant outlaws as Judge Dale was, and the Longview bank had offered a $500 reward for the robbers. The Longview citizenry had chipped in another $200, making a tidy reward for lawmen accustomed to facing great danger for miserable pay. There were various newspaper reports that members of the gang had been captured, none of which were accurate. But at last, in early June, the patient officers got a break.

In Ardmore, the perennially impoverished Houston Wallace bought provisions, including ammunition, to the tune of some $200. The store owner, uneasy at such unusual purchases by the "proverbially broke" Wallace, took the bills to the United States commissioner, who wired Longview and quickly learned that the ten-dollar bills were part of the loot from the bank robbery. Wallace may have bought a wagon as well, which would have further aroused suspicion.

Deputy Marshal Lindsey followed Wallace to the express office. There, accompanied by two women who kept their sunbonnets pulled close around their faces, Wallace presented a package pickup order signed "Hines." The express agent produced the package, but Wallace refused to sign a receipt for it. Lindsey then arrested all three on suspicion of introducing liquor into Indian Territory, a federal offense, and the box was broken open forthwith. Sure enough, it contained nine quarts of red-eye.

Wallace caved in quickly. "The whiskey is not mine," he said, "It's for some people who are staying with me." The women would not say much at all, beyond giving the unenlightening names of Smith and Pruitt. They even refused to say where they lived, but Lindsey drew his own conclusions. Wallace was forthwith consigned to the local jail, and the two women were "placed under guard."

Other accounts say that an "Indian scout" who knew Mrs. Dalton watched for her in Ardmore, and when she appeared, trailed her to Bill Dalton's hideout. Writer Harry Drago's story of the capture was also different, and unlikely. In his version of the tale, the express clerk became suspicious of the package of whiskey and called Loss Hart, who confronted one of the women and "went to work on her." Whereat she "was forced to acknowledge that she was Mrs. William Dalton and disclosed where she and Bill were living."

However the news of Bill Dalton's whereabouts came to light, the deputy marshal headed for Wallace's farm. Six other U.S. deputy marshals rode with him, as well as two local officers, and they surrounded the place—a two-room shanty—early on the eighth of June.

As the officers encircled the Wallace farmhouse, Loss Hart worked his way toward a ravine in back of the house. The ravine was the only obvious escape route since it was the only path away from the shack that had any useful cover. Before Hart could get all the way to the ravine, however, a man emerged onto the house porch, saw Lindsey, and dashed back inside. He immediately reappeared and jumped out of a back window, this time with a pistol in his hand. He sprinted for the deep ravine that would give him cover. Deputy Marshal Hart shouted at him to halt, but the man turned and raised his pistol to shoot at the lawman.

Let enthusiastic newspaper writers tell the rest. According to the *Daily Oklahoman*:

> *A .44 ball, hot from the deputy's Winchester, tore into his body at the waistband near the right rear suspender button, and with two convulsive leaps he fell. Bill Dalton, the notorious desperado and bandit, met his death on the 8th inst. at Elk, I.T. C.L. Hart, a deputy marshal of the Paris district, fired the shot that sent the spirit of the outlaw to its home. . . . Hart . . . called on him to halt. Dalton half turned around, tried to take aim while running, and just then the officer shot. Two jumps in the air were the only motions made.*

The *Fort Worth Gazette* reported that Dalton went down before the "unerring aim" of Loss Hart:

*A .44 Winchester hole at the pants band on the right side of
the spinal column, near the hip, shows where the little messenger of justice had rid the country of the worst outlaw who ever
stole a horse or shot a man in the Southwest.*

Another writer put it more simply: "Loss Hart caught him on the
wing."

It's not certain that the fallen outlaw lived even long enough for
Hart to reach him. One account, however, states that the officer asked
the dying man who he was, but got nothing out of the outlaw except
defiant silence. In moments the mortally wounded man was dead.

Inside the tiny house the officers found six terrified children and
bolts of silk cloth stuffed with "numerous crisp bills and a Longview bank
sack." A couple of the children told the officers their names were Dalton.
After an initial denial, one of the two women who had been arrested in
Ardmore the day before at last broke down when she saw Dalton's body.
She then confirmed that she was Bill Dalton's wife. The body was also
identified by one of Dalton's brothers, and maybe even Frank Fischer,
brought all the way from Gregg County, Texas. Although poor Adeline
Dalton had still another sorrow to bear, most people rejoiced at Dalton's
passage. As did the *Daily Oklahoman*:

*Stretched out on a pine board in the rooms of Undertaker
Appolis on Caddo street . . . Bill Dalton . . . lies stiff and cold
. . . a .44 Winchester hole at the pants band on the right side of
the spinal column . . . and that small piece of lead has rid the
country of the worst outlaw who ever stole a horse or shot a man.*

Which may be laying it on a little thick, considering that the com-
petition for the title of "worst outlaw" included the original Dalton
Gang, the Doolin Gang, the James–Younger Gang, Cherokee Bill
Goldsby, and a flock of other lesser-known but equally vicious bad men.
The newspaper's sentiments, however, certainly reflected the general
public's rejoicing at Bill's abrupt departure from this life.

From a photograph, Houston Wallace acknowledged that his
brother was the bandit whom Deputy Stevens killed at Longview. Of the

Knight brothers, there was no trace at Ardmore. They had evaded pursuit this time, but they were headed for the same bitter end that in time awaited every man who rode with the Doolin-Dalton outfit. It took more than a year for fate to catch up with the Knights, but at last the two brothers—along with a criminal cohort, one Jim Crane—were run down on the Charles Schneider ranch along Bear Creek in Menard County, Texas.

The posse that caught up with them included Oscar Latta, deputy to Sheriff John Jones of Kimble County, Texas. In the firefight that followed, Deputy Latta killed Big Asa Knight and somebody else put an end to Crane's earthly existence. Jim Knight, badly wounded, was taken back to Longview for trial. And there the last survivor of the Longview robbers was sentenced to spend the rest of his natural life in prison. Later pardoned, he went back to his old, bad ways. In 1929 he tried to hold up a Tulsa drugstore. The proprietor objected to being robbed and put five slugs into Jim, whereof, as coroner's juries were wont to say in those days, he died.

A lot of mythology surrounds the demise of Bill Dalton, as is common with outlaw figures of the West. Several letters appeared shortly after he was killed, one of which was supposed to have come from Bitter Creek Newcomb. There was also a report of an alleged interview with Doolin. The letters and the interview all asserted that the dead man was not Dalton. And there was an unsubstantiated soap-opera story that Dalton was playing with his daughter when he was shot down by the law. At least one Dallas newspaper bought this myth: "After daylight Dalton was in the yard playing with his ten-year-old daughter, who was a cripple, on his back, when one of the posse fired and killed him."

Colonel Clarence B. Douglass, who lived in Ardmore, gave this account to the *Daily Oklahoman* of Oklahoma City:

> *Loss Hart called to the fleeing man to halt, when he sighted carefully along the barrel of his Winchester and even when he drew the bead and pressed the trigger with his steady finger and sent a .44 caliber ball hot and stinging into the vigorous body of the suspect, his only thought was that he may have been at Longview.*

In short, Hart didn't know he was shooting at Bill Dalton, only that the man who pointed a pistol in his direction "may have been at Longview."

And in a typically whiny passage in one of his books, Emmett Dalton complained of the officers shooting down his brother, asserting that they "came in for considerable public censure" because of it, and were in time fired or "drifted to other parts." There is no reason to suppose that this is anything but typical Emmett Dalton claptrap, a commodity in which his two dubious books abound.

Other accounts of the fight at Longview vary the tale more or less. In one, the Knight brothers become "Bill Jones" and "Jim Wallace." Still another account asserts that poor old Bill Dalton had retired to "a nice little farm" at Ardmore, and that the story of his forming another gang was just "another rumor." In short, he wasn't at Longview at all. The same source includes a lot of unconvincing and unlikely dialogue between the Ardmore freight agent and Loss Hart, and even has Hart handing over the crate of booze to the two women.

What remained of Bill Dalton was shipped off to sunny California, where it was duly planted in Merced County. A newspaper story from Ardmore reported the departure under a heading that solemnly announced, "Mr. Dalton Continues Dead." Amazingly, to the editorial disgust of various newspapers, a federal grand jury much later indicted Loss Hart and the rest of the lawmen with him for the murder of Dalton, "the worst outlaw ever to . . . shoot a man." The officers were released on their own recognizance, and there is no record that they were ever tried.

So perished the last of the outlaw Daltons, joining the long line of Oklahoma hoodlums killed by peace officers, or still to die under the guns of the law. Of the several members of the Dalton-Doolin gangs, the swaggering hard cases with jaunty nicknames and larger-than-life reputations, just one outlaw died of natural causes. This man, Little Bill Raidler, debilitated by his old gunshot wounds, did not long survive his release from prison. The last man to go was Arkansas Tom Jones in 1924, back in the robbing business after stretches in prison and even a spell of honest employment. With his death in Joplin, Missouri, where he was thoroughly ventilated by lawmen's bullets, passed the last of the old gang.

It is not recorded that there was any widespread mourning.

## SCARY CHRISTMAS

### *When Santa Claus Went Bad*

IF YOU'RE THINKING OF A career in bank robbing, you probably shouldn't start out in Cisco, Texas. If you choose not to heed this excellent advice, your budding vocation may be over before it gets a good start. Even if you're dressed as Santa Claus, trying to steal the hard-earned savings of the good citizens of Cisco could prove remarkably hazardous to your health. Just look at what happened in Cisco back in 1927, when Santa and a pack of verminous elves came to town on the day before Christmas Eve.

Marshall Ratliff, Robert Hill, and Henry Helms were all ex-cons who hadn't learned a thing in prison and were looking for a bank to rob. Ratliff and his equally larcenous brother had already been sent to Huntsville Prison for a bank robbery over in Valera, but they had done only a mere year in the penitentiary. To the Ratliff boys' great fortune, they were part of a small army of convicts pardoned by Texas governor Miriam "Ma" Ferguson, a distinctly odd duck who freed an average of one hundred felons a month amid charges of corruption and bribery. Hill and Helms had also been beneficiaries of Ma Ferguson's largesse, and now all three were going to try again what hadn't worked before.

Dumping this bumper crop of crooks back on the street early did nothing to reduce Texas's soaring bank-robbery rate, which was as high as three or four heists a day. Things were so bad that the Texas Bankers

Association had a standing offer of $5,000 to anybody who shot down a bank robber during the robbery. Five thousand dollars was a great deal of money in 1927.

Ratliff's brother had planned to go a-robbing with his sibling once more, but being clumsy as well as crooked, he had gotten himself arrested again by the holiday season of 1927 and was thus unavailable for duty. The fourth member of the crew was to be a safecracker, but he had gone down with the flu at the last minute, so the gang recruited one Louis Davis, who was related to Helms. In a boardinghouse in Wichita Falls, the gang did some minimal planning, then stole a car and drove off to Cisco on the morning of December 23.

It was a very cold, crisp morning, and Cisco was in a festive mood. The stores sparkled with Christmas trees and other decorations, and now, to make the holiday atmosphere perfect, Santa Claus appeared. For reasons not entirely clear, Ratliff had borrowed a Santa Claus suit from Mrs. Midge Tellet, owner of the Wichita Falls boardinghouse. For reasons again obscure, once they reached Cisco, Ratliff climbed out of the car several blocks from the gang's objective, whither he proceeded on foot, clad as the jolly old elf and followed by a crowd of children.

As Ratliff "strolled leisurely down the street," a passing woman asked him, "What store do you represent?" and Ratliff replied, "You'll find out soon enough." His answer must have seemed somewhat cryptic to this innocent citizen, but his meaning would indeed become very clear very quickly. His accomplices parked the car in an alley behind the objective, and, meeting Ratliff, entered the bank. Ratliff was still resplendent in his red suit, surrounded by Santa's little helpers.

Inside the bank, the cashier, Alex Spears (or Speer) was chatting with Marion Olson, a student at Harvard, home on vacation. Teller Jewel Poe was handling a deposit by Oscar Cliett, a grocer in Cisco. Back in the separate bookkeeping room, Vance Littleton and Freda Stroebel bent over their numbers. For a few seconds Alex Spears thought Ratliff was a harmless harbinger of the holiday season. "Hello, Santa Claus," he called, but then he realized that the man in the red suit was no joke and the merriment ceased. Ratliff's companions pushed up to the tellers' windows and demanded that they disgorge the bank's money and securities.

*Santa Claus robbery*

The room must have seemed full of outlaws and deadly weapons. Davis was "young, lean-faced, and raw-boned," while Helms, husky and somewhat older, was said by Spears to be holding "two .44 caliber revolvers." Hill, pale and slim, brandished a pair of semiautomatic pistols. The bandits lined Spears, Olson, and Cliett up against the wall in the cashier's office. There, Ratliff searched all three for hidden weapons and pocketed the bank's pistol that was resting under the counter. Cliett was chewing tobacco and asked Hill whether he could move someplace to spit. "Spit on the floor," Hill answered, and Cliett did. Also included in the group of hostages were two small girls, Emma May Robertson and Laverne Comer, twelve and ten years old.

Ratliff harvested the cash while the other outlaws kept their guns on the bank workers and customers, and all went smoothly until Mrs. B. P. Blassengame walked into the bank. With her was her six-year-old daughter, Frances, who had followed Santa inside, perhaps to tell him all her dearest wishes.

Mrs. Blassengame quickly herded Frances into the bank's book-keeping department. She was, according to one source, "screaming" to Littleton and Miss Stroebel that the bank was being robbed. Mrs. Blassengame then unlocked a door from the bookkeeping office into the alley, pushed Frances outside, and fled, ignoring threats to shoot from Ratliff and his boys. Once outside, the woman yelled mightily that the bank was being robbed. She ran into City Hall just a block away—or telephoned, depending on which account you read—and alerted the chief of police.

Meanwhile, inside the bank, teller Poe had unlocked one safe in the vault; the other was on a time lock. The two little girls, their hands raised, were pushed into the bookkeeping room with the two bookkeep-ers. Miss Stroebel had her eyes on Helms—she said later that she had never seen a robber before—until Helms told her to look away. Helms then went to stand guard at the screen door that opened onto the alley.

Now a passerby, intrigued by the bank's closed front door, pushed his face against the plate-glass window to try to see inside. Ratliff snapped a shot at the face against the glass, holing the window but missing the face. The face departed.

Mrs. Blassengame's shouts also roused a host of ordinary citizens, some of whom quickly armed themselves. Help began to appear from all directions. It included the town postmaster and his assistant, J. W. Triplitt and W. P. Coldwell, whose offices opened onto the alley behind the bank.

Chief of Police G. E. Bedford—called "Bit" in the homey Texas tradition—had been a lawman for thirty-five years. He, too, was heading for the bank with a riot gun and two officers, R. T. Redies and George Carmichael. Bedford and his men split up to cover both the front door and the alley at the back of the building. Other citizens ran to help out the police.

Even though he must have guessed that Mrs. Blassengame would summon the minions of the law, Ratliff ignored the certainty that the fat was now in the fire and went on cramming his sack with the bank's cur-rency. Then, when the shot at the curious passerby was instantly echoed from outside, and it was obvious that the bandits were in a world of trou-ble. Hill, vainly trying to discourage further interruptions, fired several more shots into the ceiling, at which more rounds were fired at the bank

1ST NATIONAL BANK OF CISCO, TX

*Marshall Ratliff*

from outside, and at last it dawned on the gang that it was high time to get out of Cisco by the shortest route.

Herding customers and bank employees ahead of them, the gang hurried out into the alley where they had left their car, only to find people shooting at them from all directions. A first-class firefight followed in and around the alley. Later, citizens counted at least 200 bullet marks on the fair face of the bank. In the rain of bullets, Spears was hit in the jaw, and a slug in the thigh nearly knocked Olson down.

The rest of the hostages ran for their lives and reached safety, though Cliett took a round in the foot on the way. He managed to find a post to hide behind, but the bandits fired at him even though he was

1ST NATIONAL BANK OF CISCO, TX

*Robert Hill*

no threat; bullets were dug out of his post after the fight. Freda Stroebel seized her chance and ran off down the alley.

For a brief moment in time, Littleton was left inside the bank alone with Hill. Hearing the din of firing outside, Littleton asked the bandit reasonably, "Why don't you surrender?" Hill's response was to push the bank man out the door into the alley; Hill was right behind him, firing a pistol over Littleton's shoulder.

The bandits tried to force Spears into their getaway car, but the cashier, blood pouring down his face, said he couldn't get into the vehicle, and the outlaws didn't insist. Olson was forced into the vehicle; the "pale desperado," probably Hill, told him, "Lean back there in the seat and shut up or I'll kill you!" Olson did as he was ordered, but slid right on across the seat, opened the door on the opposite side, and hit the ground running. "He held two guns on me," said Olson afterward, "and told me to sit there, but I told him I was going anyway and left. There were three bandits in the car when I was there and one or more other bandits was still herding people out of the bank toward the car."

Only the two little girls were left for the outlaws to hide behind.

1st National Bank of Cisco, TX

*Henry Helms*

The officers were handicapped by trying not to injure any of their fellow citizens, now running in all directions, and they paid dearly for their care. George Carmichael was shot in the head and staggered against the wall of the bank building, leaving an ugly smear of blood where his smashed skull touched the wall. Redies ran to help him, immediately drawing heavy fire from the robbers' car. On the bandit side, Ratliff was limping badly, and Davis was badly shot up in the exchange, but the gang, dragging the two little girls with them, made it to their car and roared away down the alley.

Standing at the head of the alley was Bedford, all six feet, four inches of him, but his courageous single-handed stand could not stop the gang. His shotgun jammed, and he banged the weapon against the wall of a building to clear it. He shouted to Tom Lonox, pastor of the First Christian Church, to "get some men and guns and block the street."

About then Chief Bedford was hit, but he stayed on his feet, dropped the useless shotgun, and pulled his pistol. Before he could use it, he was hit five times and went down, mortally wounded. Citizen C. A. Nosek picked up the fallen lawman's pistol and emptied it at the bandits'

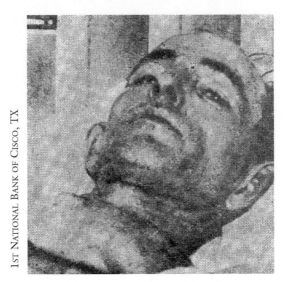

1st National Bank of Cisco, TX

*Louis Davis*

car. According to the *Fort Worth Star-Telegram,* before he went down, Bedford fired a round into Davis.

Some of the citizens were far more brave than efficient. Hill, the story goes, was horrified when R. L. Day, a restaurant owner, shoved a semiautomatic shotgun in his face. But Day had borrowed the weapon and had no idea how to use it. "How do you work this darned thing, anyway?" he wondered aloud, and turned away to try to get the shotgun working. He did manage to blow a hole in the side of the bank building, and then the bloodied bandits were in their car and racing to escape.

The outlaws soon realized that one of their tires had a bullet through it, maybe the work of A. A. Hutton, who had fired at the car's tires with the fallen Carmichael's pistol. Worse, the bandits were paying for their lack of planning, for they also discovered that they had forgotten to top off their gas tank and were running almost on empty with an angry bunch of townspeople right behind them. L. L. Hooker ran to the hardware store and borrowed a rifle and ammunition; he ran after the bandits for about a block and then hitched a ride in another citizen's car.

One robber had smashed out the rear window of the getaway car, and the outlaws were firing through the break at a swarm of angry citizens. One passerby was so close to their guns that his face was scorched by the muzzle-blast of the weapons. The outlaws were holding the little girls up as shields—ironically, Emma May was sitting on Santa's lap. Among the pursuers was Officer Redies, who stopped at the police station for a rifle and then ran down the street after the fleeing bandits. A citizen, pursuing in an automobile, stopped long enough to collect the officer, and the two joined the chase together.

The bandits were in a quandary. It occurred to them that it might be wise to get another car, and so they tried to steal an Oldsmobile belonging to a family called Harris, citizens of the nearby town of Rising Star. Fourteen-year-old Woodrow Wilson Harris—called Woody—was driving his parents and grandmother when the bandits stopped them. With enormous presence of mind, the youngster turned off the ignition and managed to stash the keys in his pocket (or throw them away, depending on which account of the raid you read).

Unaware of Woody's gutsy action, the gang hurried to move their loot, the badly wounded Louis Davis, and their hostages to the new car. Hill tried to hold off the pursuit while Helms and Ratliff transferred everything to the new car. But then the outlaws made the horrifying discovery that there was no key and the Olds wouldn't start. They must have been in a real swivet by now, for Officer Redies and the pack of townspeople were catching up to them, firing as they came. Hill was hit in the shoulder by a high-velocity round from Hooker's rifle, and the impact spun him around.

Thoroughly panicked, the outlaws abandoned Louis Davis, now unconscious. As one of the little hostages put it, "They just threw him out of the car into the street." "He's nearly dead. It's no use to take him," said one of the bandits. They piled back into their own bullet-pocked car and departed Cisco at the high lope, scattering roofing nails on the road in a vain attempt to disable their pursuers' automobiles.

Somewhere down the road they must have realized that they had left behind not only Davis, but the loot. According to one source, Helms asked his comrades as they sped down the road, "Did we get the money?" "No," said somebody, "we left it in the car." Helms's comment pretty well summed up the bandits' day: "Oh, hell!" There was sure no going back for their booty now. Sitting on the seat of the immobile Oldsmobile was more than $12,000 in cash and some $150,000 in non-negotiable securities. About then the outlaw dressed as Santa announced, "I have a bad chin." He briefly raised his Saint Nick mask to reveal blood on his chin, but replaced it when he realized that one of the young hostages was looking at him.

The bandits finally turned off the main road outside Cisco and wandered down roads ever narrower until the vehicle became stuck. Here the battered gang left behind both their car and their hostages and ran for it. The little girls were recovered unharmed by pursuing citizens, and so was the battered getaway car, studded with bullet holes, splattered with blood. In the backseat were the bandits' emergency supplies: a canteen, loaves of bread, a can of coffee, and more roofing nails.

And now the hunt was on. The Santa Claus outlaws had opened Pandora's box. Not only had they left their booty and one of their comrades behind, not only were two of them badly shot up, but they had touched off the biggest manhunt seen in Texas up to that time. Lawmen and parties of citizens were searching for them everywhere, with as many as 1,000 men covering all the roads.

With no place to run or hide, the bandits disappeared into the brush and escaped the townspeople for the moment, leaving behind only bloody bandages. Losing blood, Hill fainted only a mile or so into the woods, but the other robbers got him up and going again. One of the posses—which at times swelled to about a hundred men—was often close to them, but could not run them down. All they found was Hill's blood-soaked coat and a bag of supplies. The outlaws' momentary good luck would not last.

More and more men from several counties joined the manhunt, and the sheriff of Coryell County brought in bloodhounds, although the dogs could not keep the scent of the fugitives. Some of the searchers were mounted, and a couple of airplanes circled overhead, seeking some sign of the outlaws in the thick brush. Ranger Captain Tom Hickman was coordinating the search for the fugitives, aided by the formidable Sergeant "Lone Wolf" Gonzales, already a noted bane to criminals of all kinds.

Back in Cisco, Chief Bedford, well liked and respected, died at about 7:45 on the evening of the robbery. Officer Carmichael was also mortally wounded. News of his condition added to the anger in the town, although in the end, he would hang on another three weeks before he passed away. In addition to Spears and Cliett, the citizen casualties included: R. L. Day, who had a scalp wound; Brady Boggs, whose leg was broken by a bullet; and Marion Olson and Pete Rutherford, both with bullet holes in the thigh. Davis, the wounded outlaw, was "rushed out of the city to avoid mob violence."

A day later and now Christmas Eve, Santa Claus could go no farther on his wounded leg. The gang needed a car badly. They doubled back to Cisco, of all places, and successfully stole a new car. Then the bandits, driving the back roads, showed up at a place called the Fox Farm, the home of Davis's sister and her husband—she was also Helms's sister-in-law. Other relatives were also gathered there. It is not recorded what they thought when Davis's sister asked the outlaws, "Where's Louis?"

"He's dead," somebody answered. "We stayed with him until we all nearly got killed." But they hadn't. At just about the time that the gang was lying to Davis's sister, Davis was dying in the Tarrant County Jail in Fort Worth. On that discouraging note, the bandits stocked up on food and hit the road, but they did not get far. Spying a car carrying armed men, Helms drove off in a great hurry and managed to wreck their car on a cattle guard. They then went to a farmhouse, where Helms appealed to the farmer's better instincts. "I've had a wreck," he said, "and need a car to take my wife to the doctor."

The farmer, a man named Wylie, said he'd have his son and his nephew drive this needy man. They waited a while for the son to return with the car, but then, when the other two bandits ran from cover for the car, the nephew bailed out, leaving Wylie's son stuck with the job of bandit chauffeur. After a while, Helms, in spite of his signal lack of success at the cattle guard, took over the driving, starting a back-road odyssey that lasted almost twenty-four hours, but got the bandits nowhere.

Hiding out in a thicket during one long day, the outlaws went out after dark to steal another car. After several failures, they finally managed to steal a small coupe. They loaded Ratliff on board and bid young Wylie farewell at about 5:00 A.M. When Wylie stepped out of the

169

car, the bandits told him he was in Breckenridge, a town some 30 miles from Cisco. On running into the town, however, Wylie found he was in fact in Cisco.

Young Wylie's story made page one of the *Star-Telegram,* as he recounted his "nocturnal tour of Northern Callahan County and Southern Shackelford County . . . which ended up on the streets of Cisco the next morning. . . . They ran out of gas, and Helms twice stopped at farmhouses before they procured a new supply."

He was able to tell officers that the outlaws had again tried to reach the Fox Farm, and that the gang had talked about "planning to meet the 'father and mother' of one of the bandits . . . but this failed." Ratliff, said Wylie, was badly hurt, unable to bear weight on his injured leg.

Driving their stolen car, the bandits started to cross the Brazos at South Bend, trying to reach Wichita Falls. Waiting for them at the Brazos was Sheriff Foster of Young County and Cy Bradford, an Eastland County deputy, who was a very good hand with a gun.

The bandits turned tail and fled, with the lawmen right behind them. Santa Claus and his remaining henchmen turned aside into the breaks of the Brazos, within a few miles of the country which, as the *Fort Worth Star-Telegram* reminded its readers, "was the rendezvous of Sam Bass, the famous Texas outlaw, and his gang." The bandits abandoned their car and ran for it, and another firefight followed in a field. Bradford nailed Ratliff, who fell and did not rise, and Bradford—or maybe another officer—shot and wounded Helms and Hill as well. Whoever hit Helms and Hill, the wounds weren't enough to put them down for keeps, and both men reached cover and disappeared.

Santa Claus himself, however, was too badly wounded to run another step. He was taken into custody, and on him the officers found an astonishing arsenal: "six automatics, a Bowie knife, a double-barreled shotgun, and three pistol belts filled with ammunition." He was promptly lodged in jail, where he was comforted by his mother. Bank officials were on the way to Cisco from the towns of Bangs and Carbon to see whether Ratliff was part of the gang that had robbed their banks not long before the raid on Cisco.

The hunt for the remaining pair of robbers kept grimly on task. On the twenty-eighth, there was a report that "two men, driving at a fast rate and answering the description of Henry Helms and his companion . . . [were] reported to have broken through the cordon of police officers." The companion was thought to be "Jack Long, ex-convict and notorious criminal." The paper theorized that the two were headed for the Fox Farm, where Helms's relatives lived.

The paper guessed that the pair could not know that everybody at the farm—including a Wichita Falls doctor possibly on hand to fix the outlaws' wounds—had been taken into custody by the law. The news story added that officers had missed Helms, Ratliff, and "Long" at the farm by seconds. One of the people at the farm told officers that the third fugitive was a man he did not know, but certainly not Jack Long. Ratliff, from his jail cell, agreed.

The fugitives were now cut off from the only people who might have helped them. They probably took refuge, said the *Star-Telegram*, in what it called "a neutral rocky fortress about 4 miles square, overlooking the Brazos." After the fight in which Ratliff was captured, the lawmen closed in on the wild area along the Brazos, following fresh trails. They discovered where the outlaws had raided a corn crib and parched some of the corn over a fire, poor fare for hungry, injured men without shelter or medical aid. The pursuers also discovered a discarded "ammunition belt and scabbard for a large caliber pistol," a further indication of the deterioration of the outlaws' physical condition.

Within a few days, however, Helms and Hill, exhausted and much the worse for wear, appeared in Graham, Texas. They were arrested by local officers without putting up a fight, although Helms was carrying four pistols and Hill wore three. They had asked around town for directions to the "Texas rooms," but the second person they approached noticed two pistols under one outlaw's coat and called for the law. Hill tried to run, but he could manage no more than a clumsy stagger. Helms leaned against a building wall and then simply fell down.

Both outlaws were exhausted and bedraggled, weak from lack of food and suffering from multiple bullet wounds. Helms had been hit seven times and Hill had as many wounds, including a bullet that had torn into his jaw. Helms was "semidelirious" and running a high fever. Hill complained that Helms "got us caught. He's been out of his head for nearly two days."

Both were sent on to dwell with Santa Claus in the Eastland County Jail. Before they disappeared into their cells, however, they were photographed with a large supporting cast of lawmen and spectators. Among the crowd were Captain Hickman and the officers who actually made the capture: Jim Davis, the Graham City marshal, and Deputy Sheriff Gentry Williamson. The *Star-Telegram* rejoiced: "Avenging Fate of Bad Men Lands Weary Cisco Bandit Pair in Jail."

And so the chase was over, a chase the paper accurately called "the most relentless manhunt . . . since cow thieves were pursued by horse-riding posses." Inevitably, the *Star-Telegram* found a couple of officers who were ready to make philosophical comments on the end of the long manhunt. "The end of a trail of blood," said Sheriff John Hart of Eastland County. "It is a pity," added Ranger Captain Hickman, pointing to the disheveled outlaws, "that every criminal, vicious and petty, in Texas could not see this picture. No melodrama here—just the avenging fate of a bad man."

So the chase was over, but the story wasn't. Hill pleaded guilty to armed robbery and went off to prison. He passes from our history in the mid-1940s, when he was paroled, prudently changed his name, and apparently joined the ranks of honest citizens. For Helms, however, the bungled holdup had a grimmer ending.

He was identified as the gunman who had killed both Sheriff Bedford and his deputy, and so he faced charges of murder. He tried an insanity plea—perhaps confusing stupidity with lunacy—but it didn't work, and he passed from this life in the electric chair in September of 1929. This left Ratliff, Santa Claus himself, facing a long litany of felony charges.

In January of 1928, he was sentenced to a ninety-nine-year term for armed robbery. On his way back from court, he was heard to comment, "That's no hill for a high-stepper like me." But then, in March, the hill became a lot steeper, for he was also convicted of murder in the deaths of the two Cisco lawmen. The court accordingly sentenced Ratliff to follow Helms into the hereafter. After his appeal failed, Ratliff seems to have decided he might have better luck with acting crazy than Helms had. And so he set out to convince the world that he had taken leave of his senses.

Ratliff fooled his death-row warders at Huntsville Penitentiary completely, or maybe he really *wasn't* playing with a full deck. In any case, his mother then sought a hearing on the question of his sanity or the lack of it. All of this left the good citizens of Eastland County much wroth over the chance that Ratliff really might kill two of their friends and neighbors and get away with it.

But that was not to be. An Eastland County judge issued a bench warrant returning Ratliff to Eastland County for trial on charges of armed robbery in the theft of the Harris Oldsmobile. There, Ratliff continued with his expert lunatic impersonation and managed to convince Tom Jones and Pack Kilborn, his jailers, that he really did have a screw loose. According to one account, he managed to feign paralysis even when pricked with a needle. He persuaded the patient Eastland County warders that he was so far gone that they not only needed to feed and bathe him, but even to take him off to the toilet.

And then, on November 18, 1929, Ratliff tried to escape, probably something he had been planning from the beginning. He got out of his cell all right and ran downstairs, rummaging through a jailer's desk for keys to get him through the door to freedom. He found no keys, but did come up with Officer Jones's revolver. Running back upstairs, he met the jailers and opened fire on Jones, hitting him three times in the upper body.

Kilborn tackled the outlaw empty-handed before Ratliff could turn the pistol on him, while Kilborn's daughter, Malaque Taylor, helpless outside the jail door, grabbed her father's pistol and fired shots to summon help from the townspeople. Her formidable father needed no assistance. He overpowered Ratliff, took the now-empty pistol away from him, and beat him with it until the outlaw screamed, "Don't kill me!" Kilborn relented and put the prisoner back behind bars. Although Ratliff was back in his cell, the outlaw had mortally wounded Tom Jones. And once the town found out about that, it was the last straw.

By the next evening a mob of at least 1,000 people was thronging around the jail. To his everlasting credit, Kilborn, with the assistance of his son, tried to protect his venomous prisoner, but the crowd poured in the door of the jail and there was no holding them. Kilborn ended up on the floor with several men sitting on him, and the angry citizenry laid hands on Ratliff and dragged the outlaw into the street. According to one tale, they gave Ratliff a chance to say some last words. Those turned out to be "Forgive me, boys," a fine-sounding sentiment even if it was uttered a little late in the day. Then the mob tossed a rope over a handy guy wire between two telephone poles, tied the other end around Ratliff's neck, and hoisted away.

The citizens hadn't tied the knot very well and it came loose, dropping Ratliff to the pavement, or maybe—according to another account—the rope broke. But whether the mob went and found a stouter rope or just did a better job of tying the knot, this time they did it right. Ratliff, alias Santa Claus, expired some 15 feet above the street. It is not recorded that anybody in Eastland County mourned.

Like Ratliff, Tom Jones died that evening. What remained of Ratliff was laid out on display in an Eastland furniture store, and the door was left open for all to see the outlaw's corpse. Several thousand people did indeed troop by to look at the body, until at last a county judge put a stop to the ugly spectacle of public viewing. Although a grand jury inquired into the events of November 18, nothing ever came of it. Nobody was ever tried for the lynching, mostly because everybody in town had a total memory failure about who did what that terrible evening. What remained of Ratliff was called for by his family and taken off to burial in Fort Worth.

After the Christmas of 1927, you have to wonder what the little kids of Cisco thought about Santa.

# FIESTA IN PARRAL

## *When Dirty Dave Rudabaugh Lost His Head*

MOST OLD-TIME OUTLAWS partook of at least a little virtue, however exiguous: They loved their mothers, or they liked dogs and horses, or maybe they were kind to little children. Some, like Doc Holliday, were fiercely loyal to their friends; others, like Deacon Jim Miller, gave to the church . . . at least sometimes. A few, like Bill Doolin, were even true to their marriage vows. But it was always hard to say much of anything good about Dave Rudabaugh.

Rudabaugh was a hulking, nasty, treacherous bully, and that was on his good days. He brutalized people and stole from them. He turned state's evidence and sold out his friends. In an outlaw society not famous for painstaking personal hygiene, he was widely known for his permanent and penetrating odor. Due to his antipathy toward honest water, Dave's smell preceded him by a quarter of an hour. Not for nothing was he known as "Dirty Dave." He had, as one writer said, "the look of a man who enjoyed sleeping in his clothes." Which was putting it mildly.

Altogether, Rudabaugh was entirely without redeeming social value, as the judges say. In addition to his other grossly unattractive attributes, he had a vile temper. He lost his head with regularity, and one day his foul disposition would cause him to lose his head permanently.

During his career, Rudabaugh tried being an express messenger, a bartender, a ranch manager, and a cowboy. One account says he pushed longhorns in the massive trail drives north from Texas to the Kansas rail-heads after the Civil War. For a while, he worked for Charlie Rath, the frontier entrepreneur of Dodge City, pushing freight and hide wagons to and from the railhead. Along the way he narrowly missed the ferocious Adobe Walls fight, having hauled a load of hides out of the buffalo-hunters' outpost only days before a large band of Kiowas, Cheyennes, and Comanches attacked the place.

Driving wagons full of hides was not for Rudabaugh, even if it meant working for popular Charlie Rath. He decided he liked money more than regular work, and in time took up the outlaw business. He turned to rustling cattle and stealing horses, and may have begun his graduate work in larceny by sticking up stages in the Black Hills. Some accounts say he also rode with an outlaw gang in Texas. Considering Rudabaugh's nasty temperament, most of the tales of his lawless nature are probably true. However, he first appears as a known, wanted criminal in the summer of 1877.

In that year, the Santa Fe Railroad—or maybe it was Dodge City mayor Dog Kelley—offered a Dodge lawman ten dollars a day and room and board to run down Rudabaugh and bring him in. Wyatt Earp never did find Rudabaugh on that trip, but he made a friend. Following Rudabaugh's trail south into wild and woolly Fort Griffin, Texas, Wyatt met up with a consumptive, cold-eyed gambling man called Holliday, sometime dentist, most-time gambler, and shooter extraordinaire.

As the story goes, Doc told Wyatt that Rudabaugh had headed for Fort Davis out in west Texas. Wyatt followed the outlaw there and else-where, finally returning to Fort Griffin early in 1878. Wyatt then discov-ered that Rudabaugh had headed back to Kansas. So had Doc. He and Big-Nosed Kate had departed Fort Griffin at the high lope just ahead of a lynch mob after Doc eviscerated a local hoodlum.

Early in 1878, Rudabaugh reappeared in Kansas with a bang. Before daylight on Sunday, January 27, he and four other thugs held up a train at Kinsley in one of the most bungled holdups of all time.

Rudabaugh, a hoodlum called Roarke, and several others decided that holding up a train might make a fine payday. At first they contemplated hitting the Santa Fe train and its express car in Dodge City, but Roarke demurred. Tough Charlie Bassett was marshal in

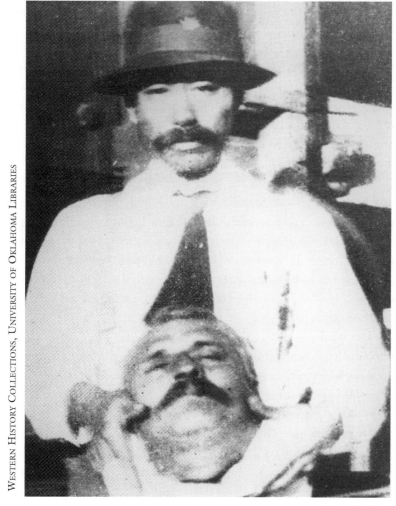

*Dave Rudabaugh's head*

Dodge just then, and Roarke wanted no part of Bassett's quick and accurate Colts.

After much palaver, the gang settled on Plan B: They would stick up the train at Kinsley, a wide spot in the road where they should meet no resistance. And so they plodded north in miserable winter weather, even abandoning the chuck wagon they had brought with them. On

January 26, 1878, the gang rode through light snow and piercing cold to snatch their bonanza from the railroad.

They obviously had not planned very well. In the dead of night, on the way into town, they stopped at a railroad worker's shack to inquire whether the train they wanted was on time. The railroad man was understandably suspicious, seeing that all his nocturnal visitors had their faces blackened. When Rudabaugh began to fondle his revolver, the railroad man took the hint: He told the gang what he could, wished them Godspeed, and went back to bed.

At the Kinsley depot, the gang held up the agent, a young man named Andrew Kinkaid. Kinkaid, cool and tough, showed the gang an empty cash drawer and convinced them that he couldn't open the safe (in which was nestled 2,000 good American dollars). When the train arrived, Kinkaid ran for his life through a shower of bullets. He tried to warn the train's engineer, but the man was clad in earmuffs against the wintry blasts and could hear nothing. He thought the agent was simply shouting a greeting.

The train was stopped, at least. But then the gang was frustrated by a tough, resolute express messenger who answered demands to stand and deliver with pistol bullets. At the same time, Rudabaugh was spraying slugs about indiscriminately, on the thesis that if you were hostile enough, nobody would be moved to interfere.

He was wrong. The crew moved the train a ways down the line and the gunfight continued. About then, an angry crowd of Kinsleyites arrived, some of them pumping a railroad handcar, banging away with everything they had. After a good deal of noisy shooting—and no casualties on either side—the gang scattered, departing into the snowy night with the posse hot on their heels. The snow covered their tracks and they were soon in the clear. They had no loot, but at least they were free.

Not for long. Determined posses beat the bushes in all directions in spite of the wretched weather. An army patrol from Fort Dodge joined in the chase as well. Worst of all, the gang drew the enthusiastic attention of a formidable young lawman from Dodge City.

Now Kinsley was less than 40 miles up the line from Dodge, and a posse led by the county sheriff, Bat Masterson, promptly ran down Rudabaugh and one other man. Even then, at only twenty-three,

Rudabaugh was said to be a veteran criminal, but he was taken without a fight. When Bat threw down on Rudabaugh and his companion, Rudabaugh started to go for his own gun. He froze in mid-reach, though, hearing the ominous "click" of posse man John Joshua Webb cocking his own weapon. "I wouldn't do that if I was you," said Webb pleasantly, and Rudabaugh quickly decided Webb was right.

During his preliminary hearing, Rudabaugh appeared "cool and collected," according to the *Ford County Globe*. Well, he should have been, for he was about to become a witness against his former comrades. As the *Kinsley Graphic* put it: "Rudabaugh . . . was promised entire immunity if he would 'squeal,' therefore he squole. Someone said there is a kind of honor among thieves; Rudabaugh don't think so."

So, as the paper said, Rudabaugh "squole," and he ratted so convincingly that his erstwhile comrades changed their pleas to guilty. Rudabaugh then hung around town long enough for Roarke to be convicted. Roarke was the last survivor of this inept mob—one other gang member chose to shoot it out with a lawman and came in second.

His ratting done, Rudabaugh sanctimoniously announced that he was going straight. He may even have taken semi-honest work as a deputy during the Santa Fe-Denver & Rio Grande Royal Gorge War. And by late 1879 he did in fact go straight; he went straight to New Mexico, where he robbed and pillaged around Las Vegas. Rudabaugh would try anything, as long as it was crooked.

In all their foul enterprises, he and his fellow outlaws were abetted and protected by the Las Vegas law, none other than Dodge City officer John Joshua Webb. All past conflict forgotten, Rudabaugh now became Webb's deputy. For a while the two of them were able to cover the operations of what locals called the "Dodge City Gang," masterminded by Justice of the Peace Hoodoo Brown. The gang was an illustrious bunch of thugs—as if Rudabaugh and Webb were not quite enough, Hoodoo also commanded the services of "Mysterious" Dave Mather and several other professional uglies.

Along the way, Rudabaugh, ever adaptable, turned lynch-mob leader for a night, officiating at the *ad hoc* hanging of three local hoodlums who had killed Deputy Tom Carson, another of Hoodoo's boys. The departed were bad eggs, so no doubt justice was done . . . but skeptics might have remarked that the lynching also disposed of three rivals to the Dodge City Gang's stranglehold on Las Vegas crime.

The Dodge City Gang's happy arrangement came to an abrupt halt when Webb was arrested for the murder of Wyoming cattleman Mike Kelliher in March of 1880. Kelliher had brought a pile of money to Las Vegas to buy cattle. The size of his kick immediately attracted the gang's attention and plans were quickly made. One of Hoodoo's boys provoked Kelliher into an argument in a saloon, whereat two others, including Webb, ran into the bar, shot Kelliher down, and stole his poke. It was a big mistake.

The crime was so brutal and so obvious that even Las Vegas took umbrage, and Webb was arrested. He escaped a lynch mob by a whisker, thanks mostly to the six-gun and determined scowl of Dave Rudabaugh, who held off the mob. Webb lived to hear himself convicted of murder fair and square. After Webb was sentenced to hang, Rudabaugh tried to break his protector out of jail, showing at least a tiny spark of loyalty—or maybe Webb owed him money. In any case, Rudabaugh and another bum called Little Allen took a hack to the Las Vegas jail and got permission to talk to Webb. They then turned on Deputy Sheriff Lino Valdez and demanded the keys. Valdez, with a good deal more guts than good sense, replied, "You may kill me, but I won't give them up." "That's easy," said Allen (according to Rudabaugh, anyway), and in a blaze of gunfire, Valdez fell.

Rudabaugh and Allen ran. Webb stayed behind, although he broke out later that year, staying free until Pat Garrett recaptured him in December of 1880. Newspaper stories of Webb's recapture shed some light on the stature of Rudabaugh as an outlaw leader. When Webb was run to earth, Garrett and his posse were actually hunting Rudabaugh and, according to one account, "his notorious gang, whose depredations have been the darkest and boldest type."

The Kelliher murder had been especially brutal and clumsy, and spelled the beginning of the end for the gang, Hoodoo included. Even though the *Las Vegas Optic* minimized Las Vegas's rash of murder victims as mostly "toughs who are better out of the world than in it," the good citizens had had enough. A vigilante group organized, and posters soon appeared advising the trash of the town to vamoose or get hanged. A number of the worst criminals were warned by name, "and about twenty others" were generically cautioned to make tracks or face summary justice.

Rudabaugh, already wanted for the Valdez killing, read the omens accurately and betook himself to safer climes. This time, he stepped up to the criminal big-time. Leaving the angry citizens of Las Vegas in his dust, he fled over near Fort Sumner. There, at Whiskey Jim Greathouse's stage depot near Anton Chico, he met Billy the Kid, who was surely his kind of desperado. Rudabaugh quickly joined up with the Kid and the hard cases who made up the McSween army in the bloody Lincoln County War.

Rudabaugh fit right in. If the Kid and Charlie Bowdre and Tom O'Folliard were tough and mean, Rudabaugh was tougher and meaner in spades. According to an old friend of the Kid's, "If ever there was a living man the Kid was afraid of, it was Rudabaugh." Other old-timers said the same thing. The Kid, said one, "never dared talk to him as he did to Charles Bowdre" and the rest of Billy's gang. All of which suggests that Rudabaugh was as dangerous as he was odoriferous, even to his friends of the moment.

Rudabaugh joined the Kid and his followers in a variety of criminal enterprises, running stolen horses, holding up stages, and on one occasion robbing an army paymaster. At the end of November 1880, however, Rudabaugh, the Kid, and others were trapped by a posse at Greathouse's, some 40 miles from White Oaks, New Mexico. The posse men captured the ranch cook, out to cut some early-morning firewood, and sent him back inside with a note for the Kid, warning him that he was surrounded and should surrender. Greathouse himself came out within a few moments, bringing the scribbled reply: "Go to hell," or words to that effect. Diplomacy obviously wasn't working.

Even so, Deputy Sheriff Jim Carlyle, with more courage than good sense, volunteered to go inside and parley with the gang. It was not a good idea. Approachable at first—he even gave Carlyle a drink—the Kid's attitude changed when he saw Carlyle carrying a pair of the Kid's gloves, captured earlier in the chase. The Kid turned sullen and ugly, sneering at Carlyle: "Jim, you haven't finished your drink. Drink up, you won't be able to later on . . . your type should not be permitted the benefit of drawing even if you had a gun."

At two o'clock in the afternoon, the time for parley expired, and one of the posse men fired a single shot to signal the end of the truce.

Carlyle, perhaps expecting a general battle, bailed out of the ranch house through a window and was killed in a burst of firing. Much more shooting followed, with nobody hit on either side; and that night the outlaws got away clean.

Nobody knows to this day who really killed Carlyle. The Kid said later that neither he nor his comrades were responsible; the posse members said the same thing. Even so, nearly everybody blamed the outlaws. Greathouse's building was burned down, and a lot of angry lawmen hit the trail and pushed hard after the Kid and his cohorts.

On December 19, Rudabaugh, the Kid, and some kindred spirits visited Fort Sumner, seeking refreshment of various kinds and newspapers—maybe they wanted current news of posse efforts, or maybe they just liked to see their names in print. In any case, a Pat Garrett posse ambushed the gang, killing Tom O'Folliard. Rudabaugh, his horse mortally wounded in the melee, scrambled up behind another gang member and escaped.

Garrett stayed close behind them, tracking his quarry through the snow in bitterly cold weather. Two days before Christmas, Garrett surrounded the remains of the gang in a small rock building at Stinking Springs. The posse shivered through the night, and with the dawn, permanently ventilated Charlie Bowdre when Charlie emerged to feed his horse. The gang's horses were then either killed or driven off by Garrett's men. With no food and no escape, and a dead horse jammed in the door of their shelter, the remains of the gang surrendered, returning to Las Vegas somewhat ignominiously, in a wagon under guard.

But Rudabaugh was about as popular as the flu in Las Vegas. Lino Valdez had been well liked, and a number of citizens thought that a tall tree and a short piece of rope was about all the due process Rudabaugh had coming. Accordingly, he was jailed in Santa Fe on both the Las Vegas murder charges and a federal stage-robbing indictment. Rudabaugh was duly convicted of stage robbing and sentenced to a term of years in the county jail; he must have hoped that he'd spend the next few years in a United States prison while the state murder charges were forgotten or forgiven.

It was not to be. Rudabaugh was forthwith tried for the death of Lino Valdez. Predictably, Rudabaugh passed the buck and said that Little

Allen did the killing. He'd heard a shot and turned around, he said, and there was poor Valdez, down and dying. "I said to Little Allen, 'What did you do that for?'" This time, however, the jury wasn't having any. Neither was the judge: The penalty was death by hanging. The sentence would be carried out in Las Vegas.

And so Dirty Dave Rudabaugh's return to his old stomping ground was not a happy one. Not only was he facing a short walk to the scaffold, but the townspeople loathed him, and he knew it. As one reporter wrote, Rudabaugh: "showed a restless, uneasy condition of mind . . . retained a stolid, hangdog demeanor and showed no disposition to recognize any of his old acquaintances . . . what a change . . . now the chained culprit, doomed to the decree of justice or possibly Judge Lynch's mandate, for we hear the grumblings of men who have revenge in their hearts."

No wonder. The *Las Vegas Optic* added that Rudabaugh "looks and dresses about the same as when in Las Vegas, apparently not having made a raid upon clothing stores."

So, willy-nilly, Rudabaugh had his reunion with John Joshua Webb, again resident in the San Miguel County lockup in Las Vegas. Rudabaugh spent most of 1881 in durance vile until, in September, he and Webb, along with three others, somehow got hold of a revolver and tried to break out. They changed their minds abruptly, however, after jailer Herculano Chavez dispatched one of their number, Tom Duffy.

By early December, however, Rudabaugh was free. Along with Webb and three other prisoners, Rudabaugh managed to acquire a knife, a poker, and a pick and dig their way out, disappearing between the darkness and the dawn. Considering that the noise of somebody hammering away with a pick is a little loud even for a small-town jailer to miss, you can't help wondering whether somebody was paid to be temporarily deaf.

Rudabaugh left the Las Vegas area in haste, but to this day nobody is sure just where he went. The last months of his life, like the early years, are forever shrouded in the shadows of time. There is, however, some evidence that he turned up in Tombstone, Arizona, drawn to trouble as usual, like iron filings to a magnet.

Down in Cochise County—if he really went there—Rudabaugh chose the wrong side again, allying himself with the "cowboy faction," the party of the Clantons, the McLaurys, Curly Bill Brocious, and John Ringo. By the time Rudabaugh joined up with the cowboys, Billy Clanton and the McLaury boys were dead, but there was still plenty of shooting to do.

It may be that Rudabaugh was part of the savage nighttime ambush of Virgil Earp. Five men attacked Virgil, and four of the attackers were identified by various witnesses. One of these witnesses was gang member Indian Joe, who gave his information just before Wyatt Earp shot him full of holes. But nobody seemed to know who the fifth attacker was. He was thought to be new around the area, and nobody could, or would, give him a name. Virgil Earp was shot down on December 28, 1881. Rudabaugh broke jail in Las Vegas on the third, so he would have had plenty of time to ride south and look for more trouble.

On the other hand, years later, Wells Fargo agent Fred Dodge said cowboy adherent Johnny Barnes confessed that he had been the fifth man in the group who gunned down Virgil in the dark. Barnes is a more likely choice to have been in the band that attacked Virgil: He had been a member of the Clanton bunch for quite some time. Rudabaugh would have been a newcomer. Still, Barnes would not have been "new around the mining camp." If the other witnesses are to be believed, the fifth attacker could not have been Barnes.

Whether he was involved in the attack on Virgil Earp or not, Rudabaugh may well have been a cowboy gunman by the following spring. In the famous fight at Iron Springs, Wyatt Earp reportedly recognized Rudabaugh as one of the ambushers. In May 1882, the *Ford County Globe* told of the Iron Springs fight: "Wyatt and Warren Earp arrived some days ago and will remain awhile . . . Wyatt says after the first shock he could distinguish David Rudabaugh and Curly Bill, the latter's body showing well among the bushes."

Wyatt would surely have recognized Rudabaugh from the Dodge City days, and there is no reason for Wyatt to falsely allege that Rudabaugh was at Iron Springs if he was not.

The trouble is, in the Stuart Lake biography, the only one for which Wyatt actually provided information, Rudabaugh is not mentioned as a cowboy partisan. Describing the Iron Springs fight all those decades before, Wyatt was very clear and very specific, at least as Lake quoted him:

*From the instant I laid eyes on Curly Bill, I was seeing and
thinking clearly. Nothing that went on in that gully escaped
me, although what happened in a very few seconds takes much
longer to tell . . . I recognized Pony Deal, and as seven others
broke for the cottonwoods, I named each one as he ran, saying
to myself, "I've got a warrant for him."*

Wyatt named all of the seven to Lake. Dave Rudabaugh was not
among them.

So take your pick. You can accept the tale as related by Lake, or
you can rely on the quote from the *Globe*. There's no deciding which
account is accurate, or for that matter, whether either one of them is. If
we assume Wyatt actually gave both versions, I'm inclined to buy the
*Globe*'s story, if only because it was written when Wyatt was in his prime
and had no motive to embroider on the story of the fight. Lake's inter-
views with Wyatt were done more than forty years after, when the old
lawman was coming to the end of the trail, and when, perhaps, he
thought he might turn a dollar on the story of his life.

Whoever ambushed Wyatt, Doc, and the others at Iron Springs,
Curly Bill died there, chock full of shot from Wyatt's shotgun.
Rudabaugh, if he was part of the fight, escaped. After Curly Bill went
down, and after Wyatt and his friends killed several more of the cowboy
gang, the survivors—presumably including Rudabaugh—lost a good deal
of their interest in Arizona generally and Tombstone specifically. Mexico
looked far more promising and a whole lot healthier, and so Rudabaugh
made his way south of the border and stayed there.

At this point the mist gets thicker. Nobody is really sure how Dave
Rudabaugh finished his earthly course. One story has him marrying and
settling down. He may have turned up, a broken man, more than thirty
years later in Deer Lodge, Montana. A man named Dave Rudabaugh did
indeed appear in Deer Lodge . . . at least that's who he said he was. The
trail ends there, unconfirmed.

However, things came to a head, literally, on the eighteenth of
February in 1886. Nobody knows precisely what happened in Parral, but
this much is reasonably certain: Rudabaugh was being his customary ugly
self in a local cantina. According to one account, he pushed aside several

Mexican patrons, ordered a bottle of tequila, and spat part of it on the floor. After this warm-up, Rudabaugh moved on to play poker with some of the locals. Upset at losing and screaming that he'd been cheated, he quickly tried to change his luck by killing two of the players and wounding another. He then sprayed enough bullets around to clear the cantina and took his leave. One story tells us that he couldn't find his horse and went back inside.

But this was no ordinary night in Parral. The citizenry had had enough of this blustering bully, and a bunch of them ambushed Rudabaugh in or just outside the cantina. This time there were no other hoodlums to help him out, no excuses to make, no lies to tell, nobody to rat on, no place to run.

And so ended Dirty Dave Rudabaugh, full of holes in a town that hated his guts, mourned by absolutely nobody. Well known and generally detested throughout the southwest, Rudabaugh's demise was widely reported in such Arizona and New Mexico newspapers as the *Las Vegas Optic*. There was no hint of regret at his passing.

But like Shakespeare's Thane of Cawdor, nothing in Dirty Dave's life became him like the leaving of it—for he gave the good citizens of Parral cause to celebrate. And so they did, exuberantly. "The natives of Parral got a procession in honor of the event," as the *Tombstone Democrat* put it.

They declared a fiesta and commemorated their tormentor's demise by cutting off Rudabaugh's ugly head, scruffy mustache, hat, and all, impaling it on a pole, and parading it in celebration around and about the plaza of the town. An American photographer even took pictures of the event, including one of a citizen solemnly holding Dave's head, complete with hat, on a platter—a little reminiscent of Salome holding the head of John the Baptist.

The *Las Vegas Optic* summed up Rudabaugh's repulsive nature pretty well:

> *Dave Rudabaugh, who was recently killed at Parral, in the state of Chihuahua, Mexico, was what might be called an "all around desperado." He was equally proficient in holding up a railroad train or a stage coach or, as occasion offered, rob-*

*bing a bank, "shooting up" a frontier settlement, or running off stock. He indulged in these little peculiarities for a year or two in Arizona.*

Had anybody put up a headstone for Dave Rudabaugh, which nobody did, it might have read simply:

GOOD RIDDANCE.

# THE JOHNSTON COUNTY HOME GUARD

## *The Battle of Mill Creek*

ORDINARILY, JOHNSTON COUNTY, Oklahoma, was a reasonably peaceful place. Its people were hardworking and law-abiding, focused mostly on the basic, important matters of everyday life: family, work, church, and education. What crime there was in Johnston County was usually pretty small potatoes, certainly not the stuff of sensation, and certainly not a major danger to the community.

For example, in April of 1927 the Johnston County sheriff's office dealt with the following collection of bush-league offenses: twenty-one cases of selling bootleg booze—Oklahoma was dry in those days—and four cases of running a still. There was also one allegation of bastardy and two of running a disorderly house; seven cases of an intriguing offense called "disturbing religious worship"; three counts of indecent exposure; and an incident of dynamiting fish. There were also a couple cases of drunkenness, and one offense of using profane language in the presence of a female. Judging from the nature of the crimes, it seems likely that all or nearly all of them were alcohol-related. None rose to the level of a major threat to the public peace.

But serious felonies there surely were. In particular, bank robbery flowered in Johnston County. It started out with a bang in 1910, when the First National Bank of Wapanucka was invaded one night. The four culprits set off a charge of dynamite that did a great deal of damage to both the bank building and the vault. The town night watchman gallantly engaged the robbers with his pistol, apparently without effect, until he ran out of ammunition. While he ran down the street to find more bullets, the bandits took flight down the tracks of the Rock Island Railroad, madly pumping a railroad handcar down the right-of-way into the gloom of night.

Then the Bromide bank was robbed of $3,000 in 1919, and the First National Bank of Mill Creek was hit twice, in 1927 and 1931. During the 1931 raid, alert bank employees Paul Sparks and Vivian Dye noted that their visitors looked suspicious, "suspected they weren't looking to make a deposit . . . [and] positioned themselves to react as necessary." Sparks and Dye took refuge in the vault immediately, leaving the robbers to rummage through the bank's assets.

While the robbers were ransacking the cash drawer, a customer walked in, a long-time resident named P. W. "Pappy" South, a rancher. Pappy was intent on only one thing, a drink from the bank's water cooler. He got it, knocked it back, and walked out onto the street, apparently without noticing the two bandits. Once they had cleaned out the drawers, the outlaws left the bank and drove away, at which point the bank employees left the vault and gave the alarm.

The police duly tracked down and arrested Arthur Fraley and Luther Goodall. The two managed an escape from the Johnston County jail before they could be brought to trial, but they did not stay free very long before they were run down close to Sulphur, Oklahoma, and hauled back to jail. Duly tried, *exeunt* Fraley and Goodall, sent away by the court for ten years.

A little more than one year passed before the really memorable attack. On March 9, 1932, about 2:30 on a cloudy, cool afternoon, three men drove up outside the First National Bank of Mill Creek. Mill Creek was a small farming town, much injured—like the rest of the state and the country—by the Depression. A dollar meant a great deal to these hard-working people, and maybe that accounts for what happened that afternoon—or maybe it was just that Oklahomans tended to be tough and proud and not at all inclined to suffer being pushed around without pushing back.

The bank robbers were intent on relieving the citizens of Mill Creek of their small savings. The people of Mill Creek, as it turned out, weren't having any, especially as this was the third time somebody had tried to rob the First National, albeit without noticeable success. It was only a year since Fraley and Goodall had made their unauthorized withdrawal, and here were three more heavily armed bandits, out to try to bust the little bank again.

Little Mill Creek must have seemed quiet and peaceful to the outlaws as they drove into town. The robbery would be a piece of cake. For all that any of the outlaws could see, Mill Creek was just an ordinary little midwestern town, going about its workaday business. The hardware store was open, where Mr. Henry Howell stocked not only hardware, but just about anything else a family might need, including groceries, dry goods, and coffins. Boss Armstrong and Bennie Reynolds ran competing barbershops on opposite sides of Main; Barnes's Drug Store was open for business, and so was Glenn Clark's cafe on the north side of the street. Clark's was also a billiards hall.

The *Mill Creek Herald* was getting ready to publish its next edition—you could subscribe for a whole year for just a single dollar, a good deal even in those far-off days. Across the street from the First National, Syrian immigrant Frank Stie ran his general merchandise store. Frank was a wonder: He spoke not only English and a couple of Arab tongues, but Choctaw and Chickasaw as well. On the north side of Main, Will Young's garage was open, helping local automobiles run like new. It was an ordinary working day in Mill Creek, a Wednesday like every other Wednesday.

The three robbers could not know that this public-spirited little town had raised a unit of "home guards," as they were proudly called. After the 1931 robbery, the secretary of the Oklahoma Bankers' Association, one Eugene Gumm, had telephoned Charley Penner, the bank's cashier, suggesting that the bank install an alarm system. Penner rounded up some of the citizens of Mill Creek and told them the bad news: If they were robbed again, their anti-robbery insurance would be canceled and they would have to close.

Penner told fellow citizens, however, that the bank would buy both the alarm system and a stock of weapons if the citizens would pitch in and help protect the bank from any more attempts to rob it. The community agreed. The bank bought weapons—one 1897 Winchester riot gun is still in existence in Mill Creek—and the bank kept its word on the silent alarm network, too.

The alarm could be fired from any of the tellers' stations, or by removing a stack of currency—one bill on top of a pile of neatly cut paper—from a cash drawer. The alarm would not sound inside the bank building itself, but it would ring in Frank Stie's store, the Will Young garage, and Howell's Hardware Store. The alarm was up and running that early spring day, and the volunteers were on the job, vigilant and armed to the teeth.

In the best bank-robber style, two of the outlaws pushed into Mill Creek's only bank that afternoon, while the third man remained just across the street in the getaway car, a black 1929 Chevrolet coupe. One of the inside men was Fred Hamner, about forty-one years old. He was later described as having been a sometime sheriff at Wewoka, but he had fallen from grace and was now in big trouble with the law. At the moment he was free during the appeal of multiple convictions for car theft. Hamner seems to have been the leader of the gang, and beside him into the bank walked one Luther C. Smalley, called "Blackie."

Behind the wheel of the car waited the getaway driver, Adam Richetti, an ex-con and friend of Smalley and his wife. Richetti was a small-time punk working on being a big-time punk. The son of a hard-working, law-abiding immigrant family, he started getting into trouble before he finished the seventh grade and never looked back. He had already done time for robbery up in Indiana.

In time, Richetti would become an associate of hard-core criminals Pretty Boy Floyd and George Birdwell. One day he would stand accused of participation in the "Kansas City Massacre" in June 1933, in which a bunch of machine-gun-toting crooks cut down and killed four lawmen and the prisoner they were transporting, Frank "Jelly" Nash. In the autumn of 1938, Richetti made a one-way trip to the gas chamber for the murder of one of the officers killed in Kansas City.

But that was in the future, and just now the outlaws must have thought they had an easy payday. Smalley and Hamner "made several passes by the windows," which Penner, the cashier, alertly noticed. He turned to the other bank employees, Vivian Dye and Paul Sparks: "Get ready to put your hands up," he told them, and then Hamner and Smalley were inside the bank with drawn pistols. Or maybe, as the *Daily Oklahoman* reported, it was a "woman's intuition" by Mrs. Dye that alerted the bank . . . "her hunch was that two of the men . . . who passed the bank twice were about to stage a holdup."

Once inside the bank, the outlaws walked straight in behind the teller's window, waving pistols in the faces of Mrs. Dye, Penner, and Sparks. "Lie down on the floor," they commanded, and Hamner began to scoop money—a little over $800—from the cash drawer, stuffing it into a black satchel brought along for the purpose.

Once the cash drawer was cleaned out, it was time to go, and the robbers ordered Penner, Sparks, and Mrs. Dye to get up and go with them. However, instead of tamely becoming hostages, once Penner and Sparks were on their feet, they dove into the vault, pulling Mrs. Dye with them. They managed to slam the vault door before the outlaws could stop them. One of the bandits fired a round at the three bank employees just as the door closed, narrowly missing Mrs. Dye, but his shot did no harm beyond a minor gash on the edge of the steel vault door.

Another history of the raid states that the bank employees ran into the vault once the citizenry outside opened fire on the outlaws. In this version, once the first shot was fired in the street—at Richetti in the car—one of the outlaws sensibly said to the other, "Let's get outta here!" The second man replied, "Wait and we'll take these people with us," but by then their potential hostages were out of reach.

In any case, the bank employees were safely inside the vault, and the robbers were stuck without hostages. Now the outlaws' situation quickly worsened. Inside the vault, Penner fired the bank's silent alarm—a couple of histories of the raid say that Mrs. Dye had set it off when the bandits first entered. As the robbers left the bank, they spotted the citizens over at Young's Garage, and one of the outlaws snapped a shot at them. It was not a good idea, for the robber's round missed. The return fire from Young's Garage did not.

The citizen shooters were part of the "planned bank robbery watch," the volunteer force of town guards, which would account for their being armed and instantly ready to open up on the robbers. When the alarm went off, Henry Howell left his hardware store on the run, pistol in hand, leaving a startled customer standing at the counter. He ran to the second floor of Stie's shop and found a window overlooking the bank. Right across the street at the garage, Will Young, Dan Walker, and garage employee John Polly took cover behind some pillars in front of the building. Two other citizens, Hooser and Orb Bulman, hurried toward the bank.

Richetti sensed that something was wrong and pulled the getaway car up directly in front of the bank. As he saw further activity on the street, he began to blow the car's horn to warn the inside men. About then Polly fired at Richetti with his .30–30. As Hamner and Smalley came out the bank door, the volunteers opened up with everything they had, and their shooting was excellent.

Hamner, carrying the satchel of loot, took a bullet on the right side of the back of his head, a terribly destructive round that ripped through the skull and came out in front between the eyes, tearing away the front of his head in the process. "The top of his head was shot clear off," as one citizen remembered. Hamner sprawled on the pavement, deader than a nit. Smalley was also hit hard, a bullet tearing into his head above the left eye; he went down too, still alive but very badly wounded, trying to drag himself far enough to reach the weapon he had dropped.

Nobody knew who had fired the deadly rounds that put both bandits down, and it didn't matter much. "Nearly a dozen Mill Creek citizens were in the 'guard' which opened fire," the Oklahoma City paper reported: "Whose shots took effect was not known definitely and, according to Penner, would not be made public by the posse if determined."

Richetti drove away some distance, backed up a little, and shoved a long-barreled .32 Special Winchester rifle through the window. He began to shoot at the citizens, who now turned their attention to him and the automobile. Running across to the front of the bank, Young opened up on the Chevrolet with his shotgun. Meanwhile, the badly wounded Smalley finally managed to crawl to his pistol and raised it to fire at Young. Somebody—probably Penner coming from the bank— either bashed Smalley on the head or kicked the pistol from his hand and disarmed him. Now Smalley too was out of the fight for keeps, his head wound only one of several he took from both rifle and shotgun rounds.

Seeing both of his confederates on the pavement, Richetti stamped on the accelerator and left Mill Creek in a hurry, driving south out of town in the direction of a farm owned by Pappy South. Richetti fired repeatedly at the town's defenders on his way out, doing no damage. He fired at Stie's store seven times, missing Henry Howell, who was shooting back. Richetti also shot at a couple of rubbernecking bystanders, killing one man's hat, but leaving its owner intact. Apparently unfamiliar with the country south of town, Richetti drove into the stockyards, where he had to turn around and drive back until he found the highway, gravel-surfaced in those days.

Back in town, the county under-sheriff, Pat Trotter, was quickly on the scene and took the battered Smalley into custody. The citizens toted him across the street to the drugstore, where a local doctor named Holloway did what he could for the outlaw, pushing back a crowd of excited and curious townspeople who were uncomfortably close to the doctor and his work. The bloody and bedraggled outlaw appeared to be at death's door, but Dr. Holloway managed to keep him alive. What remained of Hamner was taken to an abandoned produce building east of the bank and dumped onto a table.

Since Richetti had driven off toward South's farm, Young and Bob Stalcup called Pappy South, asking whether he had seen anything suspicious. Pappy said he hadn't, but added that he had noticed "a roaring sound like that of an airplane." While Young and Stalcup couldn't know it at the time, the "roaring noise" was Richetti racing the Chevrolet's engine, trying to get his car out of the mud near a gate on South's farm. The battered outlaw began walking.

Deputy Sheriff Robert Donaldson and several Mill Creek citizens followed the outlaws' car, some of them driving bank man Penner's vehicle, itself holed by bullets during the battle in front of the bank. Near South's farm the pursuers found the bogged-down Chevrolet, one tire flattened by the citizens' fire and off the rim, and a bumper dragging on the ground. There was a blood trail leading away from the automobile, which they followed, first to a nearby creek, then to farmer South's barn. Pushing on to a grove of trees, Donaldson and citizen Orb Bulman found their quarry, unarmed.

Richetti was also much the worse for wear. He had taken a rifle bullet through the leg and was also punctured here and there by buckshot. He had been shot in the left arm and the back of the neck, and slightly wounded in the left leg by the citizens' heavy and accurate fire. The outlaw had had enough of the Mill Creek home guard for one day. He did not resist.

Richetti's pistol was not in evidence, but his pockets were full of .45 ammunition, and the car still held "a 12-gauge shotgun and a .30–30 rifle, both well oiled," as the *Johnston County Capital Democrat* put it. Richetti was taken back to Mill Creek and treated by Dr. Holloway. Later in the day, both he and Smalley were moved to Sulphur, where there was a hospital.

Somebody counted the bullet and buckshot holes in the Chevrolet and found twenty-eight of them, not counting the punctures in the outlaws and those in the satchel full of loot. That was pretty fair shooting, seeing that the citizenry had fired only seventeen times, granted that some of their rounds were shotgun shells full of buckshot.

Hamner's corpse, still on the table in the empty store, was oddly dressed. He was dapperly clad in a pinstriped suit, but over the suit he wore both "overalls and a lumber-jack." Perhaps he had planned to instantly change his appearance, although his colleagues had made no such preparations. Over in Seminole County, it developed, Hamner was well known, presumably a reference to his five convictions for car theft (then on appeal), or maybe to his earlier stint as a lawman. Richetti was at first thought to be Smalley's brother, and the *Johnston County Capital Democrat* reported that both men were residents of Sulphur, in next-door Murray County, and that they had earlier lived at Wewoka.

The superintendent of the Mill Creek school, a hardy soul named McGibboney, passed word of the robbery attempt to his teachers. The kids already knew there was excitement downtown, as they could see all the activity around the bank from the school windows, even though they could not hear the firing. Accordingly, the school held an assembly, and afterward McGibboney took all the students downtown to see the edifying evidence that crime didn't pay at all. They visited the scene of the crime and saw the riddled bank facade and the blood-spattered sidewalk in front.

The schoolkids went on to view the unpleasant remains of Hamner. Some students did not go inside to see the corpse, apparently somewhat put off by the sight of brains scattered on the floor, but most wanted to share in the excitement. "We wouldn't have missed it," said one in later years. Late in the day some of Hamner's relatives showed up to recover what was left of the bandit leader. The remains were taken off to Wewoka, his home, and he disappears from history.

Nobody expected Blackie Smalley to survive, but he would. On March 19 both wounded outlaws were well enough to travel from the hospital at Sulphur. The journey wasn't long: They were moved to the county jail in Tishomingo to await trial and a trip to prison. Convicted, Smalley had only to travel on to McAlester Prison, just a short trip down the road. He was sentenced to forty years for his part in the Mill Creek debacle and started serving his sentence early in April 1932. He was only forty-six years old. The Mill Creek home guard held an emergency session and voted to keep their identities secret, seeing some reason to fear retaliation. Sure enough, said the local history, *The Life and Times of Mill Creek,*

> *relatives and friends of the bandits came to Mill Creek the next day and let it be known they intended to take care of the shooters. Obviously carrying weapons, the avengers were not aware of the fire power trained on them at all times.*

Nobody in town would give information to any stranger. One such interloper, hanging around Bennie Reynolds's barbershop, bragging about taking revenge on the home guard, suddenly discovered that one of the barber chairs was occupied by City Marshal Doug Halley. When he had heard enough of this bigmouth's bombast, Halley turned on the stranger. "Mister," he said, "I'll give you a piece of advice. . . . And if you're smart you'll take it. Better than that, I'll give you an order. You get your ass out of Mill Creek and don't you ever come back."

That sort of straightforward counsel from the law had its effect. The recipient of Marshal Halley's succinct directive disappeared forthwith, and incidents of strangers vowing revenge decreased, but several of the home guards received threatening letters from time to time. Among these was Young, the garage owner, who carried a big .45 revolver in a shoulder holster for years afterward and did not answer the door after dark. Henry Howell also went about his business armed, and the story goes that poor John Polly became so anxious that he would occasionally wake during the night and blaze away with his .30–30, convinced that somebody avenging the robbers was trying to break in and murder him.

The reward money must have been some comfort to the harassed defenders, albeit a small one, since it was split between a number of them. As the March 10 edition of Oklahoma City's leading paper, the *Daily Oklahoman*, quipped, "Dead Bank Robbers Have a Value," and indeed they did. The biggest reward was reserved for any robber killed during the holdup itself or in pursuit immediately thereafter, so Hamner qualified the shooters to receive $500 from the Oklahoma Bankers' Association. The Association paid up promptly, sending its check down to Mill Creek before the middle of March. Richetti and Smalley, being still alive, were worth only $100 each.

Perhaps understandably, harassed Oklahoma bankers clearly preferred their bank robbers dead. The Mill Creek robbery had, after all, been either the twelfth or thirteenth bank robbery in Oklahoma that year, a year that still had two-thirds of its days to run. One Oklahoma bank had already been robbed three times, and there had been three robberies in the state in a single week.

On March 21, the *Daily Oklahoman* printed a photograph of many members of the home guard over the caption "Bandits: Meet Mill Creek's Reception Committee." Many of the men were displaying their weapons, and Charlie Penner was holding in his hand the reward check, ready for presentation to the victors. Had anyone of evil disposition really been devoted to avenging the bandits' debacle, they now knew who was responsible. But it developed that the anonymous threateners were going to stay that way; they were all mouth and no action.

The *Oklahoman*'s story, about half humorous and half admiring, had this to say about the defenders of the town:

> *Bad, bold bandits will have to learn the latest in dodging and pivoting before they can escape whizzing bullets of the Mill Creek Vigilante Committee . . . . Out of the attic and cellar came the rusty shotguns and the wives returned the pistols*

*from the bridge clubs and the kiddie's targets were borrowed.*
*. . . They became William Tells of the shot gun. They could*
*uncap the sheriff's confiscated beer bottles at 50 paces. . . . This*
*organization of death-defying men . . . are not boastful of*
*their accomplishments. They regret that such a tragedy should*
*befall their little village. . . . Theirs is an active organization.*
*For too often in the past has Mill Creek been disturbed by*
*marauders. Now the whole citizenry sleeps peacefully in the*
*knowledge that they are being protected. . . . The possemen will*
*decide how the [reward] shall be distributed. They say they will*
*buy more bullets. . . .*

Some folks never learn. Just about a year later, lawmen raided the Smalley farm and flushed out Clarence Garatley and Coleman Rickerson, fresh from a bank robbery at Comanche, Oklahoma. Clarence had the sense to give it up, but Rickerson tried to fight and ended up dead.

Amazingly, Richetti served only a little more than four months for the Mill Creek robbery. He was released on bond—some said the $15,000 sum was furnished by Pretty Boy Floyd—and promptly jumped. He ended up running with Pretty Boy Floyd and began his apprentice-ship with the famed outlaw by robbing a dance hall in Wewoka, Oklahoma, in 1932.

Smalley, his partner, would never breathe free air again. He was murdered by fellow inmates in prison, finishing the job the Mill Creek home guard had begun. The formidable Floyd, Richetti's bank-robbing partner, left Oklahoma not long after his closest confederate, George Birdwell, was killed by the citizens of Boley, Oklahoma, during a failed holdup. Like the rest, however, his days were numbered: "Sooner or later," said the voice of the Oklahoma Bankers' Association, "he will take his place with the others in the silent city of the dead or behind the bars of the state penitentiary." For Floyd, it would indeed be the silent city of the dead. He died in the dirt of an Ohio field in October 1934, shot down by a mixed posse of state and federal officers.

The Mill Creek Bank persevered for years, prudently installing a remote system by which a teller could open the front door, which other-wise remained locked. But then hard times beset the town, and today very little remains. The bank building is gone now, along with most of the rest of Mill Creek, including the market, the Masonic Hall, and the lawyer's office. But among the older residents, at least, the proud memory of courage and civic pride remains evergreen.

## HOME-TOWN HEROINE

### *The Courage of Clara Aggas*

THE BANK OF MORRIS, OKLAHOMA, had been robbed more times than anybody in that stout little town wanted to remember; that was twice—twice too many—and both times the bank had been held up by the aristocracy of the bank-robbing business.

The first robbery occurred in September of 1931, when two gun-wielding punks pushed into the bank and demanded the citizens' money. It was not long after 11:00 that morning, and bank manager H. L. Mullins was on his way out the door for lunch when he noticed that the bank's clock had run down. He was reaching up to wind it when he felt the hard, cold muzzle of a .45 Colt revolver in his ribs.

The bandits herded Mullins, accountant Graham Smith, and brand-new teller Clara Aggas together in the bank's office. The three could only stand helplessly by while one man covered them with a pistol and the second outlaw stuffed a bag with cash. The pair then hurried out the door, climbed into a black Model A Ford, and disappeared with nearly $2,000. In their haste, the robbers left behind a bag of gold worth another $300.

Later the same day, three men—at first thought to be the same hoodlums—hit a bank in nearby Hitchita. They struck while only a single female teller, who had endured two prior holdups, was on duty—and got away with between $800 and $1,000. On the next day, Okmulgee County sheriff Don Stormont arrested one Roy Nicholson over in

Henryetta and got a confession. Following up, he arrested two other local losers, Nicholson's partners at Hitchita. This trio was not, however, the same men who had held up the Morris bank.

The Morris bank employees solved that mystery two days later when they pored over mug shots and unanimously identified the robbers as none other than the notorious holdup man Charles Arthur Floyd—better known to the newspaper-reading public as Pretty Boy—and his equally dangerous partner, the foul-tempered George Birdwell. To Clara Aggas and Graham Smith, the discovery that they'd been held up by the king and crown prince of bank robbers was about as upsetting as the robbery itself. The whole event was a great sensation in little Morris.

But even such a cosmic happening eventually becomes sterile history, and so the excitement faded away until a couple of months later, when history repeated itself. It happened on December 23, in the heart of the holiday season. Clara Aggas had gone to lunch. Mullins and Smith had just returned from eating, and there were four customers in the bank when a black Ford coupe pulled up in the street in front. Smith looked up from his desk to see two men neatly dressed in suits enter the bank. He knew they were not local people, but one of them did look familiar. It took a moment for the bank man to realize that he was looking into the eyes of Pretty Boy Floyd and George Birdwell.

The headline in the *Morris News* put it succinctly: "Morris Again Visited by Same Pair of Jovial Bank Robbers." It's easy to be a jovial bandit when you're carrying a submachine gun. The outlaws were enjoying themselves. One of the robbers smiled at the bank employees and customers. He and his partner "were back for a return engagement," he said. Floyd, brandishing a .45 pistol, asked Smith, "How was business since we were last here?" a jest entirely lost on Smith. "Everybody be silent and stand still," Floyd said before vaulting over the counter, as he had done back in September, and sweeping up some $1,100.

Again Floyd tried to be funny, playing to his captive audience. He and Birdwell were "taking a collection up for needy widows and orphans," he said, and this time his somewhat labored buffoonery received a nervous laugh from some of the customers. For Mullins and Smith, who'd been through all this before, the whole episode was about as funny as an open grave.

*Clara Aggas*

The collection and the comedy now over with, the two bandits herded the employees and customers outside in front of them, lined them up along the north wall of the bank building, and climbed into their car. Waving at people on the streets, the bandits drove slowly out of town and, as they had before, disappeared.

The whole town of Morris was mortified, and so was the bank's insurer. A town meeting was called, and the citizens not only vowed that their bank wouldn't be held up again, but also took some practical measures to make sure it wouldn't happen. The bank installed a silent alarm, and the downtown merchants decided to bring their guns to work and organize themselves into a local defense force. A number of them selected convenient firing positions covering the bank and agreed to man those positions if bandits should again appear.

Sure enough, as the *Morris News* wearily reported, "Morris State Bank Robbed Third Time During 8 Months."

Early in May of 1932, still another Ford coupe appeared—a stolen one, this time—carrying three punks: Roscoe Ernest, called Red; Troy Kittrell; and another man still nameless. They had already robbed Hershel Blackburn's drugstore, where they had made off with a measly $25. Now they were ready for big game, or so they must have thought.

The job must have looked easy. At 11:15 in the morning, nobody was on duty at the bank but young Clara Aggas, who had already been through this misery once. Ernest stayed behind the wheel of the Ford. Kittrell and the nameless man pushed inside, unmasked, waving pistols. One of them stayed on guard by the bank door; the second confronted Clara. "Give us all the money," he ordered the teller, and Clara had no option but to comply. But Clara, as courageous as she was young and pretty, wasn't about to give up her employer's money easily.

And so she started gathering money in the bank's vault. That was where most of the cash was, of course, but it was also where the alarm button was located. She pushed it, and then went on calmly, and slowly, bringing the bandits their loot. Knowing that help was now on the way, she dragged out the process as long as she dared, until finally she had gathered the last bill and delivered it. "Come with us," the robbers ordered, pushing her out the door toward their waiting car, a useful hostage in case of trouble.

The alarm, silent inside the bank, went off in both the town marshal's office and a nearby gas station. Marshal I. Z. Thompson hurried to the service station, where he grabbed his Winchester and joined Barron Skinner, the service station owner, who was waiting with his shotgun. At the hardware store across the street, Forrest Bradley picked up his rifle and took his firing position at a second-story window overlooking the front door of the bank. At the same time, other armed citizens were running to their chosen fighting stations. The town's defenders were ready.

Red Ernest, waiting in the car, saw Marshal Thompson behind the service station and opened up with his shotgun. The round tore through a plate-glass window, and Thompson was hit in the arm, nicked by shards of glass and a couple of shot. Bradley, at his second-story window, answered with two .30–30 rounds, and Ernest went down with a bullet in his head, slumping over in the car seat.

The gunfire in the street brought the two inside bandits out on the run. "Ahead of them," as the *Morris News* put it, "they were pushing Miss Aggas, using her as a shield from the fire of Morris citizens." Bradley, afraid of hitting Clara, could not get a clear shot at the robbers.

Clara saw Ernest slumped over the wheel in a great puddle of blood, and about then everybody in town who had a gun cut loose at the two outlaws. According to the *Daily Oklahoman*'s account of the raid, somebody—maybe Forrest Bradley, maybe Marshal Thompson—sent a bullet into one of the two remaining bandits, and he slumped to the pavement next to the vehicle. Marshal Thompson agreed it was likely that either he or Bradley had hit the second robber.

> *I saw the man sitting at the wheel of the car, and as I started to fire, either he or somebody in the street, I never did know which, fired at me and wounded me in the right arm. I aimed at the driver and fired, and either Bradley or myself killed him quickly. . . . [One outlaw] climbed into the car in such manner that he was clear away from Miss Aggas, and I took careful aim and fired at him. I believe the bullet took effect, and am told that at the school corner, the third man had to take the wheel and drive the car because the second one was wounded. . . . He drove slowly, as though he wasn't able to drive rapidly, and [the] other fellow helped him steer the car.*

The third robber, according to the Oklahoma City *Daily Oklahoman,*

> *using Miss Aggas as a shield, stooped and picked up his wounded companion from the sidewalk, shoved him into the*

*back seat, [and] lifted the dead bandit from the driver's seat*
*into the rear.*

As the firing grew heavier, a projectile—or more than one—slammed into Clara Aggas, tearing gaping wounds in her shoulder and jaw. A round had, according to the *Morris News*, "torn away part of her chin." The town's defenders were deeply concerned that the injury was caused by a stray round from one of their weapons, but the Oklahoma City paper would headline, "Kidnapped Girl Shot by Thug." Later, a welcome report from her treating physicians indicated that Clara's face

*was badly powder-burned, and that the bullet that went*
*through her jaw, chin, and into her right shoulder could not*
*have been fired from more than six or eight feet distant,*
*[relieving] the worry of Morris citizens who killed Ernest and*
*feared they had unwortedly [sic] shot Miss Aggas. She was*
*wounded as the bandits thrust her into their car.*

Store-owner Bradley, watching the drama in the street over his rifle sights, said later,

*I saw Miss Aggas and one robber walking out of the bank, but*
*I didn't dare fire. She was jumping around, but he held her*
*close to him. She yelled when she was forced into the automo-*
*bile. The getaway was made in a hurry. The dead robber was*
*thrown into the rear of the car; the wounded man was in the*
*back seat, and the other man, using the girl as a shield, took*
*the wheel. As the car sped out of town, the two robbers, guns in*
*hand, answered gunfire from Thompson and me. After the*
*girl got into the car we didn't dare shoot to hit for fear of*
*wounding her.*

As the town defenders tried to get a clear shot at the fleeing outlaws without endangering Clara, the bandits tore out of town as fast as the Ford would move, one of the outlaws holding Clara on his lap. Fearful that Clara would be hit again, the citizenry ceased fire. Carl Bay, standing on his porch with a rifle and a clear shot, held his fire at his sister's urging, and the outlaws fled Morris without further damage.

Outside town, the robbers roared southward and then, a couple of miles from the village of Coalton, turned down a dirt road and stopped. There they switched cars and drove off, abandoning Clara and Ernest—dying or dead—in the getaway car. Bloody and badly hurt, Clara crawled several hundred feet to a hard-surface road on sheer courage and determination.

There, lying by the roadside, she was found by two citizens who were passing by in pursuit of the robbers. One was Baron Skinner, who happened to be Clara's fiancé, which may account for his close pursuit of the outlaws. He loaded her into his car and roared away for Okmulgee, where there was a hospital. The news of her injury hit Clara's mother, already ill, so hard that she was reported in critical condition.

Jack Ary, chief of police at the town of Drumright, drove into Morris, where he and others made a positive identification of Ernest, described in a newspaper story as a "wandering evangelist and small-time thief," a peculiar pairing of occupations. Ary had known the dead man for fifteen years, the chief said, and knew he "had been wanted in connection with robberies in Creek County."

Other observers could give little in the way of a description of the remaining outlaws, except to say they were "of the 'hard type.' Two of the men were middle-aged while the third was in his twenties." The bandits' abandoned car turned out to have been stolen in Okmulgee the night before, by three men who held up a man and his girlfriend out for a friendly drive in the man's new automobile.

That night officers saw two men, apparently the fugitives, and watched as they ran into some woods bordering a field, carrying guns and a sack of money. Officers entered one side of the field as the bandits left it. Since both men were running, the lawmen concluded that the bandit wounded in front of the bank could not have been badly hurt. Clara agreed: She had heard nothing during the outlaws' 9-mile flight from Morris to indicate that either man was seriously injured.

Throughout the whole ordeal, Clara Aggas was, as the kids say, a class act. On May 28, an Okmulgee newspaper interviewed her in her hospital room and told her story under a large photograph of her in happier times. The newspaper called her "beautiful," and it did not exaggerate. They called her "plucky," and that she surely was, for it was her deliberate foot-dragging, all alone with two hoodlums, that gave the townsfolk time to grab their weapons.

*I began to comply with their order, and I knew that the burglar alarm was located right where most of the money was hidden away in a little cabinet, so I went there first, and as I took that money out I tripped the burglar alarm. Then I worked as slowly as I could in getting the rest of the money together so that the men who answer the burglar alarms could get their guns trained on the bank.*

Although lawmen across three counties searched and put up roadblocks, they came up empty. It was several weeks before Kittrell was run down in Detroit, where he confessed to local officers his involvement in the Morris robbery. He turned out to be a local boy who hailed originally from Dewar, Oklahoma. County Sheriff Jim Stormont duly traveled to Detroit to return Kittrell to his home state. Once in an Oklahoma jail, Kittrell went into a "poor-pathetic-me" apologia for the crime.

He helped rob the bank, he admitted, but he sure didn't want to do it. "I was forced," he whined, "I had no choice. I was threatened to make me take part in this heinous crime and threatened into robbing the drugstore too." He claimed he was bullied by Ernest—who was conveniently silent, being very dead—and by the unknown bandit, whose name, again conveniently, Kittrell said he never knew. "Fat chance," the court said, listening to this twaddle, and gave him twenty-five years in prison.

Nobody ever recovered the bank's money, nor did anyone ever learn who the badly wounded bandit had been. Indeed, he may have been dead in the shrubbery somewhere, although, as glib as Kittrell was, chances were he would have led officers to the corpse. The Oklahoma Bankers' Association duly ponied up the $500 reward for a dead bank robber. Kittrell was worth absolutely nothing, it turned out, for at that time the association didn't pay for outlaws on the hoof, only corpses.

For gallant young Clara Aggas, the next months were an agony of surgery and skin grafts for the terrible damage done to her face. At first she could not talk clearly, but she was at least able to tell the police that this time Floyd was not involved in the robbery, and she gave some help to officers pursuing the fleeing outlaws. Her lower jaw partly shot away, she underwent two operations immediately, with more painful and protracted repairs still to come. But she stuck it all out with great courage, as she had stuck out the ordeal of the robbery and the pain of her wounds. She spent months in Philadelphia, where doctors rebuilt her chin and jaw with skin grafting, a procedure new to medicine in those days.

It is pleasant to relate that in due course she married her fiancé and savior, Baron Skinner, and lived to enjoy eighty-eight years of life. At her death just before Christmas in 1994, her long obituary in the *Tulsa World* listed among her survivors three daughters, six grandchildren, and four great-grandchildren. It is perhaps understandable that she never returned to work at the bank.

The beleaguered Morris bank stayed in business, prudently installing steel bars and bulletproof glass to cover the tellers' stations. It also wisely kept only small amounts of cash on hand in Morris. Most of the bank's money remained in Okmulgee. In 1984, disaster of a different kind savaged Morris, as a tornado ripped through the town, leaving behind it many dead and injured, and the bank in ruins. Rising phoenix-like from its destruction, the bank was rebuilt. It still carries on transacting business for the town's resilient locals.

No doubt Birdwell and Pretty Boy Floyd enjoyed their comic-opera robberies of the Morris bank. It is easy enough to make jokes at the expense of frightened, helpless people who are wondering whether they're going to die in the next minute or so. But the outlaws' merriment did not last long. Birdwell tried to rob the bank in the Oklahoma community of Boley in 1932, taking on the tough citizens of that town, and ending up permanently dead. Two years after Birdwell was buried, Pretty Boy Floyd died alone in the dirt of an Ohio field, cut down by a posse commanded by the famed "G-man," the FBI's Melvin Purvis.

There is no record that he laughed after that.

# A QUIET TUESDAY IN WISCONSIN

## *The Tough Citizens of Menomonie*

WHEN PEOPLE THINK OF the wild outlaw days of the nineteenth century and the first third of the twentieth, they generally think about Texas and Oklahoma, the Kansas cow towns, Tombstone and Deadwood, Creede and Las Vegas, and later on, Chicago and Kansas City. All of those places had their outlaw reputation, to be sure, and it was well deserved. Oklahoma, for example—Indian Territory and Oklahoma Territory, as it then was—was the very heart and soul of the Wild West, even into the twenties and thirties.

But Minnesota and Wisconsin? In Minnesota, the Twin Cities for a while harbored career hoodlums as ruthless as those who infested any other spot in America. One of them was Frank Keating, originally of Chicago. He had gotten twenty-five years' hard time in Leavenworth Prison for a robbery gone bad. He had robbed the U.S. mail of some $135,000, but all it got him was a long time to think about what had gone wrong.

Keating and a hoodlum named Tommy Holden took an unauthorized departure from durance vile in February of 1930, walking casually out of the prison gates using a couple of trustee passes. The story goes that the passes—stolen, of course—were given to them by bank robber George Kelly, better known to the newspaper-reading public as Machine-gun Kelly. Once back on the street, Keating and Holden returned to their

*Winfield Kern's Restaurant*
*(note bullet holes in glass)*

natural vocation and hobby, the robbing of banks, and they decided to set up shop in the Twin Cities.

They needed associates for what they had planned, and at one time or another, they would work with some of the most famous names in felony. Alvin "Creepy" Karpis was one sometime gang member, as was Freddie Barker, vile son of an even viler mother, the egregious Ma Barker. Still another associate of the Keating Gang was none other than Frank

"Jelly" Nash, later killed during the famed Kansas City Massacre, in which several law officers also died.

Back in those wild old days, you could buy a fully automatic weapon without the complex licensing and background checks required today. A Thompson submachine gun would cost you about $250, and you could even purchase it by mail order. The Thompson quickly became a favorite with robber gangs because of its high volume of fire and its consequent power to intimidate. Keating and his cronies liked the Thompson, too, and took one along on October 20, 1931, when they went to raid the Kraft State Bank up in Menomonie. They chose the morning hours of the business day to do it, certain that the bank vault would be open and ready for their withdrawal.

This fall morning, Keating and three other men descended on the Kraft State Bank for what would be Wisconsin's thirty-fourth bank robbery in that year alone. The four thugs drove up in a big, black Lincoln—bandits of those days liked lots of size and horsepower in their cars. They parked in the 400 block of Menomonie's Main Street, ironically right in front of the Frank Hintzman emporium. Hintzman's offered not only furniture for the living, but funeral services for the dearly departed. Good customers, Hintzman's might have said, are forever. You have to wonder whether Keating and his crew, parking in front of an undertaker's, were at all superstitious.

In the best bandit tradition, the driver, Frank Webber, stayed with the getaway car and kept the engine running. Webber was a convicted bank robber who had already done time in Salt Lake City and was later appropriately described by the *Minneapolis Star* as "a notorious police character." He was, the *Star* would announce, "a pal of Frank 'Bubbling Over' Dever, notorious Minneapolis gunman now serving in prison for an $85,000 diamond robbery here."

With Webber poised to collect the other robbers when they fled with their loot, Keating, Tommy Holden, and Charles Harmon walked down Main Street about a half block to the Kraft State Bank. It was 9:15 A.M., and the bank had just opened its doors for the day's business. Some patrons were already being served by a large staff: President William F. Kraft; his sons, James and William R.; daughter Vera; cousin Ruby Kraft; teller Mrs. A. Schaefer; another assistant cashier named Hendrickson; and Madelyn Gullickson, the bank's stenographer.

At first, the raid went smoothly. The three bandits forced the bank employees to lie on the floor, and lifted, according to the *Dunn County News,* more than $90,000 in cash and securities. The *Minneapolis Star* reported that the take was about $130,000, most of which was, however, in non-negotiable securities. So far, so good. Having quickly stripped the tellers' drawers of ready cash, the bandits turned on the bank's president and cashier, William Kraft. "We want the rest of the money," they said.

"Sorry," said Kraft, "you've got all there is," but his explanation neither soothed nor deterred the two bandits. One of them shot Kraft's nineteen-year-old son James, an assistant cashier, in the shoulder, and continued to demand more money. Apparently infuriated by Kraft's refusal to produce more money and convinced he was lying to them, one of the outlaws shot William R. Kraft, another son, twice as he lay helpless on the floor of the bank. Later reported in "grave" condition, William would survive.

About then the bank's alarm went off, tripped by an observant bank security officer. The alarm was loud enough for Webber to hear a half block away, and he reacted immediately. Pulling away from the curb, he stopped the car in the middle of the street in front of the bank (there was a truck parked next to the curb) and jumped out with a submachine gun. He opened both left-hand doors, stood between them, and opened fire, periodically pumping a burst of tommy-gun fire down the street to chill the enthusiasm of anybody who might think about coming to the rescue of the bank men.

Inside, the roar of the outlaw's .45 in the close confines of the bank must have sounded like the last trumpet. After that, and all the racket from the submachine gun out in the street, there could be no doubt that everybody in town had to know there was trouble at the bank. It was therefore imperative to get clear of the bank, and the town, as quickly as possible, money or no money. The bandits grabbed Kraft's wounded son, James, and teller Mrs. Schaefer as shields, and pushed them out of the bank doors, headed for Webber and their getaway car.

There was already a good-sized crowd of angry citizens outside, and in the confusion, Mrs. Schaefer stumbled and fell. As the bandits ran

*Menomonie, Wisconsin*

on toward their car, she seized her chance and ran for shelter. She made it, but young James Kraft was either less enterprising or less fortunate, or, probably, too badly hurt to run. He remained a hostage as the gang scrambled into their car and left town at high speed.

The bank guard who pulled the alarm, Vernon Townsend, normally spent his days in a special observation post above the tellers' cages. Surprisingly, Townsend did not fire on the robbers during the proceedings inside the bank. He had, he said later, strict instructions not to open fire inside the building. Instead, as the bandits ran from the building, he pulled the alarm, then ran to the roof and opened fire on the car from that vantage point. Townsend seems to have hit the vehicle's gas tank, at least, and maybe one of the robbers as well.

By this time some of the citizens had found weapons and began to bang away at the fleeing bandits. Winfield Kern, owner of a nearby restaurant, opened fire at once, driving bullets through his own plate-glass window in the process. Ed Grudt looked out a second-story window at the Gregg Music Store in the Farmer Store Building and started shooting as well. Return fire from Webber's tommy gun knocked glass and framing out of the store windows, but missed Grudt clean. Ed Kinkle scored at least one hit, putting a hole in the rear window of the outlaws' car. Kinkle said later that he heard somebody yell, "Ouch!" as his bullet struck the car.

As it was later learned, Kinkle did indeed hit the getaway car, and it was probably at this time that he or one of the other citizens put a bullet into Frank Webber's eye, a wound that would prove at first horribly painful, and later, fatal. The under-sheriff, Jack Harmon, reported a further gunfight on the road "a short distance from Menomonie," near a town called Hayner, and it may have been during this exchange that Webber was hit.

The *Star* wrote that Harmon had "unloaded a round at the car," and that "simultaneously one of the fugitives slumped in his seat." The *Dunn County News* added that, when last seen, "the driver was bleeding profusely at the mouth and some who saw the car claimed that one of the other two in the car was wrapped in a blanket as if he, too, had been wounded."

The big Lincoln roared away from this hornet's nest of a town, racing east on U.S. Highway 12, then turning off onto County Road B. As they fled, the outlaws threw handfuls of flat-headed nails onto the pavement, in the vain hope of disabling the tires of the pursuers' automobiles.

As a car-mounted posse streamed out of town in hot pursuit, they found Webber's corpse along the road, some 8 miles from the town. The *Dunn County News* reported cheerfully that the outlaw's "right eye and temple were torn by a bullet. The dead bandit wore a steel vest for protection and carried two revolvers. The fleeing bandits also threw out a loose steel vest when they hurled their dead accomplice onto the road."

The *News* reported the finding of the body in great detail, even noting that:

> *On the left arm of the dead bandit is a tattooed figure of a naked woman. The underwear of the dead man has the figure of a double eagle sewed on, giving the impression that the man was either of German or Austrian descent . . . an examination of his hands indicated that he had done little manual labor.*

Tragically, a man hauling cream also found the body of young Kraft, shot in the back of the head by the bandits and dumped in a nearby ditch, maybe out of frustration, maybe simply in revenge for the extinction of Webber. Neither nails nor brutality stopped Sheriff Ike Harmon and a steadily growing posse, who continued to search for the outlaws without coming up with them.

Once the town and the area around it heard about Kraft's murder, citizens by the hundreds from six counties joined peace officers in hunting for the outlaws. Hearing news of the robbery, Police Chief Louis Frenstad ran from a courtroom where one Frank Sweeney was being tried for drunk driving. An aircraft was pressed into service to scout from above, though without result. Meanwhile, the remains of the gang sped north. They stopped least once north of Menomonie, for a woman hunting there—or a fourteen-year-old girl, or both—saw a car with a shot-out windshield, halted by the roadside while two of its occupants bandaged a third man.

The injured bandit was surely Charles Harmon, a Texan who had done time in his home state for robbing a poker game. He had also earned himself a stretch in the hard-time federal prison at Leavenworth, Kansas, for robbing the Davenport, Iowa, post office. And in Leavenworth, that finishing school for hoodlums, he met Fran Keating and eventually left prison with him and without the consent of the warden.

The other bandits' amateur first aid had done precious little good, for before long Harmon's body turned up beside the road at a place called Shell Lake. It was thought that one of Ed Grudt's four rounds had caused the wounds in the dead man's knee and neck, or maybe he was hit in the fight reported by Under-sheriff Harmon, although the *Dunn County News* speculated that Charles Harmon might have been murdered by his own companions. In any case, before he died, the story goes, the remaining robbers finally stopped the Lincoln, found a spot to lay Harmon down on the ground, then left him bandages and iodine and a handful of stolen securities just in case he survived his wounds. He didn't.

Besides Harmon's remains, the pursuers also found part of the robbers' armory, a submachine gun and two handguns. The remaining outlaws were gone, still scattering nails on the roads, replenishing their gasoline from cans stashed in advance here and there around the countryside, much the way the Wild Bunch had hidden fresh horses along their escape routes.

Harmon was identified by Ruby Kraft as the "little fellow who strode politely into the bank last week, saying, 'Good morning, everybody.'" "He was very polite," Miss Kraft said, "and did not act hard." Hard or not, he was identified as the robber who held up a bank messenger in Duluth and got away with $100,000. Still another banker said he thought the dead man had also been part of a gang that had robbed a bank in Colfax on September 3. The trail of the Colfax robbers, he said, led in the same direction in which the Menomonie outlaws had fled; therefore, "there must be a gangster resort near there where they go for protection after their holdups."

At last the searchers found the bandits' automobile, abandoned and burned some 6 miles east of a town called Webster. Its rear window had indeed been shot out, and the backseat was soaked with blood. There was no sign of the surviving bandits, but a witness had seen "two men pile cornstalks in the car," while another farmer reported seeing the pair "set fire to the car and then flee in another car that apparently was waiting to take the men further."

The day after the robbery, the *Minneapolis Star* reported a titillating, if somewhat vague, reference to a "mysterious long distance telephone call from a man in Duluth to a girl living with her father in Minneapolis, seen as the possible key to capture of the gunmen. A 'Wisconsin bank robbery' was mentioned in the call."

Apparently nothing came of this somewhat nebulous intelligence, and the two remaining holdup men were later spotted in Minnesota near Markville, moving toward the town of Sandstone, after which they disappeared altogether. The authorities searched high and low, and questioned an assortment of local villains in St. Paul, but without success. They even sent a man to Alcatraz Prison out in San Francisco Bay to interview Creepy Karpis, but there again they drew a blank. A municipal judge in Menomonie issued warrants for three men, including somebody described as "A. Bates," and the authorities diligently searched local hospitals for any sign of a stranger suffering from gunshot wounds. The search for "A. Bates" came to nothing, as did the hospital search, since the missing man was Charles Harmon, and he was even then lying quite dead beside a country road.

The two dead robbers spent some time on public view at Olson's Funeral Parlor, where crowds of citizens had a look at them, but nobody claimed the remains. Not until two weeks after the holdup were the bodies carted off to Potter's Field, where they ended up in a single grave, albeit with appropriate words by a local minister. On the twenty-ninth of November, the *Dunn County News* reported the event, complete with the text of the burial service. The paper could not resist adding, somewhat ponderously:

> *Over the same road . . . that the four fleeing bandits sped in their speedy machine following the holdup, the bodies of the two dead bandits were conveyed in the county coroner's truck at a lower rate of speed than that made by the fleeing bandit car after the robbery. The deaths and burials of the two bandits is the climax in the lives of the two men, giving proof to a statement once issued by Judge George Thompson: "a criminal life is a most unhappy existance [sic].*

By way of anticlimax, one Robert Newbern was tried twice for complicity in the Kraft State Bank robbery and murder. Newbern, described by the newspaper somewhat disparagingly as a "Minneapolis gambler and bookmaker, no permanent address," had already been acquitted of an earlier bank robbery and murder in Minneapolis, so he must have looked like a likely participant in the Menomonie crime. Newbern was convicted (another source says the first trial resulted in a hung jury), but his conviction was reversed, and at his second trial he won an acquittal. One Walter Twinning, a Hibbing, Minnesota, man, was arrested in Duluth, but Menomonie witnesses failed to identify him as one of the robbers. Three more suspects had been picked up in a town called Minong, but they turned out to be innocent Chicago men who had driven north on a fishing trip.

Keating and his buddy Holden had learned nothing from their bloody repulse at Menomonie. They quickly recruited more trash and went about robbing more banks in a number of towns in Minnesota. Their high-living days would not last long, for in less than a year federal agents located them and laid a trap.

One might have expected Keating and Holden to go out in a blaze of glory, guns in hand—the sort of spectacular last stand that spelled the end to the careers of such criminal luminaries as John Dillinger and Pretty Boy Floyd. Instead, in the summer of 1932, they and another outlaw were somewhat ignominiously bagged by the FBI, without a fight, on the Old Mission Golf Course in Kansas City. The story goes that Jelly Nash made a foursome with them on that day, but Jelly was such a lousy golfer that he was off in the farthest reaches of the rough and so escaped arrest.

Less than a year later, however, Jelly Nash was captured at Hot Springs, Arkansas, returned to Kansas City, and there, at Union Station, filled full of lead by a band of criminals. Several lawmen also died in the attack. The attackers were either trying to free Nash, or were trying to kill him to prevent him from talking to federal agents. By then, Keating and Holden were beginning life sentences. They died in prison.

## THE ROBBERS OF THE IRON HORSE

*Killers and Oafs*

THIS BOOK IS ABOUT THE townspeople who really built this nation, the ordinary citizens who beat off outlaws just as they did every other peril. Even so, it would not be complete without some reference to the great Western cottage industry of train robbing, which reached its zenith in the second half of the nineteenth century and the first decade of the twentieth. The railroad express cars were prime targets, for they often carried substantial amounts of money.

Robbing the railroads provided full employment for a goodly number of hoodlums in the years after the Civil War. In 1895, for example, there were at least forty-nine attacks on railroad express cars that actually succeeded, not to mention those that flopped or were repelled for various reasons. The train robbers ranged all the way from the really dangerous Dalton and James–Younger Gangs, to buffoons like inept, posturing Al Jennings and stupid, drunken Elmer McCurdy.

These felons were likely to mistreat express agents badly to get into the express safes, in which the really valuable loot was locked. If the agent were true to his salt, as a lot of them were, and forted up in the express car and made a fight of it, he ran a very real chance of having the car blown up and getting himself killed or maimed.

The railroads quickly went to a system of "way safes" and "through safes" in an effort to thwart repeated robberies. The express agent could get into the way safe, which contained comparatively small amounts of money for little towns along the right-of-way. The through safe, on the other hand, protected the really important money, and it was destined to go all the way through to the train's final or first major destination. Only there would it be opened by station personnel; the express agent on the train could not open it. On occasion, train-robbing gangs were able to blast open a through safe, but that took real talent, something most outlaws were markedly short of fostering.

There was, for example, the saga of a couple of members of the vaunted Wild Bunch who decided to stick up the Southern Pacific line. It happened at Sanderson, Texas, on March 13, 1912, when Ben Kilpatrick and Ole Beck (also called Ed Welsh) decided it would be a fine idea to fatten their wallets by robbing a train. Just the year before, Ben had finished ten years in prison for train robbery. You'd think he would have learned from his long time behind bars, but maybe that enforced vacation had only sharpened his appetite for express cars.

At first, indeed, things went well. The express messenger, David Troutsdale, showed no signs of putting up a fight, as so many of his compatriots did. His apparent submission—and that of his two helpers—must have pleased these two experienced outlaws: an easy payday, no trouble, no shooting, no spilled blood, no noise. No fuss at all, just money.

Troutsdale surely seemed an agreeable, pacific sort. Even with Ole Beck outside the express car, Troutsdale withstood with equanimity the arrogant Kilpatrick's bullying, which included a series of painful blows from the outlaw's Winchester. "Get a move on," said the bandit, and Troutsdale did. The agent's action was not, however, exactly what Kilpatrick had in mind. "This is the most valuable parcel in the car," said Troutsdale helpfully, indicating a package with the toe of his shoe. Intrigued, the outlaw bent down to retrieve the prize.

At this point, Troutsdale picked up an ice maul—a heavy wooden mallet designed to crush big chunks of ice into smaller pieces to keep cool the succulent oysters so beloved in the early West. The maul was lying conveniently on top of a nearby barrel of oysters, and with this handy implement, the express agent bashed Kilpatrick in the back of the head, then hit the bandit twice more for good measure, distributing his brains

*Ben Kilpatrick and Ole Beck*

here and there about the express car. Having put an instant end to Kilpatrick, the doughty Troutsdale prepared for further action.

The dead bandit had been armed to the teeth: a Winchester and not one, but two, revolvers shoved into his belt. Troutsdale kept the Winchester for himself and then handed a pistol each to his two helpers, men named Reagan and Banks. Wisely, the three agents waited for a while to see what else might happen. Nothing did. And so, unwilling to wait for further developments, Troutsdale fired a shot through the roof of the car. That got almost immediate results.

A voice was heard, a voice that called out for "Frank." The messenger could not be sure, but he assumed—quite correctly, as it turned out—that the voice belonged to Ole Beck. Peering around a pile of baggage, Troutsdale saw the outline of a head, somebody lurking behind the stacks of trunks and valises and boxes. He soon had a clear view of the lurker behind the baggage and drove a rifle bullet through him, creating a quaint third eye just above the robber's real one on the left side of his head. Thus ended the exploits of the famous Wild Bunch member and his dense companion.

The robbers who stopped a Rock Island train at Pond Creek, southbound from Wichita in 1894, had similar problems. There were at least four of them, allegedly including Charlie Pitts of James–Younger Gang fame (but Pitts had been dead since the Northfield raid back in 1876). Whoever they were, they stopped the train all right, but then the operation came unraveled in a hurry.

When their demands to open the express car were ignored by express agent John Crossland, they detonated a stick of dynamite under the door. Stunned, Crossland played for time while guard Jake Harmon slipped out the back door of the car, moved through another car, and stepped quietly out into the night. Seeing a gaggle of bandits outside the express car, including one who was brandishing a pistol, Harmon gave the shadowy pistol-waver a dose of buckshot. The pistol-man went down, and general panic and consternation followed. The rest of the bandits ran off into the gloom. One was captured immediately; two more were run down later and jailed.

Then there was the day when an outlaw gang stuck up the Southern Pacific at Fairbank station, down in Cochise County in south-eastern Arizona. The idea seems to have been to hide behind whatever citizens happened to be about the station and ransack the express car for what the bandits apparently expected to be a gratifying pile of money.

To the gang's profound unhappiness, the express messenger on the outlaws' chosen night was Jeff Milton, sometime local peace officer and Texas Ranger. Milton's reputation was like that of Texas John Slaughter's. Like that formidable Arizona lawman and rancher, Milton was a good man and a good friend, but he lacked even a scrap of compassion for outlaws. As the train stood in the station at Fairbank, Milton handed down packages from the express car.

Out of a crowd of bystanders, a voice ordered Milton to "throw up your hands and come out of there." Milton reached inside the car for his shotgun, and in vintage Milton style, answered the voice, "If there's anything in here you want, come and get it!" The response was a blast of rifle fire out of the crowd around the train. A bullet ripped the hat from Milton's head; more shots smashed into his left arm and knocked him down.

Even hurt, Milton was not the surrendering kind. He had his shotgun now, but he worried about hitting some innocent civilian if he simply sprayed a fan of buckshot at the robbers. Still, he wasn't going to give away the express company's cargo without a fight. In the event, the robbers solved his dilemma for him. Apparently sure Milton was out of action, the outlaws rushed the express-car door, obviously expecting easy pickings over the body of a dead or badly wounded messenger.

It came as a nasty surprise when Milton, shooting one-handed, opened fire with his shotgun at the first bandits to enter the car. The first outlaw through the door was "Three-Fingered" Jack Dunlap, who took eleven buckshot in various portions of his anatomy, whereof, in due course, he died. A single buckshot wounded a second bandit, one Bravo Juan Yoas, in the fanny, presumably as he turned tail to run. Yoas forthwith lost all interest in larceny.

The remaining three bandits ventilated the express car with many rifle bullets, but Milton was on the floor between two trunks, engaged in losing consciousness. While he was out cold, the surviving bandits entered the car, but found they could not open the safe: They had not been bright enough to bring along some dynamite, and Milton had thrown away the safe's keys before he drifted into unconsciousness.

Trouble of a different kind jumped out at the gang that stopped the AT and SF train number five near Gorin, Missouri, on September 18, 1894. The stopping was the easy part: All you had to do was wave a red lantern as if you were the station agent, and the train obediently pulled to a halt. The bandits wantonly opened fire on engineer Dad Prescott, badly wounding him, then went on back to the express car, where they expected to find their bonanza.

What they found instead was a car full of Santa Fe detectives who had been tipped off about the robbery. Charlie Abrams, the leader of the outlaw gang, went down full of holes and quickly expired; a second outlaw, one Link Overfield, managed to get clear, but was captured shortly afterward at Memphis, Missouri. The remaining bandits, two of them, got away clean, which tells you something about the shooting of the detectives.

A somewhat better day—or in this case, night—for the forces of the law was the twenty-seventh of March 1895. Train number three of the Cincinnati Southern Railroad was stopped by a lantern-waving figure just north of Greenwood, Kentucky, at a place where the right-of-way ran through a deep cut. The lantern-waver turned out to be a pistol-packing bandit, and he was followed by three equally villainous hard cases. The four may have been rank amateurs at the train-robbing business, for they headed straight for the baggage car, maybe thinking it was the express car.

As the bandits rummaged through the baggage car, back in the passenger cars, three men began to wonder what the delay was, and finally they walked forward to find out. They were Will Eddie, Will Altgood, and Thomas Griffin, and all three happened to be railroad detectives. Altgood, the first in line, was confronted by a bandit at the steps of the baggage car. "Hands up," ordered the robber, but Altgood went for his pistol instead, and all hell broke loose. One of the bandits took a bullet in the heart, which finished him. A second managed to survive for only two hours, shot through the lungs. Still a third was so badly shot up that he almost died.

The presence of the three detectives on the train was no accident, for they had been warned about the robbery. The informer, one Sam Fraser, was part of the gang and had ridden along on the raid that very night. Fraser had wisely elected to hold the outlaws' horses as his part of the scheme, and so he managed to stay out of the line of fire. The dead men were Jess and Tom Morrow, father and son. The wounded man, poor soul, was not a bandit at all, but a hobo who found himself in the wrong place. A fourth bandit, probably Mose Morrow, Tom's brother, got away.

Outlaws did even worse when they tried to eliminate one of their major opponents, a quiet, retiring man called Fred Hans. Hans was at various times a detective for the Union Pacific and for the federal government. In 1900 he worked for the Northwestern Railroad, which in those days ran between Deadwood and Omaha. This line frequently hauled very large shipments of gold from the Deadwood mines, and it was Hans's job to keep those shipments safe. The story goes that he was so good at his job that most outlaws steered well clear of the Northwestern.

Five outlaws Hans had been chasing paid the ultimate price for turning on the detective and laying an ambush for him. They managed to kill the detective's horse, but Hans used the animal's carcass as a fort, pulled his two pistols, and opened fire. He drove one round through an ambusher's heart and then killed a second man's horse. He put another bullet through a third bandit's brain and shot a fourth in the belly. The fifth man, now horseless, wisely gave it up as a bad job and surrendered.

Eight years before, in West Virginia, four hoodlums had tried to rob the travelers on a passenger train. It should have been easy, with four men, to stroll down the aisle collecting money and watches and rings. But it wasn't. A passenger named Henry Zelcher grabbed one of the outlaws and wrestled with him. Zelcher was shot in the abdomen, and Peter Lake, another passenger, was wounded twice when he went to help Zelcher. Still another passenger, however, Sam Matthes, knocked the gun from the robber's hand. At this junction, the conductor, a man named Zingley, produced two pistols of his own and blazed away at the bewildered outlaws. Zingley hit two of them, and the whole gang took to their heels.

Then there was the incident at Rio Puerco trestle down in New Mexico. Rio Puerco was a tiny station in 1896, down on the Atlantic and Pacific road, 30 miles south and west of Albuquerque. On an October evening, train number two contracted a mechanical hiccup west of the station and pulled to a stop. It did not take long to put the problem to rights, but as the train started up again, two outlaws swung on board, firing on a brakeman and wounding him in the hand. The engineer, Charley Ross, pulled the train to a halt.

Now there had been no reason to shoot at the brakeman—all the man had done was yell at the intruders—but the shots were to have serious consequences for the outlaws. First, warned by the shooting, the express messenger, L. J. Kohler, put out his lights, locked the express car door, and readied his revolver. And back in one of the passenger cars, U.S. deputy marshal Will Loomis picked up his shotgun and sent a newsboy back to his dunnage for a handful of shells.

As the bandits approached, Kohler peered through the door of the car and Loomis walked through the darkness toward the head of the train. At first, Loomis could not get a clear shot and waited, afraid he might shoot a train crewman in the gloom. But then one man, obviously an outlaw, stepped away from a knot of men gathered around the express-car door, and Loomis took his shot. The shotgun charge knocked down the bandit, one Cole Young, but the outlaw pulled himself to his feet and fired two wild shots at Loomis, or more probably at the flash of his shotgun. Loomis fired the other barrel and Young went down for keeps, rolling down the embankment in the darkness.

After a certain amount of further confused dithering, and apparently still unaware that Young was quite dead, the robbers rode off into the night, empty-handed. They were, as it turned out, the dangerous, but inept, Christian Brothers, authors of the equally unproductive comic-opera attempt on a border bank in Nogales.

Then there was the 1893 Roy's Branch holdup, unique in the annals of crime. Of six men in the train-robbing gang, half of them were working undercover for the law. Roy's Branch was a spot on the Chicago, Burlington, and Quincy just north of St. Joseph, and there the three real criminals, gang leader Fred Kohler, ex-con Henry Gleitze, and Gleitze's half brother Hugo Engel, lay in wait for what they believed would be a rich haul. They thought they were attacking a train carrying many thousands of dollars from St. Louis to Omaha. What they got was a train full of lawmen.

The outlaws also thought they had the help of three more men: William Garver, Charles Fredericks, and N. A. Hurst. The first two were ordinary citizens; Hurst was a detective. All three men had been recruited into the gang and been present at planning sessions for this raid. These three had promptly informed the railroad, which assembled an eight-car dummy train, carrying no cargo except for eighteen lawmen and the general manager of the railway.

Sure enough, as the train approached Roy's Branch, a man with a red lantern flagged down the engineer, who obligingly stopped the train. More armed men in masks then appeared, and after collecting the fireman and engineer, crowded around the door to the dummy express car and demanded admittance. They got it.

As Kohler entered the car, he gasped in surprise and raised his gun, but a policeman drove two rounds into him. The gang leader fell back out of the door, crawled a few yards along the ground, and promptly died. Engel, right behind Kohler, took a charge from a shotgun and recoiled into the weeds along the right-of-way. He died there. Gleitze, wounded, managed to get clear in the darkness, but was rounded up the next day in St. Joseph. Though he denied any involvement in the holdup, it didn't do him any good. He was newly missing three fingers on one hand and had his pockets stuffed with ammunition.

Which brings us to the champion fathead of all American train robbers, Elmer McCurdy. Back in 1911, Elmer was a very small-time bandit who led a little gang out to rob a train near Okesa, Oklahoma. Elmer's part of the split was a measly $45 in cash and a couple of demijohns of whiskey. Elmer fled from the scene of his crime on foot, and as he put distance between himself and pursuit, steadily sucked on the whiskey.

By the time sundown came, Elmer was pretty well spifflicated and sought sanctuary in a farmer's barn, where he promptly fell into a profound sleep. When he awoke, probably with a very large headache, he discovered that a posse had followed him and was now encircling the barn. In due course, the posse summoned Elmer to surrender himself unto the law, but Elmer demurred. Making the worst possible choice, he decided to fight, and the posse promptly put an end to him.

Elmer's remains were hauled into the town of Pawhuska and taken to the local undertaking parlor, and that, in the ordinary course of things, should have been the end of Elmer. Having come to the end of his short,

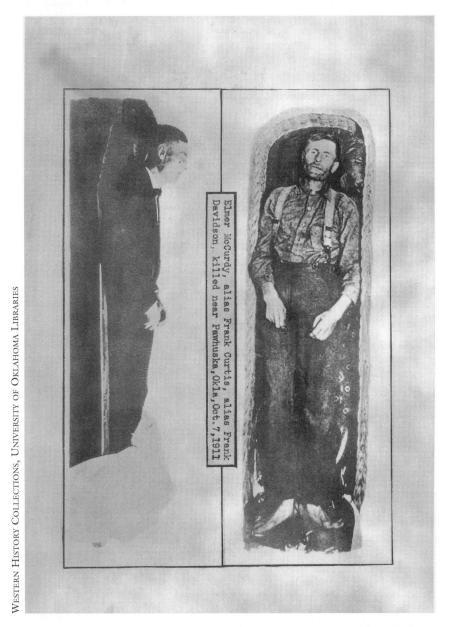

Elmer McCurdy, alias Frank Curtis, alias Frank Davidson, killed near Pawhuska,Okla,Oct.7,1911

*Elmer McCurdy*

inglorious life as a bad man, however, Elmer was about to embark upon a second career, for the undertaker, instead of embalming Elmer, apparently ossified him with some sort of arsenic solution. It seems the undertaker saw commercial possibilities in Elmer and kept him on display in his shop for years afterward: For a nickel, you could see a real, dead outlaw. Elmer wasn't much as outlaws went, but a nickel wasn't much either.

In time, however, about 1916, Elmer ceased to be much of an attraction, and so he was sold off to some sort of traveling rarity show, with which he toured for years. Thereafter, he seems to have passed into the hands of still another such display and then spent some time decorating a fun house. He even had a nonspeaking part in a movie, but then he disappeared from history for some years.

And then, during a filming of an episode of the *Six Million Dollar Man,* in a sort of warehouse of oddities out in Long Beach, California, Elmer appeared again, like the Ghost of Christmas Past. The photographer, it seems, asked his assistant to move a dummy painted in fluorescent paint, and when the assistant obeyed, the figure's arm came off. "I don't think this is a dummy," said the assistant, and so it wasn't. It was plainly human, or at least it had been at some distant time in the past. Lo, it was Elmer, returned.

A long and complicated process involving some expert detective work and very sophisticated forensic examination confirmed Elmer's identity, and at long last Elmer was restored to the land of his beginnings. At historic Guthrie, sometime state capital of Oklahoma, Elmer was returned to the soil in state, not to say pomp. Transported to the graveyard in an old-fashioned, glass-sided, horse-drawn hearse, Elmer was laid to rest in a nice gesture by a couple of public-spirited organizations dedicated to preserving the history of the West. One of his graveside neighbors was Bill Doolin. Elmer would have liked that.

Somebody wrote a neat bit of doggerel for the occasion:

> *Rest in peace, dear Elmer*
> *Beneath this Okie sky,*
> *Where many an outlaw slumbers,*
> *And politicians lie.*

# BIBLIOGRAPHY

## BOOKS

Balousek, Marv. *More Wisconsin Crimes of the Century.* Oregon, Wisconsin: Wanbesa Press, n.d.

Bartholomew, Ed E. *Biographical Album of Western Gunfighters.* Houston: Frontier Press of Texas, 1958.

———. *Kill or Be Killed.* Houston: Frontier Press of Texas, 1953.

Bates, Edmond Franklin. writing as "A Citizen of Denton County," *Sam Bass and His Gang.* Denton, Texas: Monitor Books & Job Printing Establishment, 1878; reprinted by *Frontier Times,* Bandera, Texas, 1926.

Beebe, Lucius, and Charles Clegg. *U.S. West.* New York: Bonanza Books, 1949.

Brant, Marley. *The Outlaw Youngers.* Lanham, Maryland: Madison Books, 1992.

Breakenridge, William M. *Helldorado.* Lincoln, Nebraska: University of Nebraska Press, 1992.

Burton, Jeff. *Black Jack Christian, Outlaw.* Santa Fe, New Mexico: Press of the Territorian, 1967.

———. *Portraits in Gunsmoke.* Bromley, Kent, U.K.: English Westerners' Society, n.d.

Canner, J. S. *Outlaws & Peace Officers of the Frontier West.* Roxbury Crossing, Massachusetts: Canner & Co., 1964.

Clemens, Nancy. *American Bandits.* Girard, Kansas: Haldeman-Julius Pub., 1938.

Clifton, Robert Bruce. *Murder by Mail.* Ardmore, Pennsylvania: Dorrance & Co., 1979.

Cox, Edwin T. *History of Eastland County.* San Antonio, Tex.: Naylor, 1950.

Crawford, Richard W. *Stranger Than Fiction*. San Diego: San Diego Historical Society, 1995.

Croy, Homer. *Trigger Marshal: The Story of Chris Madsen*. New York: Duell, Sloan & Pierce, 1967.

Cunningham, Eugene. *Triggernometry*. Caldwell, Idaho: Caxton, 1989.

Dalton, Emmett. *When the Daltons Rode*. New York: Doubleday, Doran, 1931.

Drago, Harry S. *Outlaws on Horseback*. New York: Dodd, Mead, 1964.

———. *Road Agents and Train Robbers*. New York: Dodd, Mead & Co., 1973.

Eaton, John. *Will Carver, Outlaw*. San Angelo, Tex.: Anchor Publishing Co., 1972.

Elliott, David S. Last Raid of the Daltons. Coffeyville, Kans.: Coffeyville Journal, 1892.

Ernst, Donna B. *From Cowboy to Outlaw: The True Story of Will Carver*. Sonora, Tex.: Sutton County Historical Society, 1995.

Fellman, Michael. *Inside War*. New York: Oxford University Press, 1989.

Fortson, John. *Pott County and What Has Become of It*. Shawnee, Okla.: Herald Printing Co., 1936.

French, William. *Some Recollections of a Western Ranchman*. New York: Argosy Antiquarian, 1965.

Gaddy, Jerry J. *Dust to Dust*. San Rafael, Calif.: Presidio Press, 1977.

Gard, Wayne. *Sam Bass*. Boston: Houghton Mifflin Co., 1936.

Garrett, Pat. *Authentic Life of Billy the Kid*. Norman, Okla.: University of Oklahoma Press, 2000.

George, Todd Menzies. *Just Memories and Twelve Years with Cole Younger*. N.p., 1959.

Graves, Richard S. Oklahoma Outlaws. Oklahoma City, Okla.: State Printing and Publishing Co., 1915.

Haley, J. Evetts. *Jeff Milton, A Good Man with a Gun*. Norman, Okla.: University of Oklahoma Press, 1948.

Hanes, Bailey. *Bill Doolin, Outlaw O.T*. Norman, Okla.: University of Oklahoma Press, 1968.

Horan, James D. *Desperate Men*. New York: Bonanza Books, 1949.

Hume, James B., and Jonathan N. Thacker. *Report of Jas. B. Hume and Jno. N Thacker, Special Officers, Wells, Fargo & Co.'s Express, Covering a Period of Fourteen Years, Giving Losses by Train Robbers, Stage Robbers, and Burglaries, and a Full Description and Record of All Noted Criminals Convicted of Offenses Against Wells, Fargo & Company Since November 5th, 1870*. Privately Published, 1884.

Johnston County Historical Book Committee. *History of Johnston County, Oklahoma*. Dallas: Curtis Media Corp., 1988.

Kaye, William. *The Killing of Bill Doolin*. New York: Leisure Books, 1980.

Keleher, William A. *Violence in Lincoln County*, 1869–1881. Albuquerque, N. Mex.: University of New Mexico Press, 1957.

Kelly, Charles. *The Outlaw*. New York: Devin Adair Co., 1959.

King, Jeffrey S. *The Life and Death of Pretty Boy Floyd*. Kent, Ohio: Kent State Press, 1998.

King, Frank M. *Wranglin' the Past*. Pasadena, Calif.: Trail's End Publishing Co., 1935.

Lake, Stuart N. *Wyatt Earp*. New York: Pocket Books, 1994.

Love, Robertus. *The Rise and Fall of Jesse James*. Lincoln, Nebr.: Bison Books, 1990.

Lucia, Ellis. *Tough Men, Tough Country*. Englewood Cliff, N. J.: Prentice-Hall, 1963.

Lynch, Larry, and John M. Russell, eds. *Where the Wild Rice Grows.* Menomonie, Wis.: Menomonie Sesquicentennial Commission, 1996.

Martin, Charles L. *A Sketch of Sam Bass.* Norman, Okla.: University of Oklahoma Press, 1956.

McWhorter, Eugene W. *Traditions of the Land: The History of Gregg County, Texas.* Longview, Tex.: Gregg County Historical Foundation, 1989.

Miller, Rick. *Sam Bass & Gang.* Austin, Tex.: State House Press, 1999.

National Bank of Cisco, *The Santa Claus Bank Robbery.* Cisco, Tex.: Longhorn Press, 1958.

Nix, Evett Dumas. *Oklahombres.* Lincoln, Nebr.: Bison Books, 1993.

O'Neal, Bill. *Encyclopedia of Western Gun-Fighters.* Norman, Okla.: University of Oklahoma Press, 1979.

Owens, Ron. *Oklahoma Justice: The Oklahoma City Police.* Paducah, Ky. Turner Publishing, 1995.

Patterson, Richard. *Butch Cassidy: A Biography.* Lincoln, Nebr.: Nebraska Press, 1998.

———. *Historical Atlas of the Outlaw West.* Boulder, Colo.: Johnson Books, 1985.

———. *Train Robbery: The Birth, Flowering, and Decline of a Notorious Western Enterprise.* Boulder, Colo.: Johnson Books, 1981.

Pinkerton, William A. *Train Robberies, Train Robbers, and the "Holdup" Men.* New York: Arno Press, 1974.

Pointer, Larry. *In Search of Butch Cassidy.* Norman, Oklahoma: University of Oklahoma Press, 1977.

Pourade, Richard F. *The Glory Years.* San Diego: San Diego Historical Society, n.d.

Preece, Harold. *The Dalton Gang: End of an Era*. New York: Hastings House, 1963.

Rasch, Philip J. *Desperadoes of Arizona Territory*. Laramie, Wyo.: NOLA, 1999.

Reed, Paula. *The Tenderfoot Bandits*. Tucson, Ariz.: Westernlore Press, 1988.

Samuelson, Nancy B. *The Dalton Gang Story*. Eastford, Conn.: Shooting Star Press, 1992.

Skovlin, Jon M., and Donna McDaniel Scovlin. *In Pursuit of the McCartys*. Cove, Oreg.: Reflections Publishing Co., 2001.

Settle, William A. Jr. *Jesse James Was His Name*. Lincoln, Nebr.: University of Nebraska Press, 1966.

Shirley, Glenn. *Belle Starr and Her Times*. Norman, Okla.: University of Oklahoma Press, 1892.

———. *Gunfight At Ingalls*. Stillwater, Okla.: Barbed Wire Press, 1990.

———. *Last of the Real Badmen*. Lincoln, Nebr.: Bison Books, 1976.

———. *Law West of Fort Smith*. Lincoln, Nebr.: Bison Books, 1968.

———. *Six Gun and Silver Star*. Albuquerque, N. Mex.: University of New Mexico Press, 1955.

———. *West of Hell's Fringe*. Norman, Okla.: University of Oklahoma Press, 1990.

Smith, Leon. *High Noon at the Boley Corral*. Detroit: Leon E. Smith, 1980.

Smith, Robert Barr. *Daltons! The Raid on Coffeyville, Kansas*. Norman, Oklahoma: Oklahoma Press, 1996.

———. *Last Hurrah of the James-Younger Gang*. Norman, Okla.: Oklahoma Press, 2001.

Stanley, Francis. *Dave Rudabaugh, Border Ruffian*. Denver: World Press, 1961.

Starr, Henry. *Thrilling Events: The Life of Henry Starr, by Himself.* College Station, Tex.: Creative Publishing Co., 1982.

Sutton, Fred. *Hands Up!* Indianapolis: Bobbs-Merrill, 1927.

Tanner, Karen Holliday, and John D. Tanner, Jr. *Last of the Old-Time Outlaws.* Norman, Okla.: University of Oklahoma Press, 2002.

Toepperwein, Herman. *Western Gunfighters in Moments of Truth.* Austin, Tex.: Madrona Press, 1974.

Traywick, Ben T. *Legendary Characters of Southeast Arizona.* Tombstone, Ariz.: Red Marie's, 1992.

Wallis, Michael. *Pretty Boy.* New York: St. Martin's Press, 1992.

Wellman, Paul I. *Dynasty of Western Outlaws.* Lincoln, Nebr.: University of Nebraska Press, 1986.

West, C. W. *Only in Oklahoma.* Muskogee, Okla.: Muskogee Pub. Co., 1982.

White, Owen P. *Them Was the Days.* New York: Minton, Balch & Co., 1925.

———. *Trigger Fingers.* New York: Putnam/Knickerbocker Press, 1926.

Wilkins, Frederick. *The Law Comes to Texas.* Austin, Tex.: State House Press, 1999.

## NEWSPAPERS

*Cherokee Advocate*
*Coffeyville Journal*
*Daily Oklahoma State Capitol*
*Daily Oklahoman*
*Daily Phoenix*
*Delta County Independent*
*Denver Post*
*Denver Times*

*Devil's River News,* Sonora, Texas
*Dunn County News*
*Ford County Globe*
*Fort Worth Gazette*
*Fort Worth Star-Telegram*
*Frontier Times*
*Grand Junction News*
*Guthrie* (Oklahoma) *Leader*
*Johnston County (OK) Capital Democrat*
*Kansas City Times*
*Kinsley Graphic*
*Las Vegas Optic*
*Longview Morning Journal*
*Meeker* (Colorado) *Herald*
*Mill Creek Herald*
*Minneapolis Star*
*Morris News*
*Nogales Oasis*
*Oklahoma Press-Gazette*
*Oklahoma State Capital*
*Okmulgee Daily Democrat*
*Nacogdoches Evening Sentinel*
*Nogales Oasis*
*Rocky Mountain News*
*San Angelo Standard*
*San Antonio Express-News*
*San Diego Union*
*San Francisco Chronicle*
*Shreveport Times*
*Tombstone Democrat*
*Tuscon Daily Citizen*
*Tulsa World*
*Wichita Eagle*

## PERIODICALS

Benz, Donald, "Alias Black Jack Christian." *Old West*, Spring 1970.

Boren, Kerry Ross, "The Mysterious Pinkerton," *True West*, July–August 1977.

Breihan, Carl, "The Northfield Raid." *The West*, November 1966.

*Chronicles of Oklahoma.*

Croy, Homer, "The Bandit Who Married the Preacher's Daughter." MS.

Curtis, Olga, "The Bank Robbers Who Became Tourist Attractions." *Empire Magazine*, July 25, 1976.

Fishell, Dave, "The McCarty Gang and the Delta Holdup." *Old West*, Spring 1985.

Koch, Mike, "The Life and Times of Henry Starr." *Oklahombres*, Fall 2002.

McGaw, Bill, "Loses Head in Parral." *Southwesterner*, August 1962.

Morgan, R. D., "Triple-Header: Robbing the Morris Bank." *Oklahombres*, Spring 2001.


## LETTERS

Heck Thomas to Homer Croy, June 24, 1957 (with enclosure)
Reno Madsen to Homer Croy, January 30, 1957
Reno Madsen to Homer Croy, April 28, 1957
Reno Madsen to Homer Croy, June 24, 1957

## OTHER SOURCES

Cisco Police Department (on-line)

*Handbook of Texas* (on-line)

Indian-Pioneer Papers, University of Oklahoma Western History Collection. Accounts of Jennie Watts Cantelou; R.B. Schooley

San Diego Historical Society, Biographies (on-line)

# INDEX